South Walsham & District Cricket Club

The First Hundred Years

ALEX EVANS

To Dave,
Hope you enjoy reading this in the sun
Alex.

All rights reserved. No part of this publication may be reproduced, stored in or introduced in a retrieval system, or transmitted, in any form, or by any means (electronic, mechanical, photocopying, recording or otherwise) without the prior written permission of the publisher. Any person who does any unauthorised act in relation to this publication may be liable to criminal prosecution and civil claims for damages.

A catalogue record for this book is available from the British Library

ISBN 978-0-9926354-0-4

Copyright Alex Evans 2013

Every effort has been made that the information recorded in this book is factual correct, the publisher does not accept responsibility for any unintentional errors which may have occurred.

First published in Great Britain in 2013

Published by Alex Evans

Graphic Artist - Micky Lynne

Printing Services - Page Bros (Norwich) Ltd

PREFACE

I realise some people will say I am slightly eccentric and some will say a little sad, but one of my passions in life has been cricket and in particular South Walsham Cricket Club. From the day I started playing in 1970 to today, some 44 years on, it has always been a pleasure to play, watch or just be around the cricket club. I have made several good mates over the past years, had hundreds of laughs and whilst my playing days are all but over I still intend to enjoy the Sundays and the tours as much as I can.

It occurred to me no one ever really jots down the history of village cricket clubs which is a shame. I would love to think in a hundred years time someone might pick up a copy of these recollections and find them of interest.

I have the Walsham scorebooks going back to 1967 and seen others going back to 1949 courtesy of George C Edrich (known as Young George). Having these books certainly helps with the memories and the statistical analysis over the past 64 seasons. I have been investigating further back as far as 1908 and I am indebted to Archant for not only allowing me to copy and publish many of the Walsham reports over the years but also looking at their newspapers going back many years. I have also been to the Norwich and Yarmouth Libraries and the Norfolk Record Office in my quest for information about the club which is so dear to me.

I am greatly indebted to John Chilvers, the Eaton stalwart for helping me with this book, without him, I don't think it would have reached print, his ability for writing is way above mine, what I have been able to write down he has been able to turn it into what I believe is a very interesting story. Also to my wife's old work mate Micky Lynne who not only has produced a super cover, but has spent hours getting my book ready for the printers. John and Micky you have both been stars. Also, David Tubby for his advice and introducing me to the Edrich family, Philip Yaxley and Chris Woods for some old team photographs.

Many well known names have either played for or generally against South Walsham. John Edrich, who as a youngster, played over 50 matches. Henry Blofeld who was bowled by George Edrich for just 2 in 1954 playing for Hoveton and Wroxham, likewise Fred Roy who was involved in the development of Roys of Wroxham. Typically, another name was Colonel Ingram-Johnson from Hoveton. However, you don't get called by your title these days.

We have also met several first class players on our tours, such as Eddie Davis, Jim Griffiths, John Dye and Brian Brain, to name but a few.

There were also stalwarts of the small local clubs like Nevlle Yellop and Eric Knell from Hoveton and Wroxham, Bill Powley from Smallburgh and Billy Bishop and 'Tip' Mills of Yarmouth, John Chilvers, the Fudge brothers and Graham Best from Eaton, the Andrews brothers from Happisburgh, and the Dewings from Bradenham. I could go on.

I am indebted to the above and many past and current players of South Walsham particularly those who have contacted me over the past five years, Pat Hood, Roly Hardesty, Doug Palmer, Ivan Watts, Colin Holmes and particularly George C Edrich and Rodney Edrich who helped me with the Edrich connection. Finally, just a big thank you to my wife Hazel for her proof reading and abundant patience.

I hope those of you who enjoy cricket will find my little book of interest.

Alex Evans

Alex Evans
Horsford – July 2013

CHAPTER ONE *Early Days*

One thing is for sure: South Walsham Cricket Club has been going strong for over one hundred years. However, this is not as long as some local clubs; research has uncovered matches played in the nearby villages of Acle and Blofield in the early 1890s.

The first recorded South Walsham match was on Wednesday 1st July 1908 and resulted in a 20 run victory against Blofield: 53 all out beat 33 all out, the top scorers being W Childs (13) and F Debbage (11). The format of this game is unknown. As it was played midweek, was it an evening match - an early example of T20 - or was it an afternoon fixture, the local farm labourers being given a precious half-day off before the long hours of the harvest season? Given the relationships that generally prevailed between the farmers and their employees, one suspects that an evening game was the more likely. Did they, one wonders, adjourn after the match to 'The Ship' or 'The King's Arms'? Both hostelries had been open for business for several decades.

On the Blofield side for this first recorded game were two members of an illustrious cricketing dynasty that was to influence over forty years of South Walsham's cricket between the mid 1920s and the 1960s: the Edriches. On this occasion, the family were represented by William (snr), the father of W J 'Bill' Edrich of Middlesex and England, and Edwin, who, many years later, was to serve as the South Walsham umpire.

For this game, and all others before the First World War, the away side would have travelled by horse and cart, bicycle or would have walked to the ground. Hence, even between the wars, teams rarely played beyond a five mile radius of their village. Games were generally played on a Saturday or midweek but, unsurprisingly, there were gaps from August onwards; the harvest was still central to the success of the farming year.

No evidence has been found of Sunday games until the 1940s. Perhaps one reason for this lies in the role in the community of the man who may well have been instrumental in founding the club: Rev Francis Ranken[1]. Unfortunately, there are no surviving club records for this era, but Rev

Ranken, who became the Vicar of South Walsham in 1901, seems to have been an active player, and may well have used his considerable influence among his parishioners to encourage cricket - but not on Sundays! Pitches at this time would have been little more than a cut piece of grass in a farmer's field with a rough outfield, hence the consistently low scores. A victory by 16 runs, against the neighbouring village of Woodbastwick, was achieved despite a score of only 49, W Blake top-scoring with 20. The opposition were dismissed for 35. However, this success was balanced in a match at Salhouse: the hosts totalled 40, but Walsham could only manage 15, probably the club's lowest ever score. In the inaugural year, one opposition, intriguingly called the 'Visitors', did score 102 and then dismissed Walsham for 48; a match total of 150 was unusual in these early years.

South Walsham squad - circa 1912

In 1909, in what must be the lowest ever aggregate score in a game involving South Walsham, they were defeated by Great Plumstead by 2 runs: 21 to 19. In contrast, against Lingwood, the Walsham innings was declared on 121-5; the opposition were bowled out for 55. In only the club's second season, there is evidence of junior matches, the South Walsham youngsters beating Acle Juniors twice: 68 to 10 in the first game, and 21 to 10 in the return.

For 1910, there is newspaper evidence of four matches. In the first, a paltry total of 17 against Great Plumstead, resulted in defeat by 61 runs and a two innings game against a team called Visitors Yacht Enterprises was lost by 7 wickets. In the latter, Walsham's scores - 44 and 23 - were surpassed by the opposition's 56 and 12-3. Quite possibly, these were the same side as that identified simply as 'Visitors' in 1908. Revenge was gained over Great Plumstead, Walsham's 84 - with Blake hitting 28 - resulting in a 62 run victory. The fourth game was also a victory with Walsham hitting 102 (Dickinson 45), while Woodbastwick could only score 23.

In 1911, Walsham beat North Burlingham by 40 to 16, the Juniors also winning against the same opposition by 52 to 17. A defeat to a combined team of Blofield and Brundall by 12 runs (69 to 57) was followed by a further loss to Visitors Yacht Enterprises by 17 runs. In a two innings game, the 'Visitors' scored 26 and 74-5 declared, while Walsham could only muster 35 and 38. In the penultimate recorded match of the season, the club held what was probably an internal game - Singles versus Marrieds - which finished in a tie at 31 runs each; that 22 players could be found to take part suggests that membership was healthy. The final match of 1911 was against Mr A.G.E. Sanctuary's XI, in which his team scored 96 against Walsham's 56. Frustratingly, to date, it has not been possible to trace who the triple-initialled Mr Sanctuary was, and from where he assembled his XI.

Six games were reported in 1912, the first one being a defeat to Blofield by 11 runs (80-5 declared to 69). Rev Ranken was still playing when the club were hammered by North Burlingham 87 to 35, but they quickly gained revenge in the return fixture winning 76 to 38. Great Plumstead again proved to be too strong, winning both games 76 to 38, and 55 to 31, while Freethorpe Church achieved a narrow victory by 43 runs to 40.

Although it seems improbable that the club did not continue, there are no games recorded in the local press for 1913, nor in the early summer months of 1914. However, war was declared on 4th August 1914; this would certainly have resulted in an early end to the season for village clubs as it did for the first-class game.

1 Reverend Francis Smith Ranken: born Barnett (2nd qtr 1865), died Redlynch, nr Salisbury, Wiltshire 25 November 1942 (age 77), but buried in South Walsham. The second son of John Smith Ranken a Scottish-born East India Merchant who married a Welsh lady, Clara (nee ?) and had six children. Education: Highgate School and Queens College, Cambridge 1884-87. Clerical posts: Curate of Liskeard 1888-1891, Curate of St. Just-in-Penwith (Cornwall) 1891-1903, Curate of St. Augustine's (Bermondsey) 1893-1900, Rector of South Walsham St. Lawrence with St. Mary 1901-1935 and Rural Dean of Blofield 1919-1931, Diocese of Salisbury 1935-1942. He married Kathleen Margaret Humphries, although there is no record of their marriage producing children. Thanks are due to Mike Davage for researching this biographical material.

CHAPTER TWO *Interlude - World War I*

For four years, cricket took second place to the contest with 'Kaiser Bill'. This pause gives us the space to reflect on the village of South Walsham in the early years of the century. There were roughly 10,000 villages in England, over 500 of them being situated in Norfolk, and although none could lay claim to being the 'typical English village', South Walsham could be said to have been representative of an archetypal medium-sized community. Over a century earlier, the quality of the land had been highlighted by the agricultural writer Arthur Young, prior to the enclosure of the village in 1801. There is every reason to suppose that, in the early twentieth century, the predominantly arable land continued to be fruitful. Farm labourers constituted the biggest occupational group for adult males, families were large, transport was limited and a sense of local identity was still powerful.

The wholly self-sufficient village had always been mythical, but there was a range of skills and trades which meant that everyday needs could be met without a trip to Acle market or an adventurous expedition to Norwich. In a population of around 500 in 1883, Kelly's directory had recorded, as well as six farmers: two Church of England ministers, two shoemakers, two grocers, two blacksmiths, two carpenters, a coal dealer, a draper, a tailor, a saddler, a plumber, a butcher, a sub-postmaster, a school mistress and four others identified as shopkeepers or general dealers. Perhaps a rather bigger enterprise was Press Brothers, described as a company dealing in coal, seed, cake and manure and engaged in milling both in South Walsham and Upton.

The two established public houses were balanced by a Temperance Club, showing that this particular Victorian/Edwardian institution had penetrated rural Norfolk. The village school had been built on its current site in 1865. The relative isolation of the village was maintained by its separation from the railway system; a line through the village was planned in 1883, but was never built. Presumably, its potential backers decided that it was unviable.

That the village was served by two Church of England ministers was the consequence of an ecclesiastical division into two parishes: St Lawrence and St Mary (later combined). The significance of this for villagers is difficult to gauge although, as suggested in Chapter 1, it was from St Lawrence that the cricket club drew its guidance. The Rev Frances Ranken (1865-1942), graduate of Queen's College, Cambridge moved to the village in 1901 and held the living for 34 years. He left in 1935 to take up a post in Salisbury but, clearly, South Walsham was where his heart was, as, when he died in 1942, he was buried at the St Lawrence with St Mary Church. A plaque in the church commemorates.

Such was the tightly-knit nature of the early twentieth century village that even those families that did not lose a husband, father, son, cousin or friend would have known several of those who perished in the deserts of Palestine, at sea or in the mud of a Flanders trench. However, the Established Church did not enjoy a monopoly of the spiritual loyalties of the village, as a Primitive Methodist chapel had been built at Pilson Green - a hamlet within the village - in 1869. The 'Primitives' were a force in many Norfolk villages. They offered a less deferential form of worship and were often linked, in their leadership circles, with nascent agricultural trades unions.

The impact of the First World War was felt in every one of England's 10,000 villages. It is an unusual village that does not have a memorial to the fallen of both world wars, the numbers recorded for the Great War generally being higher than those in the conflict against Nazi Germany. South Walsham is no exception: only three villagers perished in the Second World War, as against fourteen in the earlier conflict. The names could well include some of those who had played for the cricket club in their formative years. In addition to the war memorial, a roll of honour is displayed in the church which lists 120 names of those men connected with the village who took up arms in the conflict. Four carried the surname Blake - quite possibly, one of these was the leading run scorer of the pre-war village side - in addition to five members of the Curtis and Cutting families, six Ebbages and eight Jermys. One hopes that those who fell as well as those who survived were, on occasions, able to muse on their past memories or future prospects of home, a summer's afternoon and the camaraderie of a village cricket match.

CHAPTER THREE *Cricket Resumes!*

In the aftermath of the Great War, it appears that no matches were played in 1919 or 1920, but, in addition to the disruption caused by the war, even more deaths had resulted from the pan-European flu epidemic. Little wonder that the resumption was not immediate.

1921

The first post-war match of which there is evidence, took place against Acle on 7th May 1921 and resulted in a 68 run win for South Walsham: 95 to 27, with H Emmerson - a World War One survivor - taking 7-5. A week later, Walsham went down to Cantley by 59 runs (103 to 44).

These matches were played within the framework of the newly formed Freethorpe and District League. Games on Saturdays and the league consisted of eight teams: Burlingham, Cantley, Acle, Halvergate, Freethorpe, Reedham, Beighton and South Walsham.

In the game against Beighton, the players representing Walsham were: R Whitehand, W Blake, W Emmerson, A Falgate, F Debbage, C Jermy, H Frere, W Cooper, A Goffin, L Moore and R Bland. In the absence of H Emmerson, following his success against Acle earlier in the season, Beighton won the game by 8 runs (64 to 56) with Blake hitting 23 for Walsham. As with several other games, the full scorecard does not exist, only the run scorers are mentioned and bowlers and catchers are unattributed. The return league game against Beighton was also lost (89 to 44), but a win was achieved against Freethorpe by 28 runs (80 to 52).

Walsham also played a few friendlies, beating Buckenham and Hassingham by 83 runs (134 to 51) with Cooper hitting 30 and Moore 26. They also defeated Moulton by 72 to 43. This was balanced by a loss to Ranworth (70 to 45).

1922

League cricket continued in 1922, Walsham again losing to Beighton by just two runs (37 to 35) when, intriguingly, an F Futter top scored with 12 for Walsham. Ninety years later a Futter (Garth) still represents his home village but, unfortunately, to date, it has not proved possible to establish whether they are related.

1923
In July 1923 the game with Freethorpe, as with most games, was a low scoring affair, Walsham winning by 26 runs (68 to 42). It seems clear that Walsham, and other villages in the Freethorpe/Acle area, were at the bottom of the cricketing ladder. The Norfolk Junior Cup was the major village competition of the time but it was never won by a local side and Walsham didn't even enter it.

1924
This season saw Walsham play league fixtures against: Halvergate, Cantley, Blofield, Acle, Freethorpe, Reedham and Lingwood. It appears that Burlingham and Beighton had fallen by the wayside. The points system was very straightforward: two points for a win, one for a draw or abandoned and no points for a defeat. Walsham never reached a three figure score: losing to Cantley (57 to 20), beating Reedham (95 to 30), and losing narrowly to Freethorpe by 2 runs (40 to 38) but more heavily to Acle by 41 runs (65 to 24).

1925
In a significant change in the local cricketing scene, Hassingham became members of the league, with Blofield dropping out. It seems likely that Blofield were upwardly aspiring and sought new fixtures to test themselves at a higher level. Their village history describes inter-war cricket in Blofield as 'strong', one indicator being that, unusually, they fielded two teams.

Meanwhile among the village minnows, South Walsham lost to Lingwood, where the opposition declared on 45-7 only to bowl out Walsham for 37. A win by 11 runs against Hassingham (49 to 38) was balanced by a loss in the return fixture by 16 runs (46 to 30). The 'hammering' of local rivals Acle by 60 runs (75 to 15) was followed by a 45 run loss to Freethorpe (81 to 36).

At the end of the season, the following article appeared in the Yarmouth Independent **'REST DEFEAT CHAMPIONS'**

'On Saturday at Reedham, Halvergate as champions of the Freethorpe and

District League in which they won twelve and lost two of the season's fixtures concluded the season with a match against the Rest of the League, but lost 102 runs to 63. The winning side comprised of selected players from the other teams of the League: Cantley, Freethorpe, Reedham, Acle, South Walsham, Hassingham and Lingwood which finished their league programme in that order. Between innings, Lady Frere of South Walsham presented the cup to the captain of the Halvergate team with a gold medal to each of the players and was heartily thanked on the motion of the Rev J Sheppard Ward, secretary of the champion team.'

This fascinating report highlights several important features about village cricket in the Acle area in the early inter-war years:

* Gt Yarmouth's second newspaper considered the achievement of winning the league to be newsworthy

* the Freethorpe and District League was now sufficiently well-established to justify the award of gold medals (surely not real gold?) to the winners

* a member of the local gentry, Lady Frere, could be prevailed upon to make the awards - she was probably the mother of H Frere who represented South Walsham in 1921 and was almost certainly related, if only through marriage, to Sir Bartle Frere (see note below)

* the continuing association of the clergy with cricket, the Rev J Sheppard Ward being the Halvergate secretary

While local cricket was rising in stature, the history of South Walsham Cricket Club was also about to be enhanced by the arrival of a scion of the legendary cricketing family: the Edriches.

Note: Sir Bartle Frere was a colonialist in Cyprus and Gibralter who retired to South Walsham Hall in 1922. According to Amos's village history, he "joined in all the activities of the village." He was also a magistrate (Blofield bench), the High Sheriff of Norfolk and a County Councillor. During World War II he was County Controller of Air Raid Precautions. His family left South Walsham in 1947; he died in 1953 at the age of 90.

CHAPTER FOUR *The Edriches and the first 'golden age'*

In Chapter 1, it was noted that in South Walsham's first ever recorded match, against Blofield in 1908, the opposition contained two members of the cricketing-farming Edrich family. However, in 1925, a member of the clan - George Herbert Edrich - moved into South Walsham.

Born in 1897 in North Burlingham, he was one of eight children of Harry Edrich and wife, Elizabeth. George had previously played for Lingwood, Blofield and Stalham before his arrival in the village. He was a very useful cricketer, and it was said by those 'in the know' that, had he not been such a successful cattle auctioneer, he could have 'gone places' in cricket. He played for the representative side of East Norfolk and continued to be associated with South Walsham for the next forty years.

He also played for Ingham and, at their ground, for the All Edrich XI, whose charity games from the early 1930s to the mid 1960s, became a prominent feature of the Norfolk cricket scene. He was sufficiently committed to Ingham Cricket Club to be involved in helping them to purchase their ground in 1950. However, from a South Walsham perspective, as will be detailed later in this account, his crucial importance to the club's history was his role in the club's move to its present ground in 1948.

He served for many years on South Walsham parish council, with a lengthy period as chairman. After the Second World War, he spent some time in Australia and New Zealand, recuperating from a serious illness, but returned to South Walsham, where he died in 1982 at the age of 84 at his home, Glebe Cottage. He was probably Walsham's oldest player, playing his last game in August 1967 at the age of 70.

1926
From 1926, George or 'Uncle George', as he was frequently referred to, made a considerable difference to the strength of the Walsham side, although evidence of his first season is almost non-existent. Only one game was recorded, a victory over rivals Acle by 62 runs (90 to 28). There was no

record in the local press of the final league table.

1927
Blofield Heath entered the league in 1927, when Walsham again beat Acle, declaring on 119-8 before dismissing the opposition for 55, H Emmerson taking 5-21. In the return game, Walsham again came out on top by 30 runs (71 to 41) with 'Uncle George' taking 6-14. Towards the end of the season, a published league showed Walsham in a mid-way position having won six and lost six.

During this season, a 'League Cup' appeared, but it received scant publicity and was probably a mid-week league, with a membership of: Acle, St Edmunds, Woodbastwick, Halvergate, South Walsham, Upton, Ranworth, Blofield Heath and the interestingly-named Acle Unionist Hall. The competition appears to have been short-lived.

1928
Upton joined the league in 1928 but, again, few scorecards appeared in the press. In those games that were recorded, Walsham beat Cantley by 38 runs (65 to 27) and defeated Blofield Heath by 52 runs (107 to 55), with H Emmerson taking 4-23.

1929
Five results appeared for this season. Walsham again beat Acle 114 to 48 with W Emmerson taking 5-20, but Acle gained revenge in the reverse fixture by 47 runs (88 to 41). Walsham went down by 15 runs to Halvergate (61 to 46) but defeated Upton by 52 runs (106 to 54). They also played a friendly match against Ranworth and won by 46 runs (81 to 35).

1930
Three games were recorded. A victory over Blofield Heath by 20 runs (55 to 35) producing five-wicket hauls for Emmerson (5-13) and Turner (5-14). Clearly, 'Uncle George' was not the only useful player in the South Walsham ranks. Indeed, Emmerson was again among the wickets with amazing figures of 8-3 when Reedham were beaten by 53 runs (95 to 38). However, they gained revenge in the return match beating South Walsham by 14 runs (77 to 63).

1931

This season marked the peak of South Walsham's first 'golden age' when the years of steady progress culminated in the club winning the Freethorpe and District League. In this year, the other members were: Upton, Reedham, Blofield Heath, Halvergate, Cantley, Acle and Freethorpe. Although a final league table doesn't appear in the local press, with a week to go Walsham were clear winners having won eleven and lost two out of their fourteen games. Interestingly, both Acle and Freethorpe were docked two points for fielding an 'unregistered player', which suggests that not only was the league run on very organised principles, but the competing villages were not above gambling on playing the occasional 'ringer'!

'Uncle George's' name appeared regularly and he seemed to be a key player. When Walsham scored a 'mammoth' 114 against Halvergate, 'Uncle George' made 60, exactly Halvergate's total score. He also hit 47 not out in a total of 75, before Reedham were bowled out for 14, Goffin taking 7-8. Another win against Reedham by 8 runs (72 to 64) was, however, less decisive than the 36 run victory over Blofield Heath (55-8 against 19). The final league game saw a 16 run defeat to Freethorpe (66 to 50). As was traditional, in the final game of the season, in mid-August, South Walsham, as champions, played the rest of the league, but unfortunately, the result is unknown.

1932

South Walsham didn't have such a good year in 1932, but they still won more than they lost. Freethorpe were champions, although the league had reduced in size, only seven teams taking part. A rival league, the Beck Flegg League - named after a local farming family, or was this an early example of sponsorship? - had started and it is likely that both Acle and Upton shifted their allegiance.

In the games that were played, results were mixed. Walsham beat Lingwood by 18 runs (53-8 against 35), while against Reedham they followed up a small total of 55 by bowling out the opposition for a mere 10 runs. A press report stated that 'Uncle George' refused to bat; the Reedham wicket was obviously not to his liking!

There were defeats to Freethorpe by 16 runs (66 to 50) and to Halvergate by 38 runs (79 to 41). However, 'Uncle George' took 6-12 as Walsham beat

Blofield Heath by 38 runs (79 to 41) and starred in a big victory against Lingwood, hitting 48 out of a total of 116 and then taking 4-8 as the opposition were bowled out for 25. Goffin (5-4) returned even more impressive figures.

However, these two victories appear to mark the end of the first 'golden age' of cricket in South Walsham - a less successful period was about to begin.

CHAPTER FIVE *The Pre-War Slump*

The years leading up to the Second World War appear to have been very difficult for cricket in South Walsham. Indeed, the club, as constituted in the 1920s and early 1930s, may technically have gone out of existence in 1936.

1933
In two recorded games, South Walsham beat Lingwood by 102 runs (164 to 62) and this was followed by defeat against Cantley by 19 runs (107 to 88), despite the best endeavours of Emmerson who took 6-20 and top-scored with 27.

1934
In this season, Lingwood were again beaten by 15 runs (52 to 37), but Halvergate were victorious by 55 runs (102 to 47). Walsham also lost to Blofield 2nds by 22 runs (70 to 48), but this was followed by a rare draw against Cantley. They declared on 80-6, South Walsham replying with 57-5. However, whether rain played its part in this game is not clear.

1935
The only three matches recorded in 1935 were all defeats; by 74 runs to Freethorpe (130 to 56), 76 runs (116 to 40) against Halvergate and 3 runs (85 to 82) against Lingwood, a side that Walsham had beaten regularly in previous seasons. The first 'golden age' was clearly receding into the past.

1936-38
For the final pre-war seasons, not only were South Walsham not members of the Freethorpe and District League, but the league itself was floundering, continuing with just five member clubs. Indeed, it seems probable that a separate South Walsham club ceased to exist, as the only references to be found during these years were matches played as a joint Ranworth and South Walsham side. What may well have happened is that Walsham lost their ground and games were played at Ranworth.

In a game against Lingwood, in 1936, Ranworth and Walsham scored 68 and then skittled the opposition for 28, with Jimmy Curtis and Jack Foster taking

4 wickets apiece. These two names cropped up quite regularly during the 1930s and appear in a photograph of the team with a well-known local cricketing name - Maurice Watts. Another South Walsham player of this period was an E Pollard. Although it isn't definite, it seems to be highly probable that this was the Ernie Pollard who was still involved in maintaining the ground in the early 1970s.

No references to games played in 1937 and 1938 have been found, although it is quite possible that there were matches played on the Fountain Ground at Ranworth.

1939
However, in 1939, just before the outbreak of the Second World War several games were recorded. Norwich shoe factory side, Southalls, were beaten by 6 runs (69 to 63) with Foster taking 3-17 and Jermy 6-22. What appeared to be new opponents - Rollesby - were comfortably beaten by 52 runs (103-7 against 51). In this game, Maurice Watts hit 56 while Jack Foster took 6-8. Another win followed by 36 runs (57 to 21) against Blofield Heath, Hurren taking 5-10. Walsham also beat Railway Social by 31 runs (89 to 58), Hurren again picking up a good haul with 4-22.

South Walsham squad - circa 1934

Success continued in this final pre-war season, the return game with Blofield Heath ending in another victory for Ranworth and South Walsham by 30 runs (79 to 49), with 'Uncle George' scoring 55. Later in the season, the highest known Walsham score to this point was achieved with 185 against an H Parsons XI, T Mingay scoring 94. The opposition were bowled out for 105, Hurren taking 4-22. The final recorded game of the season was against the very impressive sounding North Norwich Imperial Junior League. However, their name must have been more impressive than their cricketing prowess as Ranworth and Walsham won by an innings and 31 runs. An innings of 164, with Maurice Watts scoring 70 and Jack Foster 34, was followed by bowling out the city side for 52 and 81, Watts taking 5-11 in the first innings. The only recorded defeat in 1939 seems to have been a quite heavy one of 41 runs to Rackheath (64 to 23).

With Watts, Foster, Mingay and Hurren in their prime, Walsham - with or without Ranworth - might have been ready to embark on a second golden age. However, six years of militaristic rumblings from Herr Hitler were about to climax in an invasion of Poland, precipitating the Franco-British declaration of war on 3rd September 1939.

CHAPTER SIX *Interlude - World War II*

Although the 1939 season was coming to a close as the German tanks rolled into Poland, by the time the 1940 season would have started, the war was going through its first decisive crisis. Churchill replaced Chamberlain as Prime Minister and, a month later, Operation Dynamo evacuated over 300,000 troops in the 'miracle of Dunkirk'. Sadly, however, few would have enjoyed a game of cricket that summer other than a knock-up in their military camp.

By summer 1941, with the entry of the United States, the ultimate result of the war was probably sealed, although the invasion of Britain remained a possibility for a few more months. The success of the Battle of Britain had significantly reduced the likelihood of this but, until US troops began pouring into Europe, 'Dad's Army' had to be on maximum alert.

What would have happened if a successful German invasion had taken place and the United States stayed out of the war? Would cricket have survived a 'nazification' of English culture or was the game too deeply embedded to be suppressed? One likes to think that it was, although whether the invaders would have 'got cricket' is less likely. The world's most famous cricket book - EW 'Jim' Swanton's 1939 copy of Wisden - certainly demonstrated the game's enduring hold, even on those battling to survive the demands of a Japanese prisoner-of-war camp.

Only three soldiers from South Walsham are recorded on the war memorial. There are no details on the death of Douglas Moore, while Alfred Bull and Norman Brown were both killed in Europe, one at Dunkirk, the other three months after D-Day. Whether any of the three was a member of the cricket club is unclear although, from their unfamiliar names, it is evident that none would have been a leading pre-war player. Their deaths would have been mourned by the community, although none of the three could be buried in the village.

Other than these three casualties, what impact would the war have had on South Walsham? Amos *(A History and Description of South Walsham)* records the setting up of units for air-raid precautions (ARP), the auxiliary fire service (AFS) and the Women's Royal Voluntary Service (WRVS), and the arrival of evacuee children from Bethnal Green, leading to overcrowding in the local school. As in the rest of the country, rationing would have been in force, but greater self-sufficiency in food was easier to organise than in the towns. Norwich was heavily bombed, but villages twelve miles outside the city received no attention from the Luftwaffe. One unexploded bomb was found close to the rectory, but there is no record of damage to lives or property. The village was too close to the marshes for a viable airstrip to be constructed. No one had an 'easy war', but a quiet Norfolk village would have been a less dangerous place than many.

However, cricket and war came together, in two ways, in the nearby village of Lingwood. Firstly, it was Bill Edrich's birthplace and the pre-war cricketing sensation - 219 in the famous 10-day Test in Durban in 1938 - had dramatically enhanced his reputation for courage as a fearless fighter pilot during low-level bombing raids on Cologne, for which he was awarded the DFC. Rather less dramatically, Lingwood was also the training location for the 14th platoon, 4th company, 6th battalion of the local defence volunteers (later renamed: the Norfolk Home Guard). The platoon commander was none other than Michael Falcon, who had captained the county for the entire twenty year inter-war period. A First World War veteran, Falcon - who lived in North Burlingham - is reported to have led his men with enthusiasm and commitment. Maybe not Field Marshall Montgomery, but any comparison with Capt Mainwaring would certainly have been equally misplaced.

One question would have dominated conversation: when would the war end? However, just possibly, for some, there would be a second question. On a warm summer's evening, two or three would gather together - servicemen on leave, older men just outside the conscription age range - and speculate. When would cricket return to the village? Mid-June..... the garden of the King's Arms.....a quiet pint...... the shared view that 'this would have been a perfect day for a game of cricket'. It would come...... and one man - 'Uncle George' - was almost certainly beginning to make plans.

CHAPTER SEVEN *Cricket Resumes...again!*

8th May 1945: VE-Day. The massive national celebrations reflected the view that 'normal' life could return. In the short term, however, this was impossible and it was over a year before any semblance of 'normality' was restored. Inevitably, 1945 was to be a quiet year for cricket. Victory in Europe came too late for games to be organised or indeed pitches to be prepared; many were lost in the drive to 'Dig for Victory'. Even Lords continued to act as a major centre for the demobilisation of thousands of servicemen. There was no first-class county season, although a series of 'Victory Tests' - exhibition games involving British and Australian servicemen - was held to meet the expected demand for entertainment. The public response was enormous and heralded the beginning of a period of unparalleled popularity for the game at international, county and club level.

In common with most clubs, cricket in South Walsham resumed in 1946 when, it appears, there was a full fixture list. Returning servicemen flocked back to the game in their thousands. One of Walsham's opponents in that year were a Norwich-based side - Fitness CC - a club set up, with government support, to encourage ex-servicemen to retain their physical standards.

Walsham's pre-war link with Ranworth had been severed - the club was now described as South Walsham and District Cricket Club - and had returned to the village playing just at a ground, just off the Panxworth Road. The first recorded game was against Rackheath on 2nd June 1946. If indeed this was the first game in the village for about ten years, it must have been eagerly anticipated not merely by the cricketers but by the whole community. After six years of war, 'normal' life.....cricket.....was back!

Evidently, the quality of cricket squares had not been a high priority during the war and run scoring was at a premium. In their first recorded game Walsham were bowled out for 33 but won by 12 runs as Rackheath managed only 21, with Sutton taking 5-1 and Hurren 5-5. Two weeks later, Walsham beat City Police, scoring 36 and dismissing the Police team for only 26, 'Uncle George' taking 5-10, Sutton 3-6 and Hurren 2-5.

Higher scores were achieved in a draw against Yarmouth Town, the opposition making 119-9, Walsham replying with 90-4. Four wins followed as Gothic were beaten by 45 runs (105 to 60), Halvergate by 61 runs (74 to 13), Martham by a 33 run margin (72 to 39) and, finally, a 51 run win against the ex-servicemen of Fitness by 51 runs (137 to 86). Clearly, Walsham had some reasonable talent on which to rebuild in the post-war era.

However, it is clear that 'Uncle George' wanted this rebuilding to include improved facilities to encourage the creation of an even higher quality side to represent the village. The official historian of South Walsham recounts the key developments:

'The club rented a field on the north side of the Panxworth Road on which they met and played. In 1947 the field was no longer available and the village decided there was a need for a permanent site for their recreation. The club and the Parish Council called a meeting to discuss possible sites and ways of raising money to purchase suitable land. It was finally decided that two Glebe fields covering about eight and a half acres of high well-drained land behind the School and running across to the Acle Road would be most suitable. The Rector, the Rev J F Williams was prepared to recommend the Glebe Commissioners to accept a reasonable offer. After negotiations it was agreed between the Commissioners, the Parish Council and George Edrich and the deal was concluded. A number of auction sales and other events were arranged to raise money for the purchase and the development.' (History and Description of South Walsham - G S Amos).

The reference to auctions can be explained by 'Uncle George's' profession. He was the local auctioneer in Acle with 'Young George', being the auctioneer's clerk. Along with 'Uncle George's' son, Peter, the three Edriches played a major part in the club, particularly in the bowling department, for the following twenty years.

1947 seems to have been another season of transition. Only nine games were recorded in detail, although it appears that between thirteen and eighteen may have been played, although when Norfolk were playing Walsham didn't seem to have a fixture. 'Uncle George' would have his own XI playing Ingham in all-day games while the village side were still playing matches, albeit of a higher standard than in the pre-war era. The main players other than the Edriches were: Frank Atkins, Pat Hood, Maurice

Watts, Jack Foster, R Curtis, Ronnie Hewitt, Ernie Pollard and John Gunton.

This group were involved in a narrow defeat at the hands of Hoveton and Wroxham (64 to 41) and in the next match, a win over City Police by 39 runs (92 to 53). In this match, Hewitt (27) headed the batting while Watts took 4-13. The latter scored a half century in the return fixture with Hoveton and Wroxham as Walsham amassed 154. Unfortunately, the rain came when Hoveton were on 45-3. Curtis and Watts both passed 30 as Walsham scored 131 against Gothic who were bowled out for 86. A one run win against Old Yarmouthians (87 to 86), Pollard taking 5-29, was followed by a draw against Yarmouth, a top side at the time. Yarmouth scored 127 (Watts 4-24) and Walsham replied with 116-7, Hood hitting 66 not out.

Later in the season, Walsham beat Old Yarmouthians for a second time, although again it was very close. The opposition scored 131 (Atkins 6-43) and Walsham replied with 137-9, Hood top scoring with 43. Atkins, who must have been a very useful all-rounder, hit 95 against Fitness in a total of 170, then took 4-7 as the ex-servicemen were bowled out for 60. The final recorded game of the season was the return fixture with Yarmouth, which again ended in a draw, Walsham scored 167-4 declared with Atkins (62) again in the runs; Yarmouth finished on 143-7. Totals were getting higher which suggests a significant improvement in the old wicket off Panxworth Road as a new ground was being prepared.

There was much work to be done to the square on the new playing field and this was mainly undertaken by 'Uncle George'. Pat Hood - who played for Walsham for 21 years (1947-1968) and continued to live in the village until he died a few years ago - has recounted that the square was George's pride and joy. He worked many hours to bring it up to the standard expected of a good quality wicket.

He also planned the fixture list, moving away from the pre-war Saturdays to Sunday games, with an occasional midweek match against a touring side. George had many contacts throughout Norfolk; he had played for Walsham since the mid 1920s and had also played for Blofield as well as for East Norfolk, so it was no surprise that he could arrange good quality fixtures. Pat Hood explained that Walsham became a very strong side playing the top clubs in the region, winning some and drawing many in the era before the limited overs game. These 'top clubs' included: Ingham, Dereham, Lowestoft, St Barnabas, Harleston and Hoveton and Wroxham - all were opponents that quite often included county players. There were fixtures further afield at Hadleigh, Rye and William Browns in Ipswich. The side had a very strong Edrich influence, sometimes having six members of the family playing in the same side with Edwin Edrich umpiring and one of the Edrich wives doing the scoring. 'Uncle George's' careful preparation had set the stage for Walsham's second 'golden age'.

CHAPTER EIGHT *The Second Golden Age begins 1948-51*

Sadly, Walsham cannot claim any credit for one of the two most famous members of the Edrich clan, as W J 'Bill' Edrich (39 Test caps in a career interrupted by World War Two) never played for the club. However, Bill's equally illustrious cousin John played regularly for several years as a teenager in the 1950s (his South Walsham career is outlined in the next chapter), while Bill's brother Eric, a Lancashire regular for several seasons, played a few games in the 1940s and 1950s. However, 'Uncle George' remained the prime force behind the club. In an article in the 'Eastern Daily Press' (September 1966), it was highlighted that he had been connected with South Walsham & District CC for 40 years and that a party was held in the village hall to celebrate this. However, other members of the family were important players. Pat Hood recalls Arthur as one of the best wicket keepers of that era not to play for Norfolk.

George C ('Young George'), when interviewed in preparation for this book, looked back on these years with great fondness. He played regularly up to the mid 1960s, remembering the pace of his cousin Peter, while he trundled away at the other end. One of his anecdotes recalled an occasion when Peter was bowling at his quickest against Lowestoft. The batsman got an edge, he stuck out a hand, and the ball nestled in his hand although he claims never to have seen it.'Young George' remembered with great pride when he took all ten wickets against St Barnabas:

'with Peter bowling quickly at the other end, I had to concentrate really hard to get the last couple otherwise Peter would have claimed them.'

As we talked, the ball was sitting on a plinth on his mantlepiece. He enjoyed his playing days, but retired after being left to clear up one Sunday when the rest of the team quickly departed to the 'Kings Arms'. Instead, he bought a car and spent his Sunday afternoons driving his wife around on trips.

This history could not have been written without the help of 'Young George' as he had all the South Walsham scorebooks from 1949 to 1962. His willingness to release these has resulted in over 1,400 games being recorded on the South Walsham Cricket Club website: southwalsham@play-cricket.com. He also produced some old fixture cards and dinner menus, copies of which appear in this book.

1948
The family played a major part in the seven recorded matches of the 1948 season. In the first game, Walsham went down to City College by 52 runs (116 to 64), the local newspaper recording that Edrich, probably 'Uncle George', took 5-16. Peter Edrich took 4-57 in Yarmouth's total of 174-6, Walsham replying with just 62. Peter also took 4-10 in a win against Barleycorns who were dismissed for 48. In the final recorded game of that season - a very low scoring-affair against Norwich Nondescripts - Walsham made 41 and the Nondescripts got home by 3 wickets, despite a fine effort from 'Uncle George' who took 5-3.

However, other members of the side did make an impact, Atkins taking 4-4 in a win against Barleycorns, after Walsham had scored 107 with Watts hitting 36. In the return game, Atkins showed his all-round qualities with a score of 92* which followed a 42 against Gothic, who won a tight game by six runs (120-9 to 114) despite Hood's 4-14. Later scorebooks show that Atkins must have been a powerful player who could hit the ball a long way, many of his innings containing several sixes. His career with Walsham lasted over 20 years during which time he scored over 2000 runs. He was also a useful bowler taking around 90 wickets.

1949
Thanks to the stewardship of 'Young George', full details of all games are available from the 1949 season. Of the 14 games played, Walsham won six and lost seven. Wins were achieved against Great Yarmouth (twice), Gothic (twice), Barleycorns and Ingham, while the defeats were against St Barnabas (twice), Barleycorns, Costessey, City Police, Old Yarmouthians and Ingham. Peter Edrich topped the batting averages with 200 runs, being the only player to average over 20. In the bowling, the three Edriches - Peter and the two Georges - took 72 wickets between them. Generally, scoring remained low but Walsham did pass 150 twice, both against Great Yarmouth. In the first game, a total of 201-7 included 76 from Eric Edrich, fresh from playing first class cricket and, in the return match, Walsham won comfortably scoring 162. 'Uncle George' took 8-17 as Gothic were bowled out for 26,

while the closest match of the season was a two run win against Ingham (137 to 135).

1950
The club was probably stronger in 1950, winning ten and losing just two of their thirteen matches. Peter Edrich took 50 wickets at 5.04 per wicket and, with the two Georges, took 115 wickets in just thirteen games. With Frank Atkins taking 11 wickets that left just 10 wickets for the rest of the bowlers. Although Walsham were only able to take nine wickets against Old Yarmouthians, they bowled out every other team.

Again it was a rather low-scoring season, although the wicket was slowly improving. Only two fifties were scored, Irving Stringer - a new name - scoring 76 against Ingham, as Walsham passed 200 for the only time that season, and Ronnie Hewitt hitting 55 in a total of 158-9 when defeating Hoveton and Wroxham. The best bowling was when Peter Edrich took 8-8 as Costessey were bundled out for 32. Victories came against Overstrand, Barleycorns (twice), Hoveton and Wroxham (twice), St Barnabas (twice), Ingham, Harleston and Costessey. The defeats were against City Police by two runs (45 to 43) and Lowestoft, with the only draw being against Old Yarmouthians.

1951
This was a more even season with six wins, five defeats and three draws. Frank Atkins was the leading run scorer, hitting 345 runs in twelve innings, with a high average for those days of 31.4. In the bowling department Peter Edrich, who made two appearances for Norfolk in 1951, led the way with 41 wickets. The season started with two defeats, an 18 run loss to Ingham followed by a 10 run defeat against Hoveton and Wroxham. In the return match against Ingham, Frank Atkins hit 83 and Irving Stringer 52 in a total of 251-9, but the bowlers couldn't dismiss Ingham who finished on 139-6 from 60 overs.

Walsham suffered a heavy defeat against Harleston and drew with Yarmouth, but won the return match by 22 runs. Harleston must have been a strong side as they again hammered Walsham by a large margin. Lowestoft held on for a draw when chasing Walsham's score of 152-7 declared, finishing on 104-8. Pat Hood led the way against Barleycorns with 61 out of a total of 172-7. Peter Edrich took 6-31 in Barleycorns' reply of 131. Atkins crashed another big score - 95 against City Police - who were quickly dismissed for 33. Overstrand were no match for Walsham losing by 63 runs as 'Uncle George' took 6-18. The last two games of the season saw a comfortable win over Barleycorns followed by a five wicket defeat at the hands of Hoveton and Wroxham.

Former player, Pat Hood, recalled these post-war seasons with great affection. Aside from the Edriches, he was proud to have opened the innings with George Head, with former Police Inspector, Harry Wright - coming in at number three. A decade later, Harry became 'bag man' and scorer for Norfolk. Many of the other players were either farmers or involved in working on the land and could usually arrange their work around their games of cricket.

But it was the Edrich clan who played the key part in the post-war development of cricket in South Walsham and the family must have been aware, for several years, that a true successor to the legendary 'Bill' was beginning to make his mark in school cricket for Bracondale. As he entered his teens, he was ready to enter the more competitive world of adult cricket.

WALSHAM IN THE FORTIES

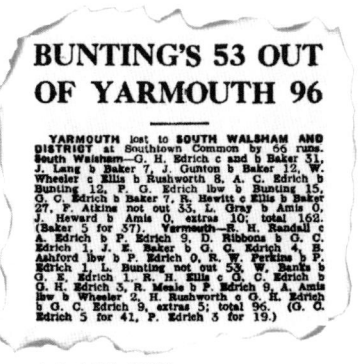

Another Good Innings by E. H. Edrich

E. H. Edrich followed his century on Saturday with another good innings at Yarmouth on Sunday. His 76 included 11 fours and helped South Walsham and District gain an easy win over Yarmouth Town.

South Walsham—E. H. Edrich b Bunting 76, J. Gunton b Bunting 0, W. Wheeler b Rushworth 2, G. H. Edrich b Baker 12, P. G. Edrich lbw b Rushworth 36, P. Hood b Rushworth 11, G. C. Edrich b Rushworth 8, P. Atkins not out 21, R. Hewitt not out 24, extras 11; total (7 wkts. dec.) 201. Rushworth (4 for 42.) Yarmouth Town—J. Ames b G. C. Edrich 0, R. Randall c P. Edrich b Wheeler 27, J. Baker c and b P. Edrich 4, W. Banks b P. Edrich 0, L. Bunting b P. Edrich 1, M. Maxwell b G. C. Edrich 0, R. Perkins c E. H. Edrich b G. C. Edrich 3, D. Harrison c G. C. Edrich b G. H. Edrich 3, P. Wright b Wheeler 3, R. Meale not out 5, H. Rushworth b G. H. Edrich 4, extras 6; total 61. (P. Edrich 5 for 4, G. C. Edrich 3 for 27.)

May 24th 1949

BUNTING'S 53 OUT OF YARMOUTH 96

YARMOUTH lost to SOUTH WALSHAM AND DISTRICT at Southtown Common by 66 runs. South Walsham—G. H. Edrich c and b Baker 31, J. Lang b Baker 7, J. Gunton b Baker 12, W. Wheeler c Ellis b Rushworth 8, A. C. Edrich b Bunting 12, P. G. Edrich lbw b Bunting 15, G. C. Edrich b Baker 7, R. Hewitt c Ellis b Baker 27, P. Atkins not out 33, L. Gray b Amis 0, J. Heward b Amis 0, extras 10; total 162. (Baker 5 for 37). Yarmouth—R. H. Randall c A. Edrich b P. Edrich 9, D. Ribbons b G. C. Edrich 1, J. E. Baker b G. C. Edrich 4, B. Ashford lbw b P. Edrich 0, R. W. Perkins b P. Edrich 1, L. Bunting not out 53, W. Banks b G. E. Edrich 1, R. H. Ellis b G. C. Edrich 0, G. H. Edrich 3, R. Meale b P. Edrich 9, A. Amis lbw b Wheeler 2, H. Rushworth c G. H. Edrich b G. C. Edrich 9, extras 5; total 96. (G. C. Edrich 5 for 41, P. Edrich 3 for 19.)

July 10th 1949

SOUTH WALSHAM AND DISTRICT CRICKET CLUB

MENU AND TOAST LIST

OF THE

FIRST ANNUAL DINNER

AT

The Sutton Staithe Hotel

On Tuesday, November 14th, 1950

at 7 p.m.

Chairman: Mr. P. Hood

SOUTH WALSHAM AND DISTRICT CRICKET CLUB

MENU AND TOAST LIST

OF THE

ANNUAL DINNER

AT

The South Walsham Kings Arms Hotel

On Tuesday, 29th January, 1952

at 7 p.m.

Chairman: Mr. P. Hood

Annual Dinner Cards for the first Annual Dinners which continued on and off until the early 1980's

---

South Walsham & District Cricket Club

FIXTURE CARD - 1949

OFFICERS—

President—
Maj. the Hon. H. R. BROUGHTON

Vice-Presidents—
Lt.-Col. H. J. Cator, M. Falcon Esq.,
Capt. C. H. Master, H. Boardman Esq.,
J. Bond Esq., F. Dunham Esq.,
W. E. Blizzard Esq., Maj. W. J. S. Fordyce,
Lt.-Col. L. V. Blacker, F. Rayns Esq.,
C. P. Watson Esq., B. Evans Esq.

Chairman—Mr. G. H. Edrich
Captain—P. Hood
Vice-Captain—M. Watts
Hon. Secretary—P. G. Edrich

Committee—
Messrs. G. H. Edrich, P. Hood, M. Watts,
P. G. Edrich, F. White, James Gray, J. Foster

Selection Committee—
P. Hood, F. White, James Gray

South Walsham & District Cricket Club

FIXTURE CARD - 1952

OFFICERS—

President—
Major the Hon. H. R. BROUGHTON

Vice-Presidents—
Lt.-Col. H. J. Cator, E. Pickering, Esq.
Capt. C. C. H. Master, F. Rayns, Esq.
Capt. E. Pennell, J. Bond, Esq.
Lt.-Col. N. V. Blacker, C. P. Watson, Esq,
Maj.-Gen. R. T. O. Carey, F. H. Dunham, Esq.
M. Falcon, Esq. J. B. Goodman, Esq.
W. E. Blizzard, Esq. John Cator, Esq.
H. Boardman, Esq. R. A. Gimbert, Esq.
B. Evans, Esq. A. Gibbs, Esq.
A. J. Symonds, Esq. C. Roofe, Esq.

Chairman—Mr. P. Hood
Captain—Mr. G. H. Edrich
Vice-Captain—Mr. R. Hewitt
Hon. Secretary & Treasurer—Mr. P. G. Edrich

Selection & General Committee—
Messrs. G. H. Edrich, R. Hewitt, P. Hood,
P. G. Edrich, E. H. Edrich, F. Atkins & J. Foster

Umpire—Mr. Edwin H. Edrich
Scorer—Mr. E. Pickering

Early Fixture Cards - unlikely to have been printed in the seasons before the Second World War.

CHAPTER NINE *A Star Is Born...*
Enter John Edrich

The second 'golden age' was, in all ways, more gleaming that the vintage years of the late 1920s and early 1930s. Dominated by the Edrich family, one name stands alone: John Edrich.

Few clubs in Norfolk can boast that a future county player spent his formative years learning the game in their ranks. Nationally, fewer still can claim to have nurtured the talents of a batsman who played 77 Test matches, scoring 5,138 runs at an average of 43.54 (higher than Atherton, Thorpe and Stewart - to name but three). Twelve centuries, twenty-four half-centuries, with a top score of 310* - one of only 21 players, including five Englishmen, to have reached this milestone - mark him out as one of the finest player of any era.

He is less frequently recalled than some of the greats, partially because his achievements were less impressive than his contemporary Geoffrey Boycott, who also has innumerable media opportunities to remind us of his heroic deeds. However, John Edrich's place in the shadows and footnotes of the game are also due to his acknowledged lack of an aesthetically-pleasing style. He was not Graveney, Dexter or Cowdrey (also contemporaries) but, like his Surrey colleague Ken Barrington, he was mightily effective.

Colin Bateman, described him as *'unflinching, unselfish, and often unsmiling while going about his business in the middle; he was a fiercely formidable opener who knew his limitations and worked wonderfully within them.'* (If the Cap Fits, 1993). His recall to the Test arena in 1976 at the age of 39 (with fellow veteran Brian Close, who was 46) to face the extreme hostility of the all-conquering West Indian attack - Roberts, Holding, Garner et al - was testimony to his reputation for courage and resilience. That he was unsuccessful in the infamous Saturday evening session at Old Trafford was unimportant to his reputation; it was universally acknowledged that only John Edrich and Close had the mental and physical toughness to withstand Clive Lloyd's fast bowling juggernaut.

An England captain - he held the reins for one Test in a tour of Australia when Lillee and Thomson were at their peak - he learned his cricket on the playing field at South Walsham, playing over fifty games, after starting as a thirteen year old in 1952. Former player Pat Hood had a bet with the old Ingham campaigner Jack Borrett that John would play for England by the time he was twenty-one; Pat lost his bet because John did not receive his first cap until he was twenty-three. It must have been a selectorial oversight! John acknowledges the club's contribution to his cricketing education in his autobiography ' Runs in the Family' and in the 1966 'Wisden', where he mentions his early days of playing cricket for South Walsham on a Sunday and Blofield Village on a Saturday. As an early indication of his outstanding application, in his first season, as a thirteen year-old, he finished top of the batting averages scoring 218 runs at 27.25.

1952

Although to some extent overshadowed by the young prodigy, Frank Atkins continued to bat well with 241 runs, while both Peter and 'Young George' took 43 wickets. Ingham hammered Walsham in the first game of the season - by 118 runs - but they came back in the next match to comfortably beat Hoveton and Wroxham by 76 runs, with Pat Hood hitting 58. There was a quick revenge against Ingham, as Walsham hit 202 while Ingham could only muster 73. Three more wins followed against Harleston, Lowestoft and Acle, before St Barnabas comfortably won by 5 wickets. Easy wins came against Ipswich Greyhounds and Barleycorns, with Atkins hitting half centuries in both games, while John Edrich passed fifty for the first time against Overstrand. In the final game of the season, Hoveton and Wroxham scored a creditable 167, despite Peter Edrich taking 8-36, but forties from 'Uncle George' and Ronnie Hewitt saw Walsham home by four wickets. In the fourteen games that were played Walsham won nine, drew two and lost two.

1953

Nationally, 1953 was a vintage year: the conquest of Everest, the Coronation, the Matthews FA Cup final and, for the cricket-loving public, the return of the Ashes after being in Australian hands for almost twenty years. And who was at the crease, with Dennis Compton, as England won at the Oval by 8 wickets? None other than Bill Edrich - the family hero - World War II pilot extraordinaire and now Ashes winner. This must have reverberated around the villages of east Norfolk where his clan farmed, auctioned and cricketed.

Resonating with national euphoria, South Walsham and District CC had a highly successful season, winning eleven and drawing three of their eighteen games. For the second consecutive season, John finished top of the batting averages with 471 runs from fifteen innings and an average of 39. At the age of 14, he also scored his first century. The chances of him emulating cousin Bill must have been the subject of many a post-match inquest in the 'King's Arms'. Keeping it in the family, 'Young George' had his most successful season, taking an amazing 66 wickets from 233 overs at an average of 6.02.

```
South Walsham & District
        Cricket Club
FIXTURE CARD   -   1953
           OFFICERS
          President—
         J. BOND, ESQ.
        Vice-Presidents—
     Maj. the Hon. H. R. Broughton
Lt.-Col. H. J. Cator      A. J. Symonds, Esq.
Capt. C. C. H. Master     E. Pickering, Esq.
Capt. E. Pennell          F. Rayns, Esq.
Lt.-Col. N. V. Blacker    C. P. Watson, Esq.
M. Falcon, Esq.           F. H. Dunham, Esq.
W. E. Blizzard, Esq       J. B. Goodman, Esq.
B. Evans, Esq.            John Cator, Esq.
C. Roofe, Esq.            A. M. Gibbs, Esq.

      Chairman—Mr. P. Hood
      Captain—Mr. R. Hewitt
   Vice-Captain—Mr. G. H. Edrich
Hon. Secretary & Treasurer—Mr. P. G. Edrich
    Selection & General Committee—
 Messrs. G. H. Edrich, P. Hood, R. Hewitt,
 F. Atkins, J. Foster, E. H. Edrich, P. G. Edrich
       Umpire—Mr. E. H. Edrich
       Scorer—Mr. E. Pickering
    Loader & Son, North Walsham
```

Despite starting with a disappointing defeat against Barleycorns by 50 runs, one of the highlights of the season followed - a one wicket win over Ingham, 'Young George' taking 6-38 as they were bowled out for 127. After a good opening stand between Ronnie Hewitt and Pat Hood, Walsham collapsed, but a young John Edrich held the innings together with 35 not out to see Walsham home. Narrow wins followed against Dereham and Hoveton and Wroxham, before St Barnabas held out for a draw, finishing on 106-8 chasing the Walsham total of 154-9 declared. However, only John Edrich reached double figures as Norwich Wanderers bowled Walsham out for 66 to win comfortably.

Walsham passed the 200 mark three times in 1953, their top score being 238-7 declared against Ingham who held on at 146-9 from 62 overs with 'Young George' taking 6-19 from 17 overs. Amazingly, in the next match, Harleston bowled out Walsham for 66 only for the home side to dismiss

Harleston for 65 with 'Young George' again taking 6-19, this time from 18.1 overs. More wins followed against Holmes Social from Yarmouth, St Barnabas and Harleston again, with Peter Edrich taking 8-26 from 11.3 overs in their total of just 53. Walsham also proved to be too good for Lowestoft: 195-8 declared against 115 all out.

The other two high scores of the season were: 223-5 declared, with Ipswich Greyhounds hanging on for a draw at 149-7, then 208-5 declared against City Police, John Edrich (109*) scoring his first century. 'Young George' soon saw off the Police with 8-39. The closing matches of the season saw wins over Dereham and Overstrand but defeat against Palmers School, a touring side from Grays in Essex. This game was well remembered by Peter Collins who played for Palmers School at the time:

'I remember the match against South Walsham very well. The name Edrich was of course very well known to all cricketers. John's reputation had preceded him. In the event we got him out for a duck, the home umpire gave him out LBW and John did little to hide his contempt for the decision. South Walsham were soon out for a very low score and we knocked the runs off for a convincing win. There was plenty of time left it being an all-day affair, so we started again. This time John spent his time pushing and nudging the ball about until applause from the pavilion signalled his fifty. He had scored this in such a quiet manner we were surprised that he had done so. The day was one of many special days we experienced on these tours.'

The final game of the season saw a comfortable win against Hoveton and Wroxham. Walsham's 1953 had more than matched the national mood.

1954

This was another successful season, with eleven wins and four draws out of nineteen completed matches. Once again it was 15 year old John Edrich who topped the batting charts, passing 500 runs at an amazing average, for those days, of 85.3. It would be another twenty-two years before Jack Denton became the second player to pass the 500 run mark in a season. Irving Stringer also scored well with 333 runs at 41.6. The bowlers were led by 'Young George' and Peter Edrich who took 56 and 48 wickets respectively, both bowling over 200 overs. After the abandonment of the first game against Barleycorns, Walsham hammered Ingham by 142 runs after scoring

212-5 declared. They then cruised to comfortable wins against Dereham, who had a youthful Peter Parfitt - later an England colleague of John Edrich - in their ranks, and Hoveton and Wroxham, with Walsham passing the 200 mark once again with 211-7. Stringer and Peter Edrich both scored fifties against St Barnabas as they were bowled out for 150, but the opposition held on at 120-8.

In the return match against Ingham 'Young George' and Peter Edrich took ten wickets between them as they dismissed Ingham for just 84. John Edrich and Stringer guided Walsham home easily by 8 wickets. Another win followed - by six wickets against Harleston - before Walsham scored one of their highest ever totals, 279-8 against King's College, Cambridge, with John Edrich and 'Uncle George' hitting half centuries. Peter and the two Georges shared the ten wickets as the students were bowled out for 83. Another touring side, North Middlesex, suffered defeat as Walsham passed the 200 mark again (218 all out) with Ronnie Hewitt hitting 78. Peter Edrich took 6-31 in the tourists' total of 127.

Returning to local opposition, a win against Holkham followed, but a 20-over match with Norwich Union ended in a 19 run defeat before a hammering at the hands of Harleston by 9 wickets, and a draw against Kingfishers (a Yarmouth club). Two wins followed against Palmers School and Barleycorns. Once again, John Edrich (101*) took a liking to the City Police bowling in a total of 238-3. The Police only managed 66, 'Young George' taking 5-9. Walsham passed 200 again with 223-6 against Dereham, who held on for the draw at 101-8. A very friendly game against the Strangers Club - a lot of the Walsham players were playing for the opposition - resulted in a 33 run defeat. The season came to a close as Hoveton and Wroxham narrowly got the better of Walsham (83 to 78). Hoveton had Henry Blofeld -

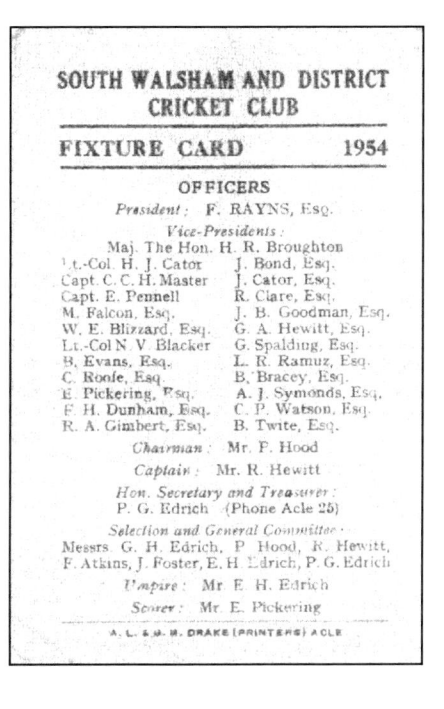

another to play first class cricket for Cambridge University, before becoming a highly distinguished cricket writer and broadcaster - in their ranks. However, he was not quite fifteen at the time and, clearly less of a precocious talent than John Edrich. He only managed two runs before being bowled by 'Young George', whose 6-21 was, however, not enough to give Walsham victory.

John was now making his mark for Norfolk and Surrey seconds and, although he played a few games in 1955 and 1956, he moved on as his talent demanded. However, his three years with the club had established the foundation of an outstanding career.

WALSHAM IN THE FIFTIES

South Walsham and District beat City Police at South Walsham by 160 runs. **South Walsham** —J. Lang b Chenery 1, J. Gunton b Reeve 7, P. Edrich lbw b Reeve 1, J. Webb b Reeve 4, T. Mack b Reeve 9, P. Hood c Riches b Reeve 3, F. Atkins c Martin b Foulger 95 (including 14 fours), J. Foster b K. Swann 24, A. Hawkshaw not out 25, A. Ling not out 4, extras 20; total (8 wkts. dec.) 193. G. Edrich did not bat. (Reeve 5 for 60). **City Police** —H. Wright c Hawkshaw b P. Edrich 8, J. Riches run out 3, G. Postance b J. Webb 0, C. Reeve b J. Webb 4, P. Chenery c G. Edrich b J. Webb 6, K. Swann c Hood b P. Edrich 4, E. Foulger b P. Edrich 0, A. Clayton b P. Edrich 0, C. Higby b P. Edrich 0, C. Martin not out 3, F. King c Foster b P. Edrich 1, extras 4; total 33. (P. Edrich 6-11, including hat trick).

August 5th 1951

Lowestoft drew with South Walsham at Denes Oval. **South Walsham** —J Gunton b Cole 6, P. G Edrich c Wharton b Cole 9, R. Hewitt c Jermy b Woosnam 20, I. Stringer b Woosnam 12, J. Webb not out 60, F. Atkins c Butcher b Strong 6, A. Hawkshaw b Butcher 6, A. Edrich b Cole 2, G. H. Edrich not out 16 extras 15; total 152-7 dec. **Lowestoft** —E. Jermy b P. Edrich 2, D. Wharton b P. Edrich 10, B. Woosnam b Webb 2, R. Patrick lbw b A. Edrich 16, P. Golding b P. Edrich 4, K. Strong b A. Edrich 6, R. Watson run out 1, R. Butcher b P. Edrich 20, B. Andrews not out 25, R. Morton not out 12, extras 6; total 104-8 (P. Edrich 4-38).

July 15th 1952

South Walsham beat Harleston by 75 runs at Harleston. **South Walsham** —P. Hood b H. Courridge 38, G C Edrich b E. Moss 0, R. Hewitt c Moss b H. Courridge 19, J. Edrich c T. Ohsten b H. Courridge 28, J. Lang b H. Courridge 0, A. Edrich c R. Youngs b H. Cour-

Scoring 28 runs for South Walsham against Harleston at Harleston yesterday, 15-year-old J. Edrich completed 1000 runs for the season.

ridge 13, F. Atkins c D. Courridge b D. Woodbridge 43, D. G. Edrich c H. Courridge b S. Taylor 4, Williams run out 2, C. Newman b H. Wright 10, J. Foster b H. Wright 1. D. Pluckrose not out 1, extras 7; total 166 (Courridge 5-36). **Harleston** —R. Youngs b P. G. Edrich 0, F. Courridge b G. C. Edrich 6, D. Woodbridge c A. Edrich b P. G. Edrich 4, S. Boot b P. G. Edrich 21, L. Bond c P. G. Edrich b G. C. Edrich 1, S. Amoss c C. Newman b G. C. Edrich 7, T. Oh'ten b G. C. Edrich 0, H. Wright st A. Edrich b P. Hood 25, E. Moss lbw b C. Newman 5, S. Taylor c Hewitt b G. C. Edrich 3, H. Courridge not out 11, J. C. Edwards b G. C. Edrich 3, extras 5; total 91 (G C Edrich 6-30). J. Edrich, 15 years old completed 1000 runs this season).

July 5th 1952

South Walsham beat Barleycorns at South Walsham by 104 runs. **South Walsham** —P. Hood c Skinner b Barley 29, G. C. Edrich c Stevenson b Youell 8, J. Lang b Barley 7, G. H. Edrich c Blyth b Barley 3, J. Gunton b Barley 8, F. Atkins c Lanham b Tomlinson 54, T. Mack b Tomlinson 6, A. Edrich not out 12, P. G Edrich not out 9, extras 9; total (7 wkts. dec.) 145. (Barley 4-43). **Barleycorns** —B. Skinner b G. C. Edrich 26, J. Holt Wilson b G. C. Edrich 0, F. Larking b G. C. Edrich 1, G. Stevenson c P. G. Edrich b G. C. Edrich 0, P. Reeves c Mack b P. G. Edrich 0, C. Lanham lbw b G. C. Edrich 0, D. Barley c A. Edrich b G. C. Edrich 1 Tomlinson c G. C. Edrich b P. G. Edrich 1, R. Blyth b P. G. Edrich 0, A. Youell c P. G. Edrich 1, P. James not out 10, extra 1; total 41. (G. C. Edrich 6-14, P. G. Edrich 4-26).

August 10th 1952

Lowestoft lost to South Walsham by 80 runs. **South Walsham** —R. Hewitt c Capon b Jermy 55, G. H. Edrich run out 36, J. Edrich c D. Wharton b Roper 36, I. Stringer b Baldry 16, K. Mayhew c Nickells b Jermy 4, J Gunton c Cook b Jermy 19, F. Atkins b Roper 5, T. Mack not out 11, P. Edrich lbw Jermy 0, G. C. Edrich not out 4, extras 9; total (8 wkts. dec.) 195. (Jermy 4-34). **Lowestoft** —M. Macpherson c G. H. Edrich b G. C. Edrich 1, A. Nickells c and b G. C. Edrich 8, E. Jermy c P. Edrich b Mayhew 30, R Capon b P Edrich 39, P. Wharton c and b Mayhew 0, D. Wharton b Mayhew 0, P. King b G. C. Edrich 8, R. Watson b G. C. Edrich 0, J Baldry b G. H Edrich 19, F. Cook lbw G. C. Edrich 5, L. Roper not out 1, extras 4; total 115. (G. C. Edrich 5-40).

July 19th 1953

CHAPTER TEN *The Edrich Era Continues...*
but without John

1955

This was not such a successful season: only five wins and five draws from seventeen games completed. The leading run scorer was not an Edrich as George Head had been persuaded to join the club. In his first season George scored 394 runs. He was well-known around the Norfolk cricket circuit playing for other clubs such as Dereham and St Barnabas. In all he played sixty times for Walsham during the 1950s; he also kept wicket claiming over 40 victims. 'Uncle George', Peter Edrich and Pat Hood all passed the 240 run mark in the season and 'Young George' bowled 297 overs - no one has bowled so many before or since - taking 61 wickets at 11.0, with Peter picking up 41.

The season started with a defeat at Ingham, as Walsham were bowled out for 131 in 50 overs, Ingham knocked off these runs with only one wicket down. Comfortable wins followed against Dereham, Lowestoft and St Barnabas, Peter Edrich taking six wickets in the Dereham and Lowestoft games setting easy targets for the Walsham batsmen. The St Barnabas match was very much a highlight of the season and the career highlight for 'Young George' who took all 10 wickets: six bowled, three caught and one lbw. Walsham scored 160-9 declared with St Barnabas all out 71, 'young George's' figures being 15.3-5-25-10.

Walsham lost again to Ingham before beating Barleycorns at Barton Turf by 84 runs, both Peter and 'Young George', bowling unchanged, taking five wickets - no taking the foot off the gas in those days. A draw with St Barnabas followed, 'Young George' only managing four wickets this time and defeat came against Harleston, who dismissed Walsham for 84 and easily knocked off the runs. Another highlight of the season was the all-day game against Hadleigh, where Walsham scored an impressive 269-8 declared in 61 overs, Peter Edrich making his highest score of 124 not out. Hadleigh responded with 198-9 from 50 overs, with 'Young George' taking 6-71, all bowled.

Narrow defeats followed: against Lowestoft (153 to 139), and Ipswich

Greyhounds who chased down 139 to win by 2 wickets. More impressively, 'Uncle George' and George Head both scored fifties in Walsham's total of 172 against Hoveton and Wroxham. In a tight match Hoveton finished on 171-9 with John Blofeld - Henry's brother and later a High Court judge - hitting 82. However, Arthur Edrich took two timely stumpings to save Walsham from defeat.

Defeats came at Dereham, by one wicket, despite 5-42 from Peter Edrich, while a mid-week match was lost to the tourists of Palmers School. Several Hoveton and Wroxham players guested for Walsham that day, including Henry Blofeld who, unfortunately, managed to score only two. Frank Atkins led the way with 76 not out in a six wicket win over Barleycorns and there was an honourable draw against the Strangers Club. Another tight draw occurred against Hoveton and Wroxham. Walsham were bowled out for 105, Hoveton finishing on 77-9 in 42 overs, with 'Young George' and Ken Mayhew bowling unchanged. The latter was a useful performer who had played for Norfolk just after the Second World War. He played on and off for Walsham from 1953 to 1967: 98 games for over 1200 runs and 136 wickets - a useful, but hardly dramatic, record for an ex-county player.

1956
This season saw the return of John Edrich for six games, in which he scored 360 runs at 97.5; the only other batsman to pass 300 runs was Irving Stringer. Peter Edrich was again the leading wicket taker with 64, while 'Young George' spent part of the season on the injured list and played only a few games. However, it was a successful season - eleven wins and three draws from nineteen completed matches - 'Uncle George' relying on his many contacts to put out a strong side. As usual, the first fixture was against Ingham, who had some excellent players at this time, many of whom played for Norfolk. They included Ted Witherden, Norfolk's professional for seven years. He played for Carrow on Saturday, but they didn't have Sunday fixtures, possibly a legacy of the Colman family's nonconformist views on Sunday sport. Walsham only managed 125 and lost heavily, Witherden making an impact with both bat and ball.

Defeat followed at Dereham, but Lowestoft, who only managed 45, were hammered, and a 77 run win against St Barnabas put Walsham back on track. Peter Edrich picked up thirteen wickets in those two games. Walsham fared better in their return match with Ingham. Chasing 194-7 they managed

140-5 with John Edrich, putting in an appearance to bolster the batting, top scoring with 48.

Ipswich Greyhounds once again beat Walsham in a tight match, this time by just one wicket. The 200 mark was passed against Hadleigh, who collapsed against the bowling of Ken Mayhew who took the first five wickets in a total of just 92. Another hammering by Harleston was followed by a comfortable win against Dereham, Irving Stringer scoring 57 in a total of 201-5 declared. Guest player R Tomkys took 7-28 in reply as Dereham were bowled out for 116. Lowestoft were clearly struggling at the time as they managed just 36 in a one-sided game, while the first President's game ended in an honourable draw.

John Edrich (116*) returned against Hoveton and Wroxham, which led to an easy victory by 124 runs. More wins followed over the Strangers Club and Hoveton and Wroxham for the second time. However, Hadleigh were a sterner proposition on their home ground as they won by 37 runs. The final two games finished in victories against Fakenham and St Barnabas, John Edrich scoring half centuries in both matches.

1957
This season saw Walsham playing eighteen games, with six wins and six defeats. Ken Mayhew finished top of the batting averages, but only Irving Stringer (218) passed the 200 run mark. With 'Young George' still not playing regularly, Peter Edrich, Ken Mayhew and Brian Cator were the only three bowlers to bowl more than 100 overs. Peter took 48 wickets at 8.6, while the remainder were shared between six other bowlers.

The season started with a draw against Ingham. Chasing 171-6 declared, Walsham could only manage 97-6. Peter Parfitt, who had joined the Middlesex staff the previous year proved that, as a young professional playing alongside legends like Denis Compton and Bill Edrich, he was now rather too good for club cricket when returning to play for Dereham. Walsham were bowled out for 110 - Mayhew hitting 50 - with Parfitt taking three wickets. He then hit 77 not out as Dereham won in just 18 overs.

A draw followed against Barleycorns and then a defeat at Lowestoft. An exciting game against St Barnabas saw the home side hit 186-9 declared, 'Uncle George' making 42. 'Young George' then did his best to win the game with 5-41 from 20 overs, but St Barnabas held on at 170-9. There was a defeat against Ingham by 27 runs in a low-scoring game and another defeat at the hands of Harleston, despite Peter Edrich's 6-40.

In a high-scoring game against Hadleigh, 'Uncle George' led the way with 64 in a total of 220-8 in 67 overs. Walsham bowled just 46 overs back at Hadleigh as they finished on 151-6. A five run defeat against St Barnabas was followed by a rare win against Harleston, who managed only 69 with Peter Edrich and Tony Pennington both taking five wickets. Walsham's batting struggled, but they got home by 2 wickets. A similar result occurred at Lowestoft, who scored 99 - Peter Edrich taking 7-47 - Walsham replying with 100-8.

Walsham beat two old rivals in close encounters: Hadleigh by 16 runs (123 to 107) and Hoveton and Wroxham by 2 wickets. Chasing 88 - Brian Cator had taken 5-18 - Walsham battled their way to 89-8. John Edrich made one of his increasingly rare appearances hitting 101 in a total of 183-9 against the Strangers Club, who were bowled out for 107. A comfortable 7-wicket win against Palmers School followed, but the season petered out with the last two games failing to finish due to the weather.

1958

This season proved a little more successful with seven wins and five draws from seventeen games completed. Peter Edrich seemed to be concentrating on his batting, scoring 387 at an average of 29.8. Basil Tibbenham also scored 251 runs, including the only century of the season - 105 against Strangers Club - which helped Walsham to an easy win. He was well known locally, playing most of his cricket for St Andrews Hospital and Acle and was a fine, free-scoring opening bat, but this was his only century for Walsham in around seventy games. Wickets were shared between Peter Edrich (41), Tony Pennington (33), 'Young George' (31) and Brian Cator (21).

The season started well with a good win over Ingham. Peter Edrich hit 54 in a total of 161, and then 'Young George' took 7-29 as Ingham managed just 126. However, Walsham were no match for Dereham, losing by eight wickets. A draw against Barleycorns was followed by three defeats: by 53 runs against Lowestoft, who now seemed a force again; 70 runs against St Barnabas with Walsham cleaned out for 57; then, in a close match with Ingham, losing by 3 wickets (110 to 111-7) with Peter Edrich and Tony

Pennington bowling 49.2 overs before Ingham secured their win.
Two low-scoring draws with Harleston and Dereham were followed by a very tense one wicket defeat against Hadleigh. Walsham scored 117 from 60 overs, Hadleigh replying with 118-9 from 44 overs. In the two matches against Hoveton and Wroxham, one was drawn as Hoveton held on at 87-9 when chasing 110, but the other was lost by 61 runs (193 to 132).

As the season drew to a close, there was another draw against Barleycorns and a comfortable win against Houghton in which 'Young George' took 5-55 as the opposition declared on 136-9. Peter Edrich then led the way with 52 not out in a seven wicket win. In the final game, Fakenham failed to make a hundred with Peter Edrich once again catching the eye with 4-8 from 9 overs. John Edrich hit 43 as Walsham romped home.

1959
Nineteen games were played: eight wins, two draws and seven defeats from the seventeen games completed. Three players passed the 250 run mark: Pat Hood (365) led the way followed by Peter Edrich (305) and Basil Tibbenham (284). Peter Edrich had a very productive season with the ball, taking 58 wickets at 9.8; Brian Cator, Tony Pennington and 'Young George' all passed the twenty mark..

With the first game against Ingham abandoned, Walsham soon got into their stride with a 43 run win against Dereham. Edriches were to the fore: Peter (50) and 'Young George' (5-22). They were then hammered by Lowestoft, only to narrowly beat St Barnabas by 16 runs with Peter Edrich taking an incredible 8-23 from just 12 overs. Ted Witherden led the way for Ingham with 86 as they scored 203-5 declared and, despite a gutsy 49 from 'Uncle George', Walsham were dismissed for 156.

Pat Hood made the highest score of his South Walsham career when he hit 120 out of 190-7 against Harleston, who were beginning to fade as a top side. They collapsed to just 50 all out, Tony Pennington taking 7- 20 from 9 overs. However, Civil Service Crusaders, a touring side, proved to be very strong knocking up 224-7, only Brian Cator (69*) and Basil Tibbenham (36) putting up resistance as Walsham fell well short.

In an exciting all-day game at Hadleigh, Walsham battled to 174 from 62 overs, but an excellent reply of 176 -8 from 50 overs saw the Suffolk side home. Harleston suffered again in a low-scoring game. Walsham made only 46, but Harleston were all out in 12 overs for just 17, Brian Cator taking 7-5 from 6 overs. Only five Harleston batsmen got off the mark. The Lowestoft and Dereham games were drawn before Hadleigh gained another win, this time by 34 runs, in a low scoring game (136 to 102).

Defeat against Hoveton and Wroxham owed much to Henry Blofeld (69), who had just left Cambridge University after only two years and without completing his degree. Walsham then went on a three match winning streak: hitting 235-6 against the Strangers Club who replied with only 85; defeating Palmers School by 113 runs, Maurice Watts making 126 out of 265-4 declared; winning comfortably against Barleycorns with Ken Mayhew (84) hitting his top score for the club, before 'Young George' picked up 5-26 to dismiss Barleycorns for 115. In the two final games Hoveton and Wroxham won again, this time by 15 runs (81 to 66), but the final game of the season ended with a win over Fakenham, thanks to Peter Edrich (7-50 and 53*).

The Edrich era continued but, as the 1950s gave way to the 1960s, the second golden age of South Walsham cricket was beginning to draw to a close. However, before the slow decline is explored in detail, it would seem to be appropriate to engage in a retrospective consideration of cricket in the 1950s.

WALSHAM IN THE FIFTIES

Lowestoft lost to South Walsham at Lowestoft by nine runs. **South Walsham**—G. C. Edrich lbw b Woosnam 4, G. H. Edrich c and b Perkins 24, C. Stringer b Perkins 28, J. Edrich c Jermy b Perkins 10, P. G. Edrich c Patrick c Fordham 34, F. Atkins b Perkins 7, A. Eades c and b Jermy b Fordham 20, J. Lang b Woosnam 9, T. Mack c Baldwin b Fordham 2, C. Newman not out 0, J. Foster st Baldwin b Woosnam 0; total 137. (Perkins 4–36.) **Lowestoft**—P. Baldwin lbw b F. G. Edrich 0, D. Wharton b G. C. Edrich 5, L. Jermy b P. G. Edrich 1, B. Patrick b G. C. Edrich 4, R. Perkins c G. C. Edrich b P. G. Edrich 75, D Fordham c and b C. Newman 32, A. Knight b P. G. Edrich 2, B. Bedford b G. C. Edrich 3, B. Woosnam b G. C. Edrich 6, R. Morton not out 1, J. Cole c Atkins b P. G. Edrich 0, extras 2; total 128. (P. G. Edrich 5–40. G. C. Edrich 4–49.).

July 20th 1952

Dereham drew with South Walsham at Dereham. **South Walsham**—G. Head run out 40, R. Hood c Chamberlain b Masters 6, J. Edrich c and b Webb 52, J. Stringer c Merrison b Cook 51, G. H. Edrich b Cook 53, R. Hewitt not out 6, K. Mayhew st Cordle b Brand 8, extras 7; total (6 dec.) 223. **Dereham**—T. Thompson c Stringer b Mayhew 42, L. Potter c Hood b R. G. Edrich 0, D. Chamberlain c Hood b R. G. Edrich 7, R. Perkins b G. C. Edrich 14, G. Merrison c and b R. G. Edrich 1, J. F. R. Cook lbw R. G Edrich 0, W. J. Webb not out 5, C. C. Cordle b G C. Edrich 4, F. G. Masters not out 6, extras 8; total (8 wkts.) 101.

August 15th 1954

South Walsham lost to Ipswich Greyhounds by 2 wickets. **South Walsham**—G. Head c Boulter b Waples 35, P. Hood c Gosling b Nightingale 10, R. Hewitt c Waples 0, P. G. Edrich c Studd b Burman 11, G. H. Edrich b Nightingale 37, P. Wright c Burman b Nightingale 21, A. Hawkshaw b Perkins 1, A. Edrich not out 12, D. Edrich b Nightingale 1, J. Foster st Studd b Perkins 2, G. C. Edrich c Studd b Nightingale 1, extras 8; total 139. (Nightingale 5–36.) **Ipswich Greyhounds**—J. Hamond lbw G. C. Edrich 28, D. Hale b G. C. Edrich 46, P. Crane b Hood 14, F. Gosling lbw G. C. Edrich 17, M. Philpot b Hood 10, P. Boulter c A. Edrich b Hood 2, C. Burman b Hood 2, C. Perkins c A. Edrich b G. C. Edrich 1, C. Studd not out 5, R. Waples not out 5, extras 10; total (8 wkts.) 140. (Hood 4–44, G. C. Edrich 4–45.)

July 24th 1955

South Walsham drew with Hoveton at South Walsham. **South Walsham**—G. Head c Harrison L Nickerson 63, P. Hood b Tink 11, R. Perkins lbw Tink 0, P. G. Edrich lbw Parker 3, P. Wright st Harmer b Nickerson 10, A. Edrich b Parker 1, G. H. Edrich not out 56, P. Atkins c and b Smith 0, G. C. Edrich c and b Tink 1, J. Foster c Parker b Nickerson 19, D. Edrich lbw Tink 0, extras 8; total 172. (Tink 4–30, Nickerson 3–36.) **Hoveton**—N. Yallop c G. C. Edrich b G. H. Edrich 45, F. Roy lbw G. C. Edrich 2, J. Blofield c and b P. G. Edrich 82, D. Nickerson b P. G. Edrich 2, D. Savory lbw G. C. Edrich 23, S. Harrison c D. Edrich b G. H. Edrich 5, A. Tink st A. Edrich b G. H. Edrich 0, M. Nickerson c Hood b G. H. Edrich 0, K. Smith not out 0, C. Parker st A. Edrich b G. C. Edrich 0, N. Harmer not out 1, extras 11; total 171-9. (G. C. Edrich 3–59. G. H. Edrich 4–23.)

August 7th 1955

South Walsham drew with Stranger's Club at South Walsham. **South Walsham**—G. Head c Simpson b Wharton 12, P. Hood b Colman 31, R. Perkins c Webb b Wharton 11, R. Hewitt c Eades b Webb 42, F. Atkins c Simpson b Eades 16, G. H. Edrich b Webb 43, P. Wright b Wharton 0, F. G. Edrich c Webb b Colman 22. D. Edrich b Wharton 0, J. Foster c Crossley b Colman 0, G. C. Edrich not out 4, extras 4, total 179. (Wharton 4–76.) **Stranger's Club**—F. Law c Atkins b G. C. Edrich 16, J. Wharton lbw Hood 6, R. Ashworth c Perkins b G. C. Edrich 3, R. Colman c Atkins b G. C. Edrich 51, I. Crossley c Atkins b G. H. Edrich 9, J. Webb st Head b Perkins 3, A. Eades c and b G. C. Edrich 55, A. Payne b G C. Edrich 9, L. Rouillard not out 2, extras 2; total (8 wkts.) 156. (G. C. Edrich 5–39.)

August 28th 1955

South Walsham beat Hadleigh at South Walsham by 114 runs. **South Walsham**—G. Head c Stevenson b Eastoe 42, I. Watts c and b Brownhill 16, R Hewitt c and b Eastoe 24, I. Stringer c Nunn b Eastoe 1, K. Mayhew c K. King b Brownhill 23, P. G. Edrich b Brownhill 17, G. H. Edrich c B. King b Brown 16, extras 16; total (8 wkts. dec.) 206. **Hadleigh**—J. Stevenson c Stuart b Mayhew 14, A. Nunn c P. G. Edrich b Mayhew 29, B. King lbw Mayhew 1, J. Eastoe b Mayhew 0, K King st Head b Mayhew 5, J. Brown run out 6, P. Parker b G. H. Edrich 1, L. English b G. H. Edrich 13, C. Martin b Perkins 4, C. Claireour not out 9, F. Brownhill c Head b Perkins 1, extras 9; total 92. (Mayhew 5–16.)

July 1st 1956

SOUTH WALSHAM AND DISTRICT CRICKET CLUB

FIXTURE LIST
1955

A.L. & C.M. DRAKE (PRINTERS) ACLE

OFFICERS

President: F. RAYNS, Esq.

Vice-Presidents:
Maj. The Hon. H. R. Broughton
Lt.-Col. N. V. Blacker   W. E. Blizzard, Esq.
J. Bond, Esq.   B. J. Bracey, Esq.
Lt.-Col. H. J. Cator   J. Cator, Esq.
K. Clare, Esq.   F. Dobbs, Esq.
F. H. Dunham, Esq.   R. W. Eades, Esq.
H. M. Edrich, Esq.   B. Evans, Esq.
M. Falcon, Esq.   R. A. Gimbert, Esq.
J. B. Goodman, Esq.   G. A. Hewitt, Esq.
D. Hurrell, Esq.
C. E. Kevill-Davies, Esq
J. Mack, Esq.   Capt. C.C.H. Master
Capt. E. Pennell   E. Pickering, Esq
L. R. Ramuz, Esq.   C. Roofe, Esq.
G. Spalding, Esq.   A. J. Symonds, Esq.
B. Twite, Esq.   C. P. Watson, Esq.
W. G. Watts, Esq.   R. Youngs, Esq.

Chairman: Mr. P. Hood
Captain: Mr. R. Hewitt
Vice-Captain: Mr. G. H. Edrich
Hon. Secretary: Mr. P. G. Edrich
Team Secretary: Mr. P. Hood
(Phone Salhouse 228)
Hon. Treasurer: Mr. A. Eades

Selection and General Committee:
Messrs. F. Atkins, A. Eades, E. H. Edrich,
G. H. Edrich, J. Foster, R. Hewitt, P. Hood

Umpire: Mr. E. H. Edrich
Scorer: Mr. E. Pickering

More early Walsham fixture cards

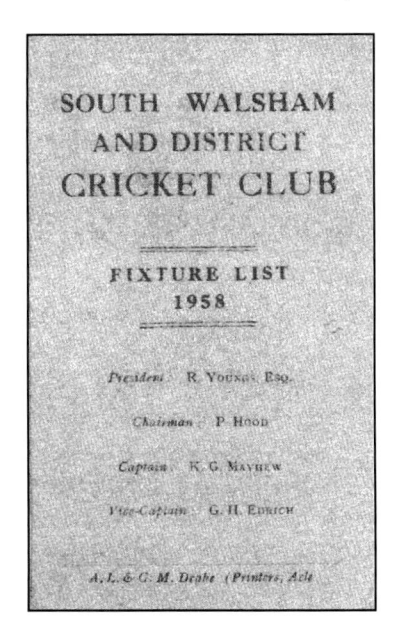

SOUTH WALSHAM AND DISTRICT CRICKET CLUB

FIXTURE LIST
1958

President: R. Youngs, Esq.

Chairman: P. Hood

Captain: K. G. Mayhew

Vice-Captain: G. H. Edrich

A.L. & C.M. Drake (Printers, Acle)

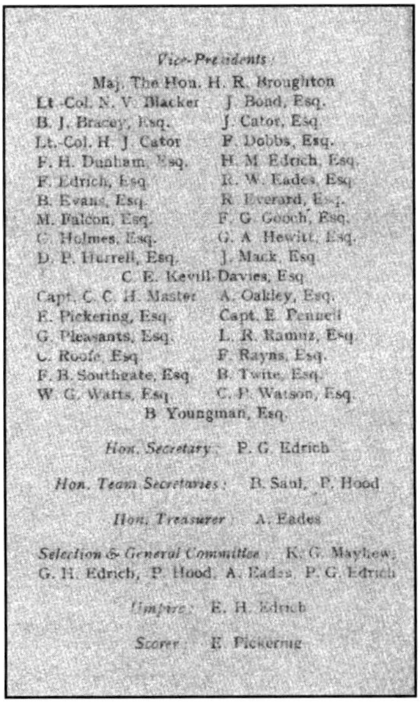

Vice-Presidents:
Maj. The Hon. H. R. Broughton
Lt.-Col. N. V. Blacker   J. Bond, Esq.
B. J. Bracey, Esq.   J. Cator, Esq.
Lt.-Col. H. J. Cator   F. Dobbs, Esq.
F. H. Dunham, Esq.   H. M. Edrich, Esq.
F. Edrich, Esq.   R. W. Eades, Esq.
B. Evans, Esq.   R. Everard, Esq.
M. Falcon, Esq.   F. G. Gooch, Esq.
C. Holmes, Esq.   G. A. Hewitt, Esq.
D. P. Hurrell, Esq.   J. Mack, Esq.
C. E. Kevill-Davies, Esq
Capt. C.C.H. Master   A. Oakley, Esq.
E. Pickering, Esq.   Capt. E. Pennell
G. Pleasants, Esq.   L. R. Ramuz, Esq
C. Roofe, Esq.   F. Rayns, Esq.
F. B. Southgate, Esq.   B. Twite, Esq.
W. G. Watts, Esq.   C. P. Watson, Esq.
B. Youngman, Esq.

Hon. Secretary: P. G. Edrich

Hon. Team Secretaries: B. Saul, P. Hood

Hon. Treasurer: A. Eades

Selection & General Committee: K. G. Mayhew,
G. H. Edrich, P. Hood, A. Eades, P. G. Edrich

Umpire: E. H. Edrich
Scorer: E. Pickering

CHAPTER ELEVEN *Cricket In The 1950's*
Gentlemen & Players

That cricket reflects society is a truism. Any activity that fired the imaginations of millions of people - and cricket was never more popular than in the 1950s - cannot but be symbiotically related to its wider setting. This chapter explores a theme that illustrated a key facet of immediate post-war cricket: gentlemen and players.

Although the 1950s was a decade when society was beginning to make incremental changes towards a more egalitarian structure - wider house ownership being the most obvious indicator of this - long-established patterns of social hierarchy retained a firm hold in many areas of life.

One of these was cricket, where the notions of 'Gentlemen' and 'Players' were so embedded in the culture of the game that several matches were played annually - including the prestigious fixture at Lords - which reinforced a distinction, which even committed anti-Marxists would have had difficulty in not perceiving as being based on social class.

Captains had to be 'gentlemen' until the England selectors took the radical step - 'revolutionary', and with Bolshevik implications, in the eyes of the average, unreconstructed MCC member - and appointed the Yorkshire professional, Len Hutton, to captain England. However, his success in tours of Australia (1954/55), where the Ashes were retained, and in the West Indies did not mark an immediate permanent change in attitudes: he was followed, as England captain, by four 'gentlemen': May, Cowdrey, Smith and Dexter - public school, Oxbridge and 'born to lead'. The lessons of two world wars were slow to penetrate the corridors of cricketing power.

Not until 1963 was the distinction abolished. No longer would a Hammond or an Edrich (Bill) have to change their status from 'professional' to 'amateur' to be regarded as 'fit' to lead their county sides. The system was riddled with hypocrisy. Trevor Bailey (Dulwich College and Cambridge), the 'amateur' captain of Essex, held a notional appointment as his county's assistant secretary for which he was paid a 'gentleman's ' salary, to enable him to retain his amateur status. For an 'assistant secretary' he played an awful lot of cricket in the 1950s.

Hutton, despite being captain of England, never captained Yorkshire. As with the abolition of the status distinction, it was the 1960s before those arch-pragmatists and steely professionals - Brian Close and Ray Illingworth - took formal control of the Yorkshire side, although in the 'White Rose' county, as elsewhere, it had long been accepted that the figurehead captain was expected to follow the instructions of his senior players on matters of tactics. Renewal of contracts, however, was a separate issue; the professional cricketer's life was precarious and could be dependent on the whims of 'gentlemen' - the captain and members of the county committee.

In local cricket in Norfolk, the distinction was equally apparent. Only the county club - or, surrogately, J&J Colman, the mustard-makers - employed a professional, generally a player who, having narrowly failed to make the grade at first class level, could do the bulk of the bowling in Minor Counties matches, coach a bit and be expected to bowl to members at net practice. 'Players' - professionals - were, on the whole, bowlers; 'gentlemen' were batsmen.

At club level, distinctions were sometimes based on the expectations and origins of a particular club. Within Norfolk, the district sides (East Norfolk, South Norfolk etc) were established as clubs for 'gentlemen'. The one remaining district club - West Norfolk - is still proud to describe itself, on its 2012 website, as 'a gentlemen's cricket club [which] is moving steadily in time towards a solid century' and for whom 'members request to play when they so wish'. Their fixture list includes: Gentlemen of Suffolk, Gresham's School, I Zingari (who else in Norfolk has a fixture against I Zingari? - the acme of 'gentleman's' cricket clubs, more exclusive even than the MCC!). West Norfolk CC still trumpet their 'strong local ties, especially with Norfolk farming families'. Clearly, cricketing democracy has yet to establish itself west of Fakenham!

The comment relating to farmers is revealing, and not without its significance to South Walsham. Farmers and auctioneers - evidently 'gentlemen' - played a key role in the club in the 1950s, providing a 'gentlemanly' dimension to a village club which seemingly, under the guidance of 'Uncle George', was seeking to establish itself as superior - in cricketing terms, and certainly socially - to its traditional pre-war opponents of the Freethorpe and District League. The 'gentlemen' among the South Walsham ranks aspired to an enhanced place in the cricketing firmament. The unmistakeable signs of aspiration are evident in two documentary sources which 'Young George' had stored in his club 'treasure house': the fixture cards and the menus from annual dinners. Sadly, neither the minutes of club AGMs nor committee meetings of the 1950s have survived, nor have the annual accounts, but the social messages of the extant documents are fascinating.

Setting aside the list of fixtures (considered below) and focusing on the front cover, the list of club vice-presidents seems to consist of the 'great and good' of east Norfolk. One is reminded that, in 1947, the club was re-established as South Walsham and District CC - this was no longer a mere village team. One of the vice-presidents was the most prestigious figure in Norfolk cricketing history: Michael Falcon, county captain (1912-46) and resident of North Burlingham. Only royal patronage would have accorded more significant recognition!

The menus for the annual dinners provide an even sharper insight into the club's vision of itself, or at least the vision of its 'gentlemen' members. The 1949 dinner was held at Sutton Staithe, 15 miles from South Walsham; only those with their own cars would have been able to attend accompanied, one assumes, by their 'ladies'. The menu, although not exciting by the standards of sixty years later, was remarkably impressive when judged in the context of post-war austerity. The most revealing feature, symbolising the nature of the occasion, was the inclusion of an emblematic series of 'loyal toasts' This was the officers' mess in peace-time, the gentleman's club in its cricketing context. There is no reference to 'formal attire' being expected as the dress code, but it is safe to assume that this was understood implicitly by all who attended.

The 'gentlemen' who led South Walsham and District Cricket Club in the post-war era would have loved their cricket, but they would have been equally insistent upon the correct social protocols being observed on and off the field. This expectation would also have been the basis for the choice of opponents. From the year-by-year account of the club's matches in the 1950s (chapters 7-10), it is evident that, in most instances, fixtures were played against the same opposition throughout the decade: Ingham, Yarmouth, Lowestoft, Barleycorns, Hadleigh, William Brown's (Ipswich). Partly, this would have been a matter of convenience - a word between captains after the game, confirmed by an exchange of letters between fixture secretaries over the winter - but, more significantly, it was based on the wish to be playing the 'right kind' of opposition, not merely in terms of cricketing ability, but also social standing.

Before league cricket introduced a rude form of meritocracy, fixture-making was governed by such considerations. Recognition of cricket based on shared values pervades the testimony of Richard English, a member of the Hadleigh family, which almost parallelled the Edriches, as he recalled playing in matches against South Walsham with his father, two uncles and a cousin in the same side. Richard, a Suffolk county player for several seasons, remembers the Walsham games with great fondness.

'I have wonderful memories of the sociability and comradeship of these encounters- no points and league tables to worry about. More important than the result of the game were the evenings in the White Hart in Hadleigh or the Kings Arms in South Walsham where, on one night in the 'Schooner race', two of the South Walsham wives joined in after removing their blouses to avoid being drenched in beer- good times.'

Whether or not the Hadleigh wives removed their blouses in a reciprocal gesture in the White Hart is glossed over, but the tone is unmistakeable. Not merely nostalgic, but redolent of 'the game' being played in the right spirit by those who shared the same sense of its meaning.

The recollections of an opposition 'gentleman' can be fascinatingly contrasted with those of a South Walsham man: Colin Holmes. He too recalls trips to Hadleigh and other games in Suffolk.

'They were always long days. We would leave quite early so we could stop for a drink before the game. We used to travel down in George Edrich's Riley Pathfinder. He was very much the man in charge.....no one queried George. We would play the game, have a few drinks in the pub after the game, then stop at the Scole Inn on the way home. They were great days and great fun.'

Great fun, but the tone is different.....'no one queried George'........the 'man in charge'; officers and other ranks are evident from Colin's account. He admits that he *'wasn't much of a cricketer'*, but he *'knew the Edriches'* and, occasionally, he *'would be asked to play at late notice.'* He was not in the circle of 'gentlemen' cricketers. In 23 games for South Walsham, he batted 14 times and scored only 25 runs at an average of 2.27, but 'Uncle George' needed the occasional 'player' to make up the numbers.

They may not have had separate changing rooms, nor entered the playing area from different entrances, nor had their initials printed differently on the scorecard - all features of the first class game - but the distinction of 'gentlemen' and 'players' pervaded the game in the 1950s from Lords to South Walsham and well beyond. But that world was about to change.

CHAPTER TWELVE *The Early 1960's...*
The Second Golden Era ends

Change did not come instantly. As the 1960s opened, cricket in South Walsham gave every appearance of continuing as it had in the 1950s: Edrich-dominated and generally successful. But, almost imperceptibly, the second golden age was drawing to a close.

1960
A wet summer resulted in season when only sixteen games being completed: seven wins, five draws and four defeats. Basil Tibbenham led the way with the run-scoring (390 at an average of 33.5) while Brian Cator and Pat Hood both passed 240 for the season. The bowling relied heavily on Peter Edrich who took 45 wickets at an average of 8.1. Only 'Young George' with 21 at an average of 12.6 also passed the twenty wicket mark.

The two opening matches were very close affairs. In the first, Ingham posted 155-9 declared and Walsham looked in with a chance of victory at 140-7 but fell five runs short. However, as Norfolk bowlers Tracey Moore and Ted Witherden took nine wickets between them, this was no disgrace. In the second game, Dereham were bowled out for 150, Peter Edrich taking 5-38. In reply Edrich also led the way, hitting 48 not out, although Walsham were dismissed for 137.

Gorleston were overwhelmed, mustering only 21 (Peter Edrich 5-5) as they attempted to chase 113-9, while Walsham hung on for a draw at Lowestoft. Set 146, they managed 100-9. A heavy defeat followed as St Barnabas rattled up 200-9, Walsham replying with 108. A rare appearance from Ronnie Hewitt (61) against William Browns also saw Peter Edrich bowl a marathon spell of 21 overs taking 4-39 in the Ipswich side's 178-9 declared, to which Walsham replied with 162-7.

The highlight of the season was undoubtedly the return match with Ingham, when Peter Edrich emulated his cousin George by taking 10 wickets in an innings (10-51 in 15 overs). Ironically it didn't prove to be enough to finish on the winning side as Walsham lost by one run (100 to 99) as a young Paul

Borrett - later a county player - took the last wicket with his first ball. Basil Tibbenham hit 76 against St Barnabas in a total of 175-9, but the game petered out into a draw, the visitors finishing on 162-4.

Walsham's top score of the season was against Hadleigh. Frank Atkins hit 55 not out in a total of 224-9 to which Hadleigh responded with 185, Ken Mayhew's six wickets securing a 39 run victory. Comfortable wins over Gorleston and Overstrand followed, before 'Young George' bowled through the innings - in the absence of Peter Edrich - against William Browns, taking 5-60 in 29 overs. However, his effort was not enough and the game was drawn. The final two games were victories as John Syrett took 5-15 against Hadleigh, while Basil Tibbenham hit 68 not out in a six wicket win against Yarmouth.

1961
Twenty games were arranged, resulting in six wins, seven draws and five defeats in the eighteen games completed. Four players passed the 200 mark: R Beeney, Frank Atkins, Peter Edrich and top scorer Brian Cator with 290 runs. Once again, Peter Edrich led the way in the bowling with 44 wickets, while Tony Pennington chipped in with 31.

The season started with the usual game against Ingham, which ended in defeat by four wickets. Pat Hood hit 46 as Walsham posted 175 against Dereham, but they never threatened the Walsham total finishing on 130-7. Two defeats followed: Walsham could only muster 75 against Gorleston and 65 against Lowestoft. There was a close game against St Barnabas as Walsham scored 194-7, Ronnie Hewitt making 76. St Barnabas replied with 178-9, 'Young George' claiming four wickets. In the return match Walsham were well beaten by four wickets. The all-day fixture with William Brown's proved a slow affair as Walsham struggled to 114 in 48 overs only for the opposition to score 98 in 49 overs, Tony Pennington taking 7-30. A draw followed against Dereham: 167-9 declared against 148-9.

Another all-day game against Hadleigh was equally slow-scoring particularly on Walsham's part. Hadleigh scored 190 in 60 overs before finally managing to winkle out Walsham for 91 in 56 overs. Two victories followed: against Gt Yarmouth and Gorleston - not yet a combined club - then a very close draw with Lowestoft, as Frank Atkins hit 79 not out in a score of 154-8, Lowestoft replying with 145-9. Brian Cator hit 81 in a total of 220 against the Strangers

Club - Walsham's top score of the season - and won by 101 runs. They also passed the 200 mark against Palmers School, but the tourists put up a stout defence with 110-5 from 49 overs. There was another close draw with Yarmouth as Walsham scored 133 and Yarmouth held on at 125-9 while, in the final game of the season, Hoveton and Wroxham proved no match for Peter Edrich who took 7-15 from 11 overs in a total of 53, which Walsham knocked off comfortably.

1962

This was an average season with seven wins and three draws from sixteen games completed, four matches being lost to the weather. Only Peter Edrich managed 200 runs, while only he and John Syrett averaged over 20. Peter also held the bowling together almost single-handedly, taking 53 wickets at an average of 9.8; no one else made an impact on a regular basis. The signs of decline were beginning to become more evident.

The season started disastrously when Ingham dismissed Walsham for 48 and knocked the runs off easily. Although the Dereham match fell victim to the weather, Walsham just hung on for draws against Gorleston and Lowestoft. The first win of the season came against St Barnabas when the visitors were bowled out for 154, Peter Edrich taking 4-49, before an excellent stand between Brian Cator (74*) and J English (57*) saw Walsham home by 8 wickets. Ingham - moving towards their 1970s status as the major club in the county - proved far too strong once again, as they made 204-8, Andy Seeley hitting a century. Peter Edrich bowled through the innings taking 5-50 from 26 overs and then top-scored (30) in a meagre reply of 126. Walsham were also well beaten by William Browns before they beat Civil Service Crusaders. Again Peter Edrich starred with the ball with 7-50 from 28 overs in a total of 155. County batsman, Ivan Watts, making a rare appearance for his home village, led the way with 51, as Walsham cruised home by five wickets.

This heralded a winning run of victories, firstly over Hadleigh, by just one wicket, Peter Edrich taking 8-55. He took five more wickets as a two-wicket win was secured against St Barnabas. Finally, in one of the matches of the season - the return game, at Ipswich, against William Browns - the home side scored 187-7 declared off 64 overs, but Peter Cator (82) and John Syrett (71*) won it for Walsham by five wickets in 52 overs. The next game against Lowestoft was drawn, but excitingly so. Lowestoft scored 152 and, when Walsham slumped to 50-8, the game seemed over. However, a 90-run partnership for the 9th wicket between Jeremy Tomlinson, a future county player, and Tony Pennington stopped the rot and came close to winning as the game ended with Walsham on 140-8.

Pat Hood scored 50 as Walsham hit 240-5 - their highest score of the season - against Hadleigh, who were no match that day as they were bowled out for 104, Frank Atkins taking 4-24. However, Great Yarmouth, who were a cricketing force in the early 1960s, beat Walsham twice: by 112 runs and then by eight wickets. The final game saw a return to winning ways. Peter Edrich was once again in the wickets with 6-28 as Hoveton and Wroxham were bowled out for 80 and the runs were knocked off for the loss of only five wickets.

1963
Walsham were beginning to falter. Many of the players, who had played together for about fifteen years, were getting old at the same time. There were no regular appearances from either 'Young' or 'Uncle' George, although Pat Hood, Brian Cator and Peter Edrich were still performing impressively, all passing 200 runs for the season. Jeremy Tomlinson batted to good effect, scoring 424 runs, including a century against William Browns. The bowling was spread around rather more than in previous years, but Peter Edrich continued to bowl the most overs (185) and still finished the top wicket-taker with 24.

In the first match, Ingham made 140-7 declared, but the game petered out into a draw as Walsham finished on 103-6. Dereham cruised to victory as Walsham only managed 93, and Lowestoft were denied a win as Ken Mayhew and Tony Pennington held out on 90-9, after Mayhew had bowled through the Lowestoft innings of 112-8, taking 5-37 from 24 overs. The next game saw St Barnabas win by 21 runs and the batting again failed at Ingham as Walsham scored just 132 against Ingham's 214, when Mayhew again took five wickets.

However, the game against William Browns proved to be the match of the season, if not the decade. Walsham must have been happy with what, at the time, was their highest ever score, 289-6 from 52 overs, Tomlinson leading the way with 128. For once, Peter Edrich had very little impact with the ball being hit for 71 from 13 overs, but John Syrett took 5-90 as the Suffolk side hit a four off the last ball of the game to win by one wicket.

Walsham finally won their first game of the season in late June, against Hadleigh. Brian Cator hit 40 in a total of 146 and Peter Edrich and Tony Pennington bowled throughout the innings to dismiss Hadleigh for 87, Pennington taking 6-34. Heavy defeats followed against Dereham and Lowestoft, then a second win, again against Hadleigh when Walsham passed 200 for the second time in the season (211-6), Peter Edrich scoring 50. Hadleigh made a valiant effort but were bowled out for 169, Brian Cator taking 5-58. The two matches against Great Yarmouth were both one-sided affairs. In the first, Walsham only managed 52-9 in 48 overs chasing 138 and crumbled in the last match of the season being bowled out for 120. Billy Bishop hit 80 not out in Yarmouth's reply (121-1) to secure a nine wicket win.

The signs of decline were unmistakeable.

CHAPTER THIRTEEN *The Mid 1960's...*
Years of Decline

1964
Nineteen games: just three wins, seven draws and five defeats with four matches unfinished due to bad weather. The decline was gathering pace; newer players were beginning to make an impact, mainly as batsmen, but the bowling was becoming threadbare.

Jeremy Tomlinson scored 327 runs in only six games, while Norman Owers finished top of the run-scoring (305) at an average of 33.9. Aubrey Hammond and Brian Cator both passed the 200 mark but, with Peter Edrich and Pat Hood playing less, Walsham were struggling. Peter Edrich still bowled most overs (121) and again took 24 wickets, but Ken Mayhew, Roly Hardesty and Brian Cator all fell short of twenty wickets.

As the usual opening fixture against Ingham was rained off, the season started against Dereham where Walsham scored a respectable 141, but Dereham cruised home by seven wickets. In a very low-scoring game, Gorleston managed 56, with five wickets for Brian Cator, but Walsham made heavy weather of it before winning by three wickets.

In a tight affair at Lowestoft, Walsham made only 80 but, despite 7-24 from Peter Edrich, Lowestoft crept home by one wicket. A high scoring draw against St Barnabas saw Walsham hit 212-9 declared, Tomlinson (64) and Hammond (48); St Barnabas replied with 180-6. There was a second win of the season as Ingham collapsed from 60-0 to 140 all out. Tomlinson again led the way with 56 not out in an eight wicket win.

A drawn game against Hadleigh followed, and then a comprehensive defeat by St Barnabas who scored 148-9 against Walsham's total of 95, Brian Cator hitting 40. For the first time Walsham had a President's Day with a few of the old players and several from other local sides. Walsham had the upper hand in a drawn game.

The return match with Lowestoft was another close affair, Tomlinson hitting 58 in a total of 168-7 declared. Ken Mayhew, who seemed to like playing at

Lowestoft, took 6-73 as they finished seven runs short of victory, with two wickets left. Gorleston held on for a draw in the next match while, against Hadleigh, Walsham hit their highest score of the season (251-4 declared), Norman Owers and Peter Edrich both passing 70. Hadleigh hit back with 224-6 in an entertaining game. Palmers School had the better of a high scoring draw, but Walsham collapsed badly to lose by 145 runs against William Browns, despite Roly Hardesty taking 6-71. Great Yarmouth once again cruised to victory, this time by 90 runs, before the final game of the season saw the third victory. Tomlinson hit 93 in Walsham's total of 183-5 against Hoveton and Wroxham who responded with a valiant 149.

1965

A further decline in fortunes: nineteen matches, only 16 completed, with just four wins, six draws and six defeats. The highlights came when Peter Edrich, concentrating on his batting at this stage in his career and in his last full season, managed to score two of his three South Walsham centuries in his season's aggregate of 453 runs at an average of 64. Of the other batsman, only Norman Owers passed 200 runs. Roly Hardesty started to emerge as the main bowler with 26 wickets at an average of 17, while Brian Cator and T Ridley took 17 wickets each.

The season started with a dishonourable draw against Ingham who scored 164-9 with Brian Cator taking 4-48. In reply, only Peter Edrich (56) and David Balls (22) reached double figures, but Walsham held out at 100-7. One of Peter Edrich's centuries was against Dereham - 105 not out in a total of 154-8 - and although Barry Battelley hit 94 for Dereham, Walsham won by 10 runs. St Barnabas held out for a draw as Walsham posted 183-5, with Edrich hitting his second century (118 not out), the Saints finishing on a disappointing 96-6. This was followed by a terrific game at Ingham. After the home side had declared on 161-8, another outstanding innings from Edrich (70) saw Walsham home by 3 wickets.

The pattern was clear. If Peter Edrich failed with the bat, Walsham would score a low total. This was certainly the case against William Browns; the Suffolk side hit 149 while Walsham only managed 81. It was the same experience against Hadleigh (148 to 89). Another draw against St Barnabas was followed by a defeat at Lowestoft, Keith Gregory taking 5-31 for the home side in Walsham's total of 122. Lowestoft cruised home by seven wickets. Gorleston also won as Walsham could only post 82 and, in a low-scoring draw, Walsham scored 134 but Hadleigh held on at 87-9, Ridley taking 5-24.

Walsham's next fixture was against a South African touring side - Bloemfontein Ramblers - who came to the UK in alternate years from 1965 to 1971, after which the apartheid issue stopped further tours. They played most of their matches in the London area, but had connections with the Mack family, three of whom had played for South Walsham. The Ramblers certainly knew how to enjoy themselves and there were many happy and noisy evenings after these matches in the Kings Arms. The 1965 match was a close affair with Walsham winning by one wicket, chasing a moderate score of 125, Roly Hardesty (4-52) starring with the ball. Roly recalled the pleasure it was playing for Walsham in the mid-sixties, although, by 1967, the club was beginning to struggle. He had particularly good memories of games against the Ramblers.

Returning to local opposition, Walsham gained a rare win over Great Yarmouth, as Brian Cator hit 70 when chasing a modest score of 128. The President's game and the return match with Yarmouth were drawn before the final game of the season saw a narrow defeat to Hoveton and Wroxham who scored 76 - Derek Blaxell (5-11). However, Walsham were bowled out for 71, Blaxell top scoring with 20.

1966

This season marked the end of the career of Peter Edrich, who played only eight games finishing in July. Over his career, he took 729 wickets at an average of 10.1, with 54 five wicket hauls. Had he not done so much bowling, it is probable that he would have scored more than 3651 runs, averaging just over 20 which, in this era, should be judged in the context of sides often being bowled out for under a hundred.

Sixteen matches are recorded in 1966, although two matches may have been played but have not been recorded. Only twelve known games were completed of which Walsham won two, drew one and lost nine. No batsman passed the 200 run mark, K Wright top-scoring with 185 runs at an average of just over 20. Roly Hardesty took 25 wickets while Brian Cator took 20. More guest players appeared, as many of the stalwarts were either playing less or had retired.

The season started with defeat against Ingham. Despite bowling out Walsham for 119, Ingham struggled to reach the total, K Rutherford (62) seeing them home by three wickets. Dereham won the next match, although it was a spirited performance by Walsham. Sandy Kennon, the former Norwich City goalkeeper, hit 86 in Dereham's total of 195. Walsham were well behind, before a last wicket stand of 55 between Roly Hardesty and R Attoe made it a close run thing, Walsham being bowled out for 177.

A hammering at Lowestoft was followed by revenge over Ingham, with Peter Edrich (5-30) rolling back the years in Ingham's total of 103, Walsham winning easily by nine wickets. An extremely low-scoring game saw William Browns win (70 to 61) before the second win of the season, K Wright hitting 93 when successfully chasing Hadleigh's score of 144. A batting collapse against St Barnabas ended in a 46 run defeat, and a first ever game against Cromer also ended in defeat. Cromer managed 128, Peter Edrich - still effective in his final season - taking 6-18, but Walsham managed just 100. After holding on for a draw against Great Yarmouth, the return fixture against Cromer was also lost (95 to 75), 'Young George' making a rare appearance to take three wickets.

The season finished with two more defeats. In a good match against William Browns, Walsham scored 197 but, despite 4-68 from Ridley, the Suffolk side got home by three wickets with four balls to spare. The final game saw Great Yarmouth score 200-5 declared, Walsham replying with exactly 100.

Decline was now all too evident, but the low point of the cycle had yet to be reached.

CHAPTER FOURTEEN *The Years of Struggle*

1967

The club was really beginning to struggle. Most of the squad had played for nearly twenty years and had retired or were ready to retire. However, deceptively, the results in 1967 were good, with ten wins in nineteen completed games. K Wright topped the scoring with 412 runs from 10 completed innings, although no one else managed to average over 15. In the bowling department, Walsham were stronger with M Owers picking up 42 wickets from just 110 overs at an average of 9.53 and Roly Hardesty and Brian Cator both passing the 25 wicket mark.

Good wins over St Barnabas, by six wickets, and William Browns, by two wickets, got the team on the winning trail after they failed to win any of their first six matches. Indeed, in one of the early matches they slumped to an all out total of 31 when chasing 124 at Ingham, who fielded five Norfolk players: Borrett, Handley, Powell, Moore and Goodwin. County opening bowlers, Tracey Moore (4-18) and Roger Goodwin (6-13) demolished Walsham inside 21 overs, but it could have been worse as the last wicket pair of Mack (9) and Arthur Edrich (6*) contributed almost half the runs!

An excellent four wicket win against Cromer saw Owers pick up 5-41, while Wright led the batting with 65 not out in a total of 170-6. Owers' 7-35 return against Great Yarmouth was another highlight of the season - he took all seven wickets as Yarmouth finished on 120-7, while George Heward, later to become Walsham's skipper, took 6-44 in a narrow defeat against regular tourists, Palmers School. The top score of the season was obtained against international opposition, as Walsham beat South African tourists, Blomefontain Ramblers, by 21 runs (195 to 174). The final game of the season saw a 24 run victory over Hoveton and Wroxham (131 to 107).

1968

This season saw a further slip in fortunes, with some of the star performers of previous years playing less: K Wright played fewer matches and M Owers, who had bowled well in 1967, did not play at all. Only three players - Mike Moreland, Gladney Wragg and Ian Sidell - managed 200 runs in the season, while Roly Hardesty was the only bowler to take more than 20 wickets. Most of the Edrich family had retired, with only Arthur putting in an occasional appearance. The team managed just two wins from twenty-one games, with several disappointing batting performances: all out for 77 against UEA, 92 against Rye and 75 against Ingham.

The first win of the season was against St Barnabas by 60 runs, with fifties from A Pank and Mike Moreland. There was a good performance against Sussex tourists, Horsham, and William Browns. Both games finished in high-scoring draws, but the team slipped to a 31 run defeat against a Peter Kilshaw inspired St Barnabas. The future county player top-scored and then took 6-35. More defeats followed, but the final game of the season did see another victory with guest Vic Newton - a pre-war Lancashire League player who had moved to Norfolk - taking five wickets as Hoveton and Wroxham were bowled out for 141. Ian Sidell and P Sanders made short work of the total, adding over 100 for the second wicket as Walsham won by 8 wickets.

1969

There was a further decline in this season: even more of the old guard either retired or left the club and only two players - Gladney Wragg (338) and Ian Sidell (235) - managed to score over 200 runs. Again only two wins were achieved. The bowlers really struggled; only two completing over 80 overs in the whole season, showing that there were now no genuine front-line performers.

A few younger players started: David Clark, from Acle, and Steven Smart. The latter was a talented all-rounder, but inexperienced at the level Walsham played as the club still had a strong fixture list. The season started well with an encouraging draw against Dereham, but the signs were worrying as Walsham struggled to field a full side. To maintain playing strength, contacts with quality players were exploited: Tony Lawes and Walter Elliott from Cromer - both on the verge of the Norfolk side - helped out and Neil Beacock, another future county performer, also guested.

The next three games ended in defeat before a high-scoring draw improved spirits, with hard-hitting Ian Sidell scored an excellent half-century. Another youngster from Acle, David Bane, started to play regularly as did Peter Fisher, who was to play a major part in keeping the club going in the early 1970s. Peter's debut coincided with the first win of the season. He failed to trouble the scorers, but Smart top-scored as Hadleigh were beaten by six wickets. Sadly, more defeats followed, including a 102 run defeat against the

Bloemfontein Ramblers when, once again, Smart top-scored with a modest 19.

Smart was from Thorpe Grammar School and it was this link - which also led to the recruitment of John Joyce and Keith Hall - together with that established with Norwich Etceteras, which helped keep the team going over the next couple of seasons. Things reached rock bottom against Ingham, when Walsham collapsed to 31 all out - for the second time in three seasons - seven players failing to get off the mark. Steve Terry (8-9) saw Walsham off in just 18 overs. Quorn Handley and Sandy Kennon quickly led Ingham home. Fixtures against clubs with a preponderance of county players were beginning to become really problematic.

One encouraging sign was the acquisition of the experienced George Heward. He had been with Acle for many year before starting to play regularly for Walsham. However, results kept going against the team other than an isolated two wicket victory against Norwich Wanderers, in which Smart again top-scored.

1970
This was the most unproductive season of all, as far as results were concerned: not a single game was won and sixteen were lost out of nineteen played. Only Peter Fisher scored over 300 runs, at an average of 18.29. Alan Sheppard and youngsters John Westgarth, David Bane and Steven Smart showed great promise, but lacked the experience to turn a score in the teens or twenties into a half-century. The experienced pair of George Heward and another newcomer, Graham Worth, bowled most of the overs taking 21 and 22 wickets respectively, while Alan Sheppard showed his all round ability with 23 wickets. Sadly, he only played for just over one season.

George Heward had been elected captain and Peter Fisher vice-captain and fixture secretary. Peter always believed in arranging the strongest fixtures possible and on good wickets. In many ways this was laudable, but it did show up the weaknesses of the side. The first game of the season resulted in defeat to a very strong Dereham side, which included four Norfolk players: the Battelley brothers (Ian and Barry), Ted Wright and Nigel Cook. To Walsham's credit, Dereham only managed 120-9 off 50 overs. Unfortunately, in reply only Smart and Sheppard managed double figures as Walsham slumped to 70 all out in 45 overs. For an early season game this was not a bad performance against a strong side, but another defeat followed, losing by 78 runs to Lowestoft.

Against St Barnabas Heward picking up three wickets and Worth four as they scored 206. Walsham started well in reply and, at 79-1, were in with a chance of at least a draw, but 6-34 by Colin Crisp led to a collapse and a 62 run defeat in an entertaining game. More defeats followed against Eye and Acle. In the next match, against Aldborough, Walsham came very close to victory. Chasing 172-7, a final total of 169-4 was frustrating. John Westgarth top-scored with 71 not out but, with wickets in hand, the game should have been won. The return game against St Barnabas, was also lost by five wickets after a collapse to 126 all out, although George Heward (42) hit his top score for the club. Another Thorpe schoolboy, Jack Denton, made his debut in this match - the eldest of three Denton brothers, who were to play for Walsham over the next forty years.

Another defeat followed against a strong North Runcton side, who scored 187 with all ten batsmen being caught. They had been 119-9 but number eleven batsman Whitelam came in and hit 42 to put the game out of reach. Don Thompson made a guest appearance and bowled throughout the innings, taking 6-57 from 24 overs while Alan Sheppard took the other four wickets. Whitelam was certainly the man of the match, taking 6-10 as Walsham were bowled out for 40, which represented somewhat of a recovery after being 16-8!

Defeat against Earlham Lodge was followed by a draw against Eye, although victory was never a serious possibility. Peter Fisher scored 35 out of a total of 67 against Smallburgh, while Ray Lusted - who became a club stalwart in the 1970s - made his debut against Yarmouth, a game which was lost by four runs. Yarmouth scored 58 and bowled out Walsham for 54 on Southtown Common; perhaps the scores reflected the quality of the wicket as much as the two teams. Graham Worth and Laurie Halls, another guest from the Norwich Etceteras connection, both took five wickets. But Ted Dix caused Walsham's downfall with six wickets, as he had when playing for Acle against Walsham just a few weeks earlier.

The highlight of the season was an excellent 45-over game against Lowestoft, who batted first and scored 219-4. Walsham's batting form suggested there was little chance of challenging this formidable total, but an opening partnership between Fisher and Garry Blake, also recruited from Acle, added 80 and a guest player from Yarmouth, John Freeman, scored a hard-hitting 62, while Bane kept the score going with 32 not out. Unfortunately it was not quite enough: the result - a one run defeat.

Arthur Edrich played his only game of the season and made the final appearance of his Walsham career in 1970 against Attleborough, scoring 10 and taking a catch while keeping wicket. It must have all seemed very different to him, playing with mostly youngsters that he didn't know. Arthur was in his fifties and, when he decided to call it a day, the final playing link with the Edrich family was lost after almost fifty years, although 'Uncle George' did serve as President from 1968 to 1976.

Defeat against Attleborough by 5 wickets - an all out total of only 63 was a meagre target - was followed the heaviest defeat of the season at Bradfield, who scored 235 with Sheppard taking 5-77. The reply - 52 all out - Sheppard top-scoring with 22, clearly showed how weak the batting had become.

Over the season lack of experience had produced too many silly dismissals. The failure to reach the hundred mark on seven occasions was clear evidence of this, while dismissing the opposition only six times in the season also showed the need to strengthen in that area, although not to win at least one game was probably unlucky.

However, the club still maintained a strong fixture list and good contacts on the cricket circuit. The spirit of the side was excellent, and George Heward - the Acle hairdresser - was an able leader, seeking to get the best out of a group of enthusiastic youngsters from the Thorpe area of Norwich and local villages. Above all, there was optimism that, out of the dark days of the late 1960s, the good times would return.

CHAPTER FIFTEEN *Cricket In The 1960's*

If the defining characteristic of cricket in the 1950s was 'gentlemen and players', the influences that were beginning to change the game in the 1960s reflected those that were pervading wider society. Of these, two interlinked matters were prominent: a rising standard of living and improved communications.

Harold MacMillan's confident 1957 assertion that *'you've never had it so good'* not only provided the platform for a third consecutive Conservative election victory two years later but, by the middle of the next decade, was undeniable. The consumer boom - washing machines, smarter furniture, kitchen gadgetry - was re-shaping many households. But the most potent symbol of the 'new age', transforming expectations and extending horizons, was the motor car.

Pouring off the assembly lines of Dagenham, Longbridge and Cowley were thousands of vehicles, bringing affordable personal transport within the means of those for whom the bicycle had previously represented independent travel. Car ownership revolutionised society and it markedly changed cricket. In one respect, it provided an alternative way of spending weekend leisure time, as highlighted in Chapter 8, when 'Young George' became disillusioned with the game, he bought a car and spent his Sunday afternoons taking his wife on jaunts around the countryside. He would not have been the only cricketer to withdraw from the game and seek alternative entertainment.

However, wider car ownership could also provide opportunities for cricketers: new fixtures, a wider circle of potential players, while the 'gentlemen' car owners of the 1950s, with their Riley Pathfinders, were no longer obliged to provide the transport for the 'players' on trips to Hadleigh or Ipswich. Car ownership was 'democratising' in its implications. Fixtures could be arranged with reduced consideration for transport costs and complications and many clubs used the opportunity to find new opposition. The social 'appropriateness' of fixtures did not totally disappear, but playing strength became a more influential criterion: democracy may have tip-toed, but meritocracy followed the motor car.

More significantly for the game, improved personal transport almost certainly enabled many 'village' clubs, including South Walsham, to keep going. 'Young George' may have opted for Sundays on the coast or visiting stately homes but, without transport, the links with Norwich Etceteras and the group of Thorpe St Andrew schoolboys which were critical to the club's survival in the dark days of the late 1960s, would not have been established.

The motor car was the iconic cultural product of the 1960s, but underlying its mass production was a vibrant economy, supporting a rise in consumer spending that embraced two items that were critical to the 1960s cricketer: kit and beer. Although 'club kit bags' continued, and still continue, to be heaved in and out of changing rooms, more 'players' were in a position to buy a treasured bat, even if they delved into the club bag for pads and gloves. (It had always been the sign of a genuine non-cricketer if he sought permission to borrow the club 'box'!). On financial grounds, individual kit had previously been the preserve of the 'gentleman' cricketer.

Beer had always been intimately associated with cricket, From 'The Bat and Ball' at Hambledon, through the 'Trent Bridge Inn' to the 'King's Arms', the convivial exploits of post-match celebration have been well documented in many sources. However, by the 1960s, the affordable two shilling (10p) pint encouraged consumption and this at a time when car ownership widened. However, the introduction of the breathalyser in 1967 was sporadic in its impact for the first few years and cricketers, both renowned and humble, travelled many miles throughout the summers of the 1960s distinctly less than sober. Censorious as the judgment of the twenty-first century mind might be on this blatant refusal to recognise the drink-driving laws, the average cricketer - and many other honest citizens besides - quite simply did not accept their legitimacy.

The 1960s was a radical decade, although it would be difficult to link cricket with some of the more obvious changes: the contraceptive pill, protest against the Vietnam War, Beatlemania. Those losing concentration in the outfield were more likely to be contemplating what kind of cakes would be on the table during the tea interval or which barmaid would be serving in the Kings Arms rather than recovering from an evening spent smoking pot. Cricket was changing - not perhaps as rapidly as society in general - but changing, nevertheless. For South Walsham, as the 1960s blended into the

1970s, the mission was self-evident - within this changing social context, to rebuild a successful side.

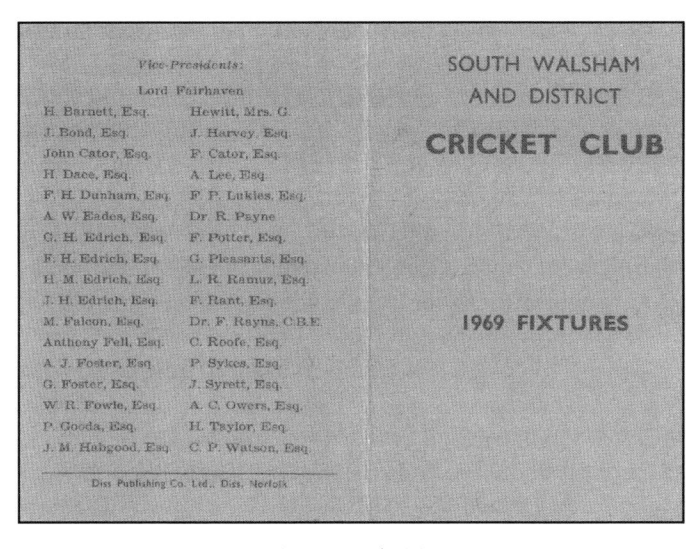

Fixture Card 1969

CHAPTER SIXTEEN *1971 - The Tide Turns*

Twenty-six games without a victory: the celebrations when this was finally achieved - in the fifth game of the 1971 season - were memorable indeed! It was against UEA, whose captain, on winning the toss, had put Walsham into bat. The previous Sunday, the two teams had met in Norwich and the students' skipper had been less than impressed by Walsham crabbing to 43-9 in 39 overs in the successful pursuit of a draw. Unaware that, for the return fixture, the Walsham line-up was boosted by the inclusion of Worth, Westgarth and new arrival Burdett, the tactic backfired. Despite the early dismissal of Peter Fisher, Westgarth (48) and Burdett (67) batted well, adding 70 for the second wicket. No one else registered double figures, but 155 was not only defendable - it could be the platform for a win.

Worth and another new recruit, Trevor Johnson, opened the bowling and reduced the students to 47-5, three wickets to Johnson and two to Worth. When they were rested, only one more wicket fell as the score advanced towards 100 but, when the opening pair were brought back for their second spells, they quickly went through the tail. 100 all out: victory at last!! A few beers were quaffed in 'The Ship' that night - post-match entertainment had shifted from the 'King's Arms' - but the students took it very well. Perhaps to them it was just a game of cricket but, for South Walsham, it was the day the tide turned.

George Heward - in his final season - continued to lead the side, but it was the newcomers, Rod Burdett and Trevor Johnson who held the key to better days. Both were playing in only their second matches, Burdett having made his debut at Heacham a fortnight earlier. He had top-scored with 58 in a tight draw which could so easily have been that elusive victory, the opposition hanging on five runs short of their 165 target with nine wickets down. Trevor Johnson began his eight-year South Walsham career against the UEA students in the fighting draw at Colney Lane which set up the famous victory the following week.

When both newcomers came together, the Walsham revival began. Rod Burdett was a splendid cricketer: a good bat as well as a useful bowler and fielder and was to captain the club before his move to Yorkshire several years later. He was instrumental in the club's renaissance but, in many ways,

Trevor Johnson's contribution was even greater. Not only was he a competitive bowler, but he encouraged players around him to battle a little more. Perhaps, like all really effective quick bowlers, he had a little bit of a 'nasty' streak. If he saw a bouncy wicket he would use it, banging it in short, with close fielders poised; he picked up lots of wickets with the batsman trying to fend the ball off. He was also sharp enough to change tactics and bowl the yorker, but there were not too many slower balls! One typical story from a game against Hoveton and Wroxham: having been hit on the head by a Johnson bouncer, the stricken batsman was sympathetically encircled by the Walsham fielders to check he was OK. The skipper of the day said to him, *'go and have a sit down and come back later in the innings.'* Only the bowler had noticed that, as he fell, the batsman had dislodged a bail and the umpire had to reluctantly give him out. It was another wicket; there were no hard feelings, it was just the way Trevor played his cricket. After the Edriches, he became the only bowler to take 50 wickets in a season twice.

In the first two games of the season, before the Burdett/Johnson inspired revival, the wrong side of a draw against Norwich Etceteras, despite a patient 48 not out by Peter Fisher, was followed by a heavy defeat against. Barleycorns who included three county players - David Stockings, Andrew Agar and Roger Schofield - in their ranks. The winning draw at Heacham, the losing draw at UEA, and then......the win!

The next game - without Westgarth, Worth and Burdett - saw a heavy defeat by 147 runs to St Barnabas, who were a strong club in the early 1970s. The following day, Bank Holiday Monday, being well-supported by two guest players, Don Thompson and John Thirtle from CEYMS, a second victory was achieved. Defending a total of only 83 against Beccles, Trevor Johnson and Thompson took 9 wickets for a total of 37 runs from 25 overs to bowl the opposition out for just 75. The third win came quickly, a Steven Smart half-century leading to a good total of 180-9 against Watton; Heward and Johnson bowled unchanged to dismiss them for just 54. Johnson took 7-26 off 10 overs, while Heward returned 3-28. In this era, there was no quarter asked or given; once you had a team down, you finished them off if you could.

A draw against Acle followed, then a heavy defeat against Sprowston. The visit of the Bloemfontein Ramblers was rather a non-event as they dismissed

Walsham for 72 in 25 overs, and knocked off the winning runs off 19 overs for the loss of only five wickets, Johnson claiming 3-20 in 8 overs. Drinking went late on into the night at the Kings Arms but it was the final visit of the South African tourists to England as their country was squeezed into sporting isolation.

More reverses followed, with a 31 run defeat against Horsford and a very poor performance at Beccles in an all-day game. The hosts were keen to avenge the earlier defeat and Walsham were bowled out before lunch for 66, only Johnson reaching double figures. The sad part of the day was not the result, but the consequences of Steven Smart's dismissal - lbw for 0. He was absolutely furious, coming off the pitch saying, *'that's it. I'm not playing anymore.'* He changed and left the team with ten men. It was assumed by all that he would get over it but, many years later, he confirmed that he never did play again. This was extremely sad; he was potentially a very good cricketer and was showing great promise, particularly as a batsman. The match was over by 3pm, Beccles winning by seven wickets.

Another defeat followed against Mundford, but Boulton and Paul were beaten by three wickets in the next match after a recovery from 56-7 led by George Heward who added 42 for the eighth wicket with Alex Evans. More defeats followed, however, including a ten run loss against Hoveton and Wroxham, despite 50 from Keith Hall and 28 from Alex Evans.

At the end of the season, the club was able to look back with some satisfaction, despite achieving only four wins out of twenty-four games. The batting was still weak, nobody averaging over 20, the departed Steven Smart topping the averages with 18.3. The bowling department was stronger: Trevor Johnson's 235 overs producing 47 wickets at 13.9, George Heward taking 34 wickets at 17.0 and Graham Worth 25 wickets at 22.2. Peter Fisher was doing a steady job behind the stumps and, after the problems of the previous few years, things were getting better. Burdett and Johnson had added substance to the side and the younger players were continuing to improve.

The club was on the up!

CHAPTER SEVENTEEN *New Players...*
New Hopes

On 7th May 1972, at 1.45 pm, a Hillman Imp swung on to the South Walsham playing field. From it emerged a man of medium height, but sturdy frame, whose most conspicuous feature was a mop of not entirely tidy hair. He introduced himself politely, almost genteelly, but there was something about the twinkle in his eyes when he smiled that more than hinted at mischief. When younger, he could in appearance and demeanour have auditioned convincingly for the lead role in Richmal Crompton's 'Just William'. The newcomer's name was John Vaughan.

He had played for Etceteras against Walsham the previous week and had scored 22 but, on his debut for the club, he made only four runs. He played in two further games in 1972, not unduly troubling the scorers on either occasion, and it seemed likely that he would drift away, as had so many others, to a summer Sunday routine of a roast joint, gardening, a salad tea and *Songs of Praise.* He would not be missed and would probably have been forgotten, other than that he had turned up for his debut wearing a pair of faune trousers.

John Vaughan

Thirty years later he retired from South Walsham cricket, after almost 500 games in which he scored over 11,000 runs and took 323 wickets and 169 catches. A club legend: the first to pass 10,000 runs and such an integral part of the team, that it was difficult to imagine what those thirty years would have been like without, not only his cricketing contribution, but his engagingly cheery presence. For if the initial assessment of his ability as a cricketer had been massively inaccurate, judgements of his capacity for mischief proved to be much more perceptive. For a vicar's son, he possessed a remarkably wide repertoire of risqué songs - probably the product of his association with Crusaders Rugby Club. He enjoyed the odd glass of port and was quite prepared to go behind the bar and either serve himself or others if the service wasn't quick enough. On the field, the game was serious, although never solemn, while off the field there was always fun.

He was not the only new recruit as the club reshaped itself over the next two years. Mike Sidell, a Cringleford doctor who had made his debut the previous year, started to play more regularly. Another recruited via the link with Norwich Etceteras, his skills would sometimes come in very useful, although the Hippocratic oath meant that 'unfortunately' he would always treat injured opposition players as well as those of his own team! Two more 'Etceteras' who began to add greater quality to the side were Dave Russen, a wicketkeeper, and Ken Kerry, a useful bat and a very slow bowler who took over the captaincy when Rod Burdett moved to Yorkshire and, until he stopped playing in 1978, appeared in 90 games, scoring 900 runs and taking 67 wickets. Others faded: Peter Fisher played very little due to injury and John Westgarth had moved to Devon so, despite the new arrivals, the batting was possibly a little weaker in 1972. The bowling remained heavily reliant on Trevor Johnson and Graham Worth.

However the key change was in the captaincy. George Heward had held the reins during the difficult years and the club owed him a major debt of gratitude. However, he was now in his fifties and, after the first few games of the season, decided to accept an invitation from his friend and former Acle teammate Stan 'Jimmy' Biss to join a new club that had been set up in 'Jimmy's back garden' in Brundall. The club was known initially as 'Vauxhall', the name being taken from the successful Biss-owned caravan park on the outskirts of Yarmouth. Taking over the South Walsham captaincy was Rod Burdett, who had become a little disillusioned with cricket at CEYMS. His batting had been important in 1971 - the year of revival - but now the club had a captain who could lead from the front. Over his three seasons before his move to Yorkshire, he scored over a thousand runs and took 66 wickets. He enjoyed a drink and a fag but, more importantly, had the cricketing knowledge and experience not only to lead but to stabilise the club.

For the first, and only, time Walsham entered the National Village Cup, the first round of which was the opening game of the season. Loddon were the opposition and Basil Tibbenham, a player from the past, and his fourteen year old son Andy helped out. Loddon were bowled out for 123, Heward and

Burdett taking three wickets each and Ken Kerry two. Tibbenham (snr) top-scored with 25 as a three wicket win was achieved, while son Andy was presented with the man-of-the-match award for his 16 not out, having come in at 69-5 and helped to reach the target. Two defeats followed before the club's one and only Carter Cup match. It was questionable whether Walsham were strong enough to enter, but Eric Bedwell, who had helped to get the competition off the ground, was one short for 32 teams and Walsham agreed to make up the numbers. It was a mistake!

The first-round opponents were Sprowston, a very useful side so when, in an all-day 60-over game, they were all out in just 21 overs for 50, the social atmosphere over the lunch interval was not particularly pleasant. Many of the Sprowston players thought that the Walsham wicket was dangerous; it may not have been good, but it certainly wasn't unplayable. Trevor Johnson, who could be a difficult bowler on his day - and this was his day - took 5-11 from 11 overs, while Dennis Ellis, an occasional player and another 'Etcetera' took 5-16 from just 4.3 overs. After lunch, despite battling hard, class told and Walsham were cleaned out for 25 in just 15 overs. Sprowston were relieved, but they still felt the need to report the wicket to the Carter Cup committee. As last minute entrants, the club were hurt and never applied for re-entry to the competition.

However, the following week, it was back to the second round of the National Village Cup against Mundford, another useful side. Walsham were bowled out for 68, Basil Tibbenham top-scoring with 26, and the game was lost by nine wickets. The mandatory competition for first-round Carter Cup losers - the Carter Plate - then pitted Walsham against Overstrand. After the first match was abandoned, the game was replayed on a difficult wicket at their scenic seaside ground. Again only a small total was achieved: 46 all out in 18 overs, Overstrand winning by five wickets with 27 overs to spare. There were no complaints, but the obvious conclusion was that the club wasn't quite up to that class of cricket.

The next two matches were drawn before confidence was fully restored with wins over Horsford and Mundford. Johnson was 'on fire', taking 5-26 in the first game and 4-23 in the second. Revenge over a rather weaker Mundford side, with Burdett scoring 50, was heartening. Another draw against Diss was followed by defeat at the hands of Vauxhall, with George Heward in the opposition. However, the better end of a draw against Lowestoft was notable for Mike Sidell and the ever-improving Jack Denton scoring half centuries. Wins were achieved against Brooke, Attleborough - with Jack Denton top-scoring with 67 not out - and Hoveton and Wroxham. The latter was close, by just 6 runs: at 65-6, and only chasing 77 to win, Hoveton were favourites, but Burdett picked up three wickets in three overs to secure victory.

Some fixtures, legacies from the club's heyday, remained very strong. In the match against Wanderers, the two opening bowlers - Flower and Beacock - were both current Norfolk players. Burdett was good enough to score fifty, but the rain came down and the match was abandoned. Two defeats against Bradfield ended the season, with two fifties from 'regular guest' Keith Hodds.

Over the season only Jack Denton (247), and Rod Burdett (297) had made over 100 runs. Of the regular players, only these two averaged over 10, while Trevor Johnson with 52 wickets was easily the top bowler once again. However, five games out of twenty had been won, mainly when he had rolled over the opposition for a small enough score for the still limited batting to surpass. In many respects it was encouraging, although progress needed to be maintained.

The 1973 season brought more new players and further incremental improvement. Peter Fisher returned from a season being injured and Doug Palmer, Paul Robinson and Graham Coan were welcomed to the club. Doug Palmer was a very useful player, who just wandered up one day and asked if he could play; over the next ten years he played 80 games, scoring nearly 1,000 runs and taking just short of a 100 wickets. He was a typical left hander who could hit the ball miles if he middled it. Paul Robinson was a young lad from the local garage, who was very rusty when he started, but improved with experience and played for five seasons. Graham Coan was very much a 'trier', playing for a couple of seasons. He had one glory moment when the side was struggling in a tour match and nobody could hit the ball off the square. Graham suddenly hit a six; everyone was stunned.

The seasonal record improved marginally in 1973: six wins, six draws and five defeats. More significantly, it was the first time more games had been won than lost since 1967. Runs were still quite hard to come by in an era when a score of 150 was regarded as unusual. Jack Denton's tally rose to

315, John Vaughan scored 211 and Rod Burdett 203. Only three bowlers bowled over fifty overs and they took the majority of the wickets: Trevor Johnson (36), Graham Worth (17) and Rod Burdett (15).

The importance of two of these players - Jack Denton and Graham Worth - deserves to be emphasised. Jack, one of the many Thorpe Grammar youngsters, continued to improve throughout the early 1970s and looked like making a big score nearly every game. It was a great shame for the club when he decided to emigrate to Australia in 1976. By then he had played 112 games, scoring over 2,200 runs. A few years ago he came back to Norfolk for his father's funeral, and those who had played with him reflected on how much he had been missed by the team for over a quarter of a century.

Graham Worth had supported Trevor Johnson very effectively for several seasons. He was a very steady bowler, but no one really knew much about him. The 'mystery man': he would turn up, play his game and go straight home. He never came down the pub, nearly always travelled to away games on his own and, when he retired from playing, he was never seen again. He 'disappeared' at the end of the 1974 season, after playing 66 games and taking 95 wickets. He was a regular number eleven batsman but, at that time, the club had about five of those!

The season had started reasonably well with creditable draws against Cavaliers and UEA, followed by a win against Hoveton and Wroxham by 16 runs, man-of-the-match, Rod Burdett, top-scoring with 36 and following this with 4-14 from 9 overs. Another win against Watton, by 19 runs, saw John Vaughan begin his run-scoring in earnest with 46 and Mike Sidell took 5-63. However, the match against Earlham Lodge was lost by four runs - 'shot ourselves in the foot' was the consensus view. Worth and Johnson quickly bowled out the opposition for 44, only for Walsham to be dismissed for 40 after being 34-3. Experience and 'professionalism' from old hands Eric Critchfield and Vic Newton, who bowled unchanged, played its part, but so did the umpiring. John Vaughan recalls:

'We were cock-a-hoop at tea and were batting nicely at about 27-0. One of our opening bowlers and vice-captain then went out to umpire. Some of us protested, because we had a feeling about what was about to happen, but too late ....he was out there in the middle, gave umpteen (three actually)

ridiculous LBW decisions that only a bowler could make, and we were all out for 40. This is the only time I could have throttled a South Walsham colleague and the person in question came close to being kicked into touch......perhaps too, we all knew that with Vic Newton etc. they had some really good players and that day we had a chance to remind them we were a team.'

Just occasionally, even the affable Vaughan could be angry and the memory obviously still rankles forty years later!

The next three games saw consecutive wins, by five wickets against Smallburgh - Denton continuing to blossom with 31 not out - by 45 runs against a struggling Yarmouth and Gorleston and a superb victory over Lowestoft by 43 runs, who were not best pleased at being beaten. Walsham posted 159-7 off 49 overs and Lowestoft were confident of victory, but they were soon 65-6 with Burdett and Ken Kerry getting the wickets. They fought back, but with Palmer mopping up the tail they slipped to 116 all out. Earlier, Palmer had also starred with the bat hitting 55. The Lowestoft Journal headline that week was *'Bad batting against indifferent bowling.'* That was sour grapes; it had been an excellent team performance and the right result.

The rest of the season was a mixed bag of the odd win and a few defeats. A hard core of just nine players meant frequent reliance on 'guests', but there was beginning to be more shape and substance to the side. A couple more regulars, particularly if they were players of some quality, could sustain the momentum of improvement. After the tide had turned in 1971, these two years had not only consolidated but pointed the way to the future.

CHAPTER EIGHTEEN *Steady Progress 1974/5*

1974 was the season in which South Walsham again started to become a team to be reckoned with. Rod Burdett continued as captain while Peter Fisher resumed the role of fixture secretary. Although six matches were lost to the weather, 32 games were arranged - the most in a season before or since. These included Walsham's first tour, of which more anon (see Chapter 20).

The Fisher philosophy was to organise the strongest fixtures possible. Not everyone agreed with this approach, some members feeling that the club should be trying to get fixtures of a slightly lower standard, while ensuring that the away games were played on quality grounds. However, he had been elected to do the job and it was only right to support him, which most players did. Sadly, he 'fell out of love with cricket', at least at Walsham, after the 1974 season. He had played 85 games scoring just under 1,000 runs and was also a tidy wicket keeper.

The 'heavy roller'

Fortunately, for many other clubs, his loss of enthusiasm was short-lived and, over the next few years, he became something of a 'have bat will travel' cricketer as he dragged his voluminous kit-bag into the home changing rooms at Earlham Lodge, Mallards, Carrow, Happisburgh and possibly others. He was last spotted, some years ago, umpiring for Bradfield. A mild eccentricity of manner was one of Peter's endearing qualities. His stay at South Walsham may not have been lengthy, but his importance in the dark days has to be acknowledged.

Another key figure in these years was Ray Lusted. Although never an outstanding cricketer, Ray gave unlimited time and energy to secure not only the club's survival but its revival. When George Heward moved on, Ray took over the role of groundsman. This was a demanding task: the club had a heavy roller, but it needed six to push it. The quality work which the square needed was not being done and it had become a little uneven.

Sadly, a lot of the work 'Uncle George' Edrich had put into it was being lost. However, Ray started to organise the wicket work a little better, and he himself put in countless hours over the next nine years to try and keep it up to scratch. An extremely good clubman, he played 177 games before his departure, in rather sad circumstances, after a game against Wisbech Old Grammarians in 1980.

The team continued to call on lots of guests, the most welcome appearances coming from Keith Hodds. Not one to raise his voice too often, but he knew his cricket and was a valuable addition to the squad albeit on a part time basis. He played a few games every season for over twenty years; his 83 innings saw him score over 2,500 runs with one century and fifteen fifties. Few players in local cricket have ever hit the ball harder. There is a tale - probably apocryphal, but almost believable - that Keith, when playing on the central pitch at the Beaconsfield Recreation Ground in Yarmouth, hit the ball over the main gates, whereupon it bounced across the main road, through the car park and had to be retrieved from the beach. In the winter, Keith kept in practice by playing centre-forward for Gorleston Hockey Club, for whom he scored over 1,000 goals in his career. It was rumoured that he hardly ever moved more than ten yards from the 'D' but, with such an impressive strike-rate, his team-mates probably excused him from too much running! Having experienced a serious illness, from which he has thankfully made a partial recovery, it was brilliant to see him score a fifty for the President's side in 2012. The previous day his hockey team had won 2-0, with Keith scoring both goals - not bad for a man of sixty two, who had been in Addenbrookes for a lengthy spell a couple of years earlier!

Although, 'guests' remained important, the 'hard core' of the side was getting bigger. The batting line up of Burdett, Fisher, Denton, Palmer and Vaughan was solid, and this was shown when, after losing the first two matches of the season, Walsham hit a really good vein of form, winning five matches in a row: two against Drayton, two over UEA and the other against Hoveton and Wroxham. Trevor Johnson took fifteen wickets in those games and John Vaughan was suddenly discovered as a bowler as well as a useful bat. Against Drayton, he bowled superbly taking 6-35 off 16 overs; he had arrived and became a key member of the attack for the next twenty-five years.

However, the next match, against Rollesby, was a salutary reminder against complacency. The opposition were bowled out for 87, but eased home by dismissing Walsham for 56; the years of low scores had not totally ended. The following game, against Watton, was the first to demonstrate John Vaughan's mischievous nature. Watton were reduced to 87-8, but the heavens opened and the game was abandoned. Quickly entrenched in a local hostelry, drinking and singing - for which we were becoming famed - took hold. Vaughan, unconvinced by the speed of service, decided to go behind the bar to assist, an action which offended some members of the Watton team. Harmless fun but, unfortunately, not everyone saw it that way.

There was a defeat against Smallburgh, the game in which Colin Denton, the 13 year old brother of Jack, made his debut; over the next few years he was to become a major player in the side. At Riddlesworth - a tiny hamlet on the Norfolk/Suffolk border where, sadly, there is no longer a cricket club - Peter Fisher's determination to secure a draw caused some consternation among the opposition. Chasing a modest total of 108, after Johnson and Vaughan had shot out the opposition, at 90-4 Walsham were coasting to victory. However, a collapse to 98-9 made Riddlesworth favourites. Many of their players thought there was a couple of minutes to go, but Fisher quickly whipped the bails off and called time. 'Friendly' cricket it might have been, but a draw was a draw!

In September the club went on its first tour and this is detailed in Chapter 20. Returning for the final few games of the season, an unsuccessful run with no more victories was recorded. The final outcome: seven wins, thirteen defeats and six draws. Jack Denton was highest run scorer, with 393 at an average of 18, while Burdett, Vaughan and Fisher all scored over 200 runs. The wickets were shared, Johnson (42) once again leading but Vaughan (25) showed his all-round ability. Another six bowlers all took at least 12 wickets, with an average under 20. It was a still primarily a bowlers' game in the mid 1970s.

There were more changes in 1975: Peter Fisher stopped playing for South

Walsham and Graham Worth retired. However, four players who came in more than filled the gaps: David Watkins who, at the time of writing (2012) is still playing, Mike Conrad, who made a major impact on the side up to 1980, Brendan Dwyer and Colin Denton who began to make his mark having made his debut in 1974 as a 13 year-old.

David Watkins is club legend number two. He joined South Walsham after John Vaughan met David's wife, Ann, when they were working in the Education Department of Norfolk County Council. She casually mentioned that her husband was looking for a club and he was invited to join South Walsham; such are the workings of serendipity. He quickly got hooked on South Walsham's way of playing cricket and, although he scored very few runs in his early innings, a famous 87 against Hull Railway Clerks set him on his way. By the end of the 2012 season he was easily the club's highest scorer with over 16,800 runs in 763 appearances, having passed the author's appearance record, and he continues to play regularly. The least said about his bowling the better, although he would insist on recognition of over 50 wickets with his occasional slow - 'spin' would be lying - bowling. However, his contribution to the club has gone well beyond the playing side. For nearly thirty years, he has maintained the square, improving it to its now excellent standard; the average score now being nearer two hundred, rather than in the 1970s, when 150 was unusual. He captained the side for several years, his sons Ben and John have played occasionally for the club and he looks like going on for several seasons yet. Perhaps the later episodes of the legend are yet to be written.

Mike Conrad, although playing for just five years, made a major impact on the club's success. He was a very good player: batsman, bowler and fielder, and was very competitive, although he sometimes struggled to understand the weaknesses of some of the lesser players. During his five seasons he played over 100 games, scored over 3000 runs and took just short of 100 wickets. He even had a go at wicket-keeping for a while, but he was just too good an outfielder to be 'wasted' behind the stumps. After Ken Kerry retired, Mike had two seasons as captain and one game, against Hoveton and Wroxham in 1977, exemplifies his approach. He tried to win the match on his own, taking 8-23 and took a catch for the ninth wicket. However, Hoveton held out for a draw, when maybe tossing the ball up might have led to a Walsham victory. But that was Mike Conrad!

For a short while, the club also enjoyed the company of Brendan Dwyer, who played until 1979. He is best described as an 'occasional regular' during these years, playing 44 games and scoring around 700 runs as well as keeping wicket for a while. However, he enjoyed league cricket and opted to spend his Saturdays with Norwich Etceteras before moving on to Ingham.

The fourth newcomer was Colin Denton, the most talented player to perform regularly for South Walsham over the past forty years. He played a few games as a quiet 13 year-old in 1974, but he gradually developed into a bowler who was good enough to be selected for Norfolk in an early season friendly against UEA in 1982, scoring 11 not out and taking 2-47. He could be a hard-hitting batsman, but it was his off-spin bowling that gained him county recognition. He used flight sparingly, but his accuracy and sharpness of turn, allied to a very pacy faster delivery, made him a formidable bowler by his early twenties. Sheer volume of wickets for Norwich Wanderers, his Saturday club, forced him to the attention of the county selectors. He got no further and stopped playing for a while, prior to a move to Yorkshire where he picked up where he had left off in some very good-class club cricket. The second of three brothers - Keith was still to arrive on the cricketing scene - South Walsham can claim to have played a key part in the development of this fine player.

Strangely, although the team was stronger than for many seasons - Jack and Colin Denton, Burdett, Johnson, Vaughan, Conrad, Sidell and Watkins - results didn't show this in 1975, as just four games were won. Some opponents were still strong sides and, although many more runs were being scored, dismissing the opposition was still proving to be difficult. The first match was lost by five wickets at Riddlesworth, after being bowled out for 76. The first win came against regular opponents Hoveton and Wroxham, with Sidell, Jack Denton and Conrad among the runs, while Johnson and Lusted picked up the wickets. An exciting draw followed against Mundford, when last man Evans had to keep out the final over with nine wickets down. A second win came against Watton, Conrad proving his worth with 50 and four wickets.

Against the University of Sussex, Walsham came up against a player called Ramnaring, who had represented Guyana and claimed to have played in the same side as Garfield Sobers, although the great all-rounder came from the island of Barbados. Unsurprisingly, Ramnaring was a class act and scored an effortless 91 not out to win the game. In one of the tightest games of the season Walsham beat Margaretting, the Essex touring team, by just three runs, with a maiden 50 for Vaughan and four wickets for Johnson.

The following week was the game that really sparked off David Watkins batting career when he scored 87 against Hull Railway Clerks, although he was first to appreciate that he was dropped about seven times! A total of 178 was high for the mid 1970s, but HRC won comfortably by six wickets. Later in the season, Paul Robinson had his finest hour when he took 5-43 against Mundford in a drawn game. Following this, Walsham scored the highest total for many years, 242-5 declared against Vauxhall. Even in those days the Biss-financed wicket was very good; Vaughan and Conrad both scored half centuries. The former Walsham stalwart George Heward, now well into his fifties, was still bowling creditably, but the Vauxhall batsmen couldn't maintain the run rate and the match petered out into a draw.

The next game, against Lowestoft, was probably the most memorable of the decade, and for many years after. Walsham batted first and, boosted by a superb 72 not out by Jack Denton and with good contributions from Watkins, Dwyer and Palmer reached 200-7 by tea. As Rod Burdett was missing, John Vaughan took charge - an experience he admitted later he didn't particularly enjoy. All seemed to be going well for Lowestoft at 129-3 when the young Colin Denton was brought into the attack. He bowled superbly to take 5-36 off 9 overs, leaving Lowestoft needing three to win off the last ball with one wicket left. They only managed a single and finished on 199-9; a tight draw is one of the most exciting of finishes - a feature lost in the win/lose format.

Colin Denton continued to bowl well for the rest of the season, particularly a mammoth spell of 4-47 off 21 overs against Old Buckenham. Strangely, in the final few matches the batting fell apart, Walsham failing to make a hundred in three successive games. However, the season's statistics saw Jack Denton (479) produce the highest aggregate for many years, with Conrad and Vaughan both passing the 300 mark. The wickets were well spread: Johnson (31) was still at the top, but the teenage Colin Denton bagged 26. The saddest aspect of the year was when Rod Burdett played his last game and moved to Yorkshire. This was a major loss to the club, but his contribution over three years had been immense and he had built a squad that could continue to improve.

CHAPTER NINETEEN *The Third Golden Age Begins 1976-1978*

With the exception of Rod Burdett, the 1976 squad was largely the same as previous years, but results changed quite dramatically. Ken Kerry, a very experienced cricketer who had played for many years for Norwich Etceteras, was the new skipper. He was a useful batsman and leg break bowler and had played a few games in previous seasons but, from 1976, he committed himself to playing regularly on a Sunday.

The first game of the season saw a splendid eight wicket win over Riddlesworth. Chasing a total of 172, the game was won with just a few balls to spare, Jack Denton being left high and dry on 98 not out when the winning runs came from two leg byes. Jack never scored a century for Walsham and this was the nearest he came, but he was very much a team man and never really seemed too bothered. Following another win against UEA, results were mixed for a while until a run of four wins in a row. Colin Denton was slowly becoming a star turn with 5-33 against Smallburgh followed by 6-24 against Essex tourists, Margaretting. Vaughan continued to be a useful all rounder with 5-24 and 30 not out against Loddon, although the game was a dishonourable draw, Walsham finishing 102 runs short of victory, after recovering from 39-7 to hold out. Generally speaking, this was not Walsham's way; trying to win always came first and only as a last resort hold out for a draw. It would also depend a little on the opposition and how they played a game; if they tried to knock heads off, a battle was accepted but, if they tossed the ball up, trying to whack it was more likely.

But games could be contentious. Some opponents did not play on great pitches: in a win on Wortham's dangerous wicket, Trevor Johnson pitched the ball halfway down the track and it rolled at pace straight along the pitch to take out middle stump. Revelling in these conditions, he took 6-23 to win the game, but, importantly, there were no injuries. In an ill-tempered game against Vauxhall, their players lost interest after Mike Conrad had run out young Jim Biss when backing up. He was immediately called back, as it was realised this was not the thing to do. However, his partner John Clarke told him he was out and should go. He then threw his wicket away and the situation became rather tense. They were bowled out for 123 and Walsham won by 9 wickets. Words were said in the pub afterwards and it was sometime before the fixture was revived; a very sad episode - but, thankfully, unusual.

Against Lowestoft, Malcolm Hill made his debut starting with a duck, but he made the top score in his second match and went on to enjoy three successful seasons. Jack Denton continued to bat well: 63 against Vauxhall, followed by scores of 61, 39, 50, 41 not out and 65 (out of a total of 90 against Kirkley's strong Alliance bowling). He made 27 in his final innings - contributing to a rare win over Bradfield - before he emigrated to Australia with his girlfriend Julie. Thirty five years later he is still there, but the club have been fortunate to maintain the family link with his brothers, Colin and Keith.

1976 had been the most successful seasons on record. Jack Denton (646 runs) topped the averages for the fifth season running, while Conrad scored over 400 and Vaughan 350. In the bowling, Johnson took 55 wickets - a record only beaten by Colin Denton in 1980 - while Vaughan, Colin Denton and Robinson all took over 20. The team was ably led by Ken Kerry and good fielding helped to secure thirteen wins and only two defeats in the twenty two games played.

This form was generally maintained in the 1977 season when the club played thirty matches. Success was encouraging people to play for Walsham as Ray Lusted's ever-improving square led to more runs being scored. The season got off to an excellent start with a five wicket win over Riddlesworth, Vaughan taking five wickets. Two more wins followed - over Lowestoft and Eaton. Conrad and Kerry both did well with bat and ball against Lowestoft, while Hodds led the way with 47 against Eaton. The next two matches - against UEA and Hoveton and Wroxham - were drawn. In the latter, Conrad, who was stand-in captain for the game, took 8-23 from 18 overs. He was probably straining too hard, when trying to pick up the last couple of wickets, but it was a splendid spell. North Walsham were beaten on a difficult track, Colin Denton making 88 not out - his highest Walsham innings - and Mike Sidell a delightful 73. An excellent game against Kirkley, with a half century from Vaughan and four wickets from Denton, was only marred by the result - a four wicket defeat.

Another unforgettable match was against Smallburgh. This was played at

Stalham High School because their normal ground was unavailable. The major problem was that the outfield had not been cut and was about a foot high. In the Walsham innings, the Smallburgh fielders were stopping the ones and it was almost impossible to score; as soon as the ball left the square it just stopped. Vaughan took the aerial route on a couple of occasions with two sixes, but most batsmen surrendered in frustration: 55 all out off 35 overs. Despondency at tea, but it was clear that it would be just as difficult for Smallburgh who were bowled out for 33, Johnson taking 7-13 in 14 overs. What a game: 88 runs and 20 wickets from 63 overs.

The now confident team came within three runs of beating a strong Sprowston side, but had to settle for a draw and also played really well against Acle, scoring 200-4 declared, with Kerry (88) and Conrad (70) adding 158 for the third wicket. Acle finished on a miserable 99-8. Against Riddlesworth, it was Walsham's turn to accept the draw. Chasing 207-1, a reply of 143-4, with Colin Denton scoring another 80, was hardly electrifying. Perhaps the most memorable feature of the afternoon was the banana and jam sandwiches.

Before a second touring adventure (see Chapter 20), Rod Burdett brought his new team, Stamford Bridge from Yorkshire, to visit Norfolk. They were a class side and scored 234-5 against a strong Walsham side. When the reply reached 68-1, the heavens opened and the teams adjourned to the pub. No-one suggested that Stamford Bridge had been saved by rain!

On returning from the tour, there were a couple of defeats before Old Buckenham were hammered by 80 runs, Hodds (75) leading the way and Johnson and Denton both taking five wickets as Buckenham were bowled out for just 65. This was followed up with a 11 run win against Wanderers when the author recalls the last Wanderers wicket

'I just stuck out an arm as the batsmen whacked it in my direction; the ball hit my outstretched hand and stuck. I couldn't believe it and neither could the batsman!'

The final game of the season was a real disaster; a 120 run defeat to Eaton, who had scored 154 and cleared out Walsham for only 34. A bowler called Mike Tooby took 6-5, with five players not scoring. Like all teams, they occasionally get thrashed for no apparent reason except the opposition just got it right on the day. John Chilvers, the Eaton captain, remembers that day:

'we regarded South Walsham at the time as high profile opposition. In only our second game against them, our main aim was to retain the fixture. Tooby was a class act and, with Conrad, Denton, Palmer and Vaughan in their side, we were chuffed indeed.'

From the Walsham perspective, it was a poor end to a good season. Mike Conrad (703) finished the season with a record aggregate of runs while Vaughan (604) and Denton (567) made major contributions. Three bowlers took over 40 wickets - Johnson, Vaughan and Denton - while Conrad proved his all round skills with 33 wickets. Eleven games were won, six lost and thirteen drawn. John Vaughan was elected player of the season.

1978 saw the return of Doug Palmer, who had spent two seasons playing almost exclusively for Norwich Etceteras, and a new player Mike Stevens, who was a useful bat but, unfortunately, only played for one season. Another newcomer to make his debut was Kim Futter, a very keen fourteen year-old who lived in the village. Kim was not of great stature, but could bowl at a good pace. He never played much with Trevor Johnson although, if they had been able to bowl together in their pomp, it would have made a quick and aggressive opening attack. However, there would almost certainly have been strong views expressed over who should bowl with the wind! Kim took over from Trevor, until he stopped playing regularly in 1999, although he did miss four seasons during the 1980s. He also proved to be a useful batsman, could hit as well as defend and was a safe catcher. At the time of writing, it is hoped he will play a few more games, particularly as his son, Caleb, is proving to be a very promising player. A few more games and Kim would have a claim to a place in the legend category!

Kim Futter

Ray Lusted continued to look after the wicket along with other stalwarts such as Watkins, Vaughan and Evans. The season started well with a winning draw against Riddlesworth, Malcolm Hill taking four wickets and David Watkins taking over as wicket-keeper. During the season these duties were mainly shared by Reeson and Conrad, which was probably not the best way of enabling someone to specialise in the role. Colin Denton continued to improve as a bowler, his four wickets helping Walsham towards the first win of the season against Hoveton and Wroxham.

South Walsham Cricket Club 1976 - Back (l - r) Vaughan, Palmer, Ellis, Denton, Lusted, Hill Front (l - r) Johnson, Kent, Kerry, Conrad, Robinson

A further win followed against Great Braxted from Essex, with Palmer picking up five wickets. However, the 1978 season was a wet one with seven matches - a quarter of the fixtures - falling foul of the weather. A third win was not achieved until the Riddlesworth return game when Kim Futter opened the bowling for the first time and took 2-19 off 6 overs. Old rivals

Smallburgh were hammered by 99 runs, with Conrad among the runs and Johnson among the wickets.

Stamford Bridge and Rod Burdett were welcomed back to Norfolk and this time Walsham held on to a draw without the assistance of the elements. Their opening bowler, Nigel West, was decidedly quick and the author recalls

'playing down the line of the stumps and hearing a fizz and then a thud as it landed in the wicketkeeper's gloves. This happened for the whole over and, by the end, everybody could see the funny side. He was probably the fastest bowler I ever faced, but Vaughan and I held on with nine wickets down.'

A draw is a draw!

Another tour to Yorkshire (detailed in Chapter 20) was followed by a fixture against Hoveton and Wroxham. Johnson and Denton soon had them on the back foot with four wickets each, and an easy win by 75 runs ensued. Wins against Wisbech Old Grammarians and Eaton were followed by defeats against Old Buckenham and Kirkley. It had been a reasonably successful season: eight wins, four defeats and the rest either drawn or abandoned. Conrad (552) finished top of the run scorers with an average of 36.8, while Vaughan scored over 300. Johnson was slowly losing his strike bowling role through age and injury; he took just 29 wickets following his 260 in the six previous seasons. Denton (34) took the most wickets, but was well supported by Palmer (27) and Hill (17).

These had been three good seasons. Could the good times keep on rolling?

CHAPTER TWENTY *The Early Tours*

In 1974 the club decided to undertake its first tour. Peter Fisher took responsibility for the organisation and arranged some tough-looking fixtures: Claygate in Surrey, Glynde and Beddingham, Newick and Horsham Trinity in Sussex and White Roding in Essex on the way home. The party was boosted by Ivan and Les Andrews, both very useful cricketers, and Jeremy Rowe, a Horsford player, who had made his Norfolk debut earlier in the season. With Burdett, Fisher, Jack Denton and Kerry in the batting it was a very strong side. Unfortunately, the Brighton area had its worst rainfall for twenty-five years during the week and, in cricketing terms, the tour was an absolute disaster.

There was no chance of playing against Claygate on the Monday while, on Tuesday, the fixture against Glynde and Beddingham resulted in a defeat by six wickets against a class side in gloomy conditions. Persistent rain meant that the next two games - against Newick and Horsham Trinity - didn't even start, although there was an excellent social day at Newick. Horsham's ground was under water and the squad didn't even travel.

To speculate on what might have happened: the Claygate game would have been tough as they had won the Surrey final of the National Village Competition, as had Glynde and Beddingham in West Sussex. Newick, however, was a small village and might have been opponents of roughly the same standard. Back, via Essex, for the final day, Walsham played very poorly on a mud heap, although the opposition did their best to make sure there was a game which was lost by five wickets.

By the end of the tour, the players had been to the pictures, tenpin bowling, Brighton dogs and indulged in lots of drinking; it was OK, but we were there to play cricket. The squad had stayed in a hotel on Brighton front, which was supposed to be owned by the actress Dora Bryan and this was the scene for the tour's highlight: Peter Fisher engaged in a political debate with Mick McGahey, the famous miners' leader, who was later to become deputy to Arthur Scargill. The discussion went on long into the night, with voices getting louder as more drink was consumed. Recollections of the details are now hazy - for some, they probably were indistinct by the following morning - but Peter's right-wing views acted as a catalyst for a full exposition of the

McGahey gospel. The life-long communist, the bogeyman of the *Daily Mail*, regaled his cricketing audience, in his uniquely growling Glaswegian tones, with tales of the disaffected as Peter tried, mainly in vain, to stem his flow.

The author's tour was not without its dramatic moments. Dave Russen, a Norwich Etceteras player who appeared occasionally for Walsham, was fielding against Glynde and Beddingham when he was hit on the head. Although he insisted he was OK, he clearly wasn't and had to be taken to Eastbourne hospital for a check-up. This was where the problems started:

'David was drifting in and out of consciousness and, as we approached Eastbourne, the car broke down. Flagging down another car - I had assumed that the hospital was close - two lovely old ladies gave me a lift to the hospital and I left David with his girlfriend. I reached the hospital, explained the situation and returned in the ambulance. When we got back, David was awake again and under the bonnet trying to repair the car. I am not sure what would have happened if he had got the car going and driven off. I think the ambulance men would have thought I was mad.

By this time, David was getting quite difficult and his girlfriend and I insisted he went to the hospital. We finally got there and David received treatment. They were a bit undecided whether to keep him in overnight, but David insisted he was OK. Back in the car park, he insisted that he would drive the car, as he did, despite the nervousness of both me and his girlfriend. When we got back to the ground, the game had finished and the lads were having a few beers. David complained that he had a headache and decided to go back to the hotel early. When he came down to breakfast the next morning, he could not remember anything from the time he had been hit on the head. It was a bit frightening really, as he had driven his car twelve miles. It was a lucky escape and taught me how dangerous concussion can be.'

The rain-affected tour had been dispiriting and there was a three year gap before the next venture - to York in 1977 - helped by Rod Burdett's contacts in the area. Opponents were: Stamford Bridge, Osbaldwick, a team that had visited Norfolk earlier in the year, Pocklington and Heworth. The tour party was strengthened by the Fudge brothers from Eaton but, generally, it was the normal Walsham squad. Again the weather intervened, but nowhere near as badly as 1974: Walsham had the losing end of a draw against Osbaldwick and were rained off against Heworth, but it was the Pocklington game which produced the drama.

On the Sunday before the tour Walsham had played Dereham whose spinner was Barry Battelley, a current Norfolk player. It turned out that he would be in the Pocklington area on the day of the fixture and, as it was known that they were going to be a strong side, he was asked to make a guest appearance. He agreed but, unfortunately, did not arrive at the agreed pick-up point, hence there were only ten players on the field as Pocklington motored to 43-1 from the first five overs. Mike Conrad, who could be a little excitable, yelled at Battelley's unused chauffeur (the author) to get changed and announced, classically, that he would bring himself on to bowl 'to slow the run rate'. He immediately went for 24 in two overs! However, the match changed when Mike brought on the spinners, Denton and Hill, who bowled 22 overs for 84 runs, which in the context of the game was an excellent performance. Pocklington finished on 207-8.

Alex Evans, left, and Rod Burdett, leading the singing on the York Tour 1980

Walsham rarely played 45-over games, but Pocklington seemed to think playing for the draw might be the Norfolk approach, so an overs game had been agreed. There was a slow start and the run rate rose, but only a few wickets were lost. Vaughan scored 64, a local wiseacre commenting that, in the local accent, he was '*solid enuff, but all bottom and.*' When he was dismissed, 90 were needed from 11 overs. Suddenly, Conrad, Nick Fudge and Hill went 'berserk', the ball being hit in all directions. One lasting memory was their left arm quickie bowling to Hill who smashed the ball straight back at him; it hit him in the middle of his forehead and went for four! A little earlier one of their players had left early, thinking the game had been won. Hill hit 33 off just 18 balls and secured a Walsham win by five wickets off the last ball. For Walsham, elation at such a great win, but not for the Pocklington players who were furious. They had taken it easy and blown it; they shut themselves in the dressing room for an inquest and it was some time before they arrived in the bar.

After this, the game at Stamford Bridge - a 53 run defeat - was something of an anti-climax. Denton took 5-38, but only he and Kerry got past 20 in Walsham's reply. However, it had been an excellent tour and it was universally agreed there would be more.

Returning to York the following year, the squad were again badly hit by the weather. Only one game was played in Yorkshire, plus one on the way home against Wisbech Old Grammarians on the Friday. On the Tuesday a fixture had been arranged against Osbaldwick, with whom a good rapport had already been established on the previous tour and when they had toured Norfolk. With heavy rain falling, a game was unlikely but, from midday onwards, pub games were accompanied by multiple portions of meat pie and mushy peas. Mike Sidell - an old rugby man - was very good with the songs and a few others joined in. The whole village seemed to turn up in the evening and a riotous time was had by all. At one point there were a few dares, one of them resulting in Mike - the respectable Cringleford doctor - running round the bar naked, despite the mixed company. A wonderful day which ended about midnight, although twelve hours drinking had left many of the party rather worse for wear.

In the game that was played, Sidell and Lusted played for Stamford Bridge as they were two men short. The Yorkshiremen clearly couldn't cope with their presence as they only managed 135-7 off 40 overs. These were knocked off with four overs to spare in a six wicket victory, thanks to Hodds and Watkins.

The game on the way home at Wisbech ended in a winning draw, after Walsham had scored 144-5. The former professional Eddie Davis, who had enjoyed a twenty-year career with Northamptonshire, successfully farmed the bowling when playing for the draw. Having 'transferred' Evans to the opposition, the opportunity to run him out was spurned by his Walsham team-mates who opted not to remove the bails. The Old Grammarians finished on 100-8 in what had been a rather unsatisfactory finish to the week. However, there was a return to Yorkshire, for a third time in 1980: a tour that will never be forgotten!

The first remarkable thing to happen on the third venture to York tour was the loss of one of the star players through injury before the first match.

There were four games planned and accommodation was again at *The Newington Hotel* - the HQ for previous tours - but it was under new ownership and it didn't seem quite as relaxed as previously. However, bags were deposited and an evening in York for a few beers, and possibly a night club, seemed the appropriate way to start the week. The squad was the core Walsham players, Steve Royal who played for one season, Keith Hodds, Nick Fudge from Eaton and Derek Holyman, who played for Cringleford, a larger than life character who helped the party move along.

On the way into town a green box, similar in shape and size to a Royal Mail post box, offered the first challenge of the evening. It was decided to have a competition as to who could leap the box. Hazy recollection suggests that Denton and Holyman managed to clear it with ease. Conrad, ever the competitor, attempted it and fell awkwardly yelling that he had done something to his leg. Luckily, Dr Sidell was in the squad. He examined it as best he could - bearing in mind that a few beers had already been consumed - and thought it was probably not too serious. The evening carried on, more beers were consumed and, eventually, the party returned to the hotel at about 1.00am. By this time, Mike Conrad was in some pain and had to be carried. Reaching the hotel, the team doctor suggested we needed to raise Mike's bed so his leg could be elevated while he slept. The 'obvious solution' seemed to be to take some of the rockery from the hotel garden and use this to raise the bed, hoping that the hotel owner wouldn't notice until there was a chance to put it all back. Such was the thinking of a group of semi-inebriated cricketers!

According to his room-mate, Conrad groaned and moaned all night and, by the time he was carried down to breakfast, Mike Sidell thought it would probably be a good idea to take him to the local A&E for a precautionary X-ray. He was accompanied by the entire squad, anxious to provide moral support, which became useful when he was told that the leg was broken in two places. Mike asked the doctor whether it was likely that he could play later in the week - he was in plaster for the next eleven weeks! There was a certain amount of laughter when he rang his wife explaining that he had broken his leg. Unsympathetically, she was not impressed when he explained the circumstances.

To add to the team's problems, on the night of the injury, Kim Futter had clearly made up his mind to drink York dry single-handed and the next day was in no position to play cricket. There were fifteen players in the squad, but this had already been reduced to thirteen before the first game at Tadcaster. Conrad was happy to umpire on crutches while Futter was banished to the score box, where he stayed all day. It was an interesting ground with breweries all the way round and the constant smell of beer. Perhaps the preparations for the first game had not been of the best and, at 39-7, embarrassing defeat loomed. However, the hosts opted to release the pressure and, with Vaughan standing firm with 62 not out and Nick Fudge playing his part with 29 not out, the total crawled to 122-8 off the allotted 40 overs.

At tea it was all very light-hearted. Tadcaster were so confident of victory that they reversed their batting order, with their two first teamers batting at 10 and 11. When they reached 63-1, the game was effectively over. Enter secret weapon, Derek Holyman: bowling at a very steady medium pace. The batsmen tried to hit him round the park, but kept getting out and he took 7-25 from 10 overs. This left the two first teamers to knock off the final 24 runs for victory. However, luck was with Walsham when the two batsmen both ended up at the same end, producing a run out and a 15 run victory. Walsham delight was matched by Tadcaster fury. As at Pocklington three years previously: an inquest in the dressing room. They were clearly the better side, but cricket is a funny game although, on both occasions, the opposition were less than amused. Another boozy night followed!

Returning to Osbaldwick, rain affected the game which was reduced to 16 overs a side. Walsham hit 118-7 - only Denton and Hodds made any significant runs - and the home side won by five wickets with three balls to spare. Conrad continued to perform well as an umpire on one leg, but rain washed out the Thursday game. Again on the way home Wisbech Old Grammarians provided the Friday opposition; the game ended in a draw, Denton top-scoring and taking four wickets.

The base for these three York tours had been *The Newington*, about a half a mile from York's historic 'Shambles'. Close by was a wonderful watering hole called *The Bay Horse,* which provided the setting for some memorable evenings.However,1980 was the last visit to *The Newington*. Their patience had probably been tested a bit too far: getting back late, waking up other guests, losing the key and general mischievous behaviour. On one visit Greg Norman, the famous Australian golfer had been staying in the same hotel when he was playing in a tournament at the nearby Fulford course. It's likely that he didn't always get a good night's sleep when Walsham were in town! Doug Palmer recalls a classic story of the tour.

'I remember rooming with Mike Sidell. We were in the hotel very drunk, and the owner closed the bar at a time we thought was pretty early. We were very hungry but, with no chance of any food, we kept the owner talking whilst Mike found his way to the kitchen. Mike reappeared and, looking a little uncomfortable, indicated that we ought to go to bed. On arriving back in the room Mike produced from under his shirt a whole side of smoked salmon. He then of course, as doctors do, produced a scalpel and proceeded to cut the fish into manageable bite sizes. The skin, which we could see as a problem in the morning, we decided was best thrown out of the window. In the morning we discovered, to our concern, hotel staff with ladders up on the roof trying to unblock the guttering. Fortunately we heard no more from the owner, although I am sure he had his suspicions.'

The author recalls another episode:

'We were out and, after a few beers, we thought it funny to wear some traffic cones on our heads while walking around York. Looking back it was a bit dangerous, as these cones were surrounding a hole in the pathway. Anyway, we were walking up the street when we were stopped by a policeman. His first words were 'It's Alex, isn't it?' I had to admit it was. We had played cricket against him earlier in the tour. We returned the cones and nothing more was said.'

Such were the joys of cricket tourism 70s-style with South Walsham!

CHAPTER TWENTY ONE *Cricket In The 1970's*
Leagues, Cups & Money

Club cricket changed quite dramatically in the 1970s. Previous chapters have highlighted the key characteristics of the two previous decades - the Gentlemen/Players divide of the 1950s and the impact of a consumer society in the socially radical 1960s - but, in terms of the shape and atmosphere of the club game, the major changes in Norfolk cricket in the 1970s can be summarised in three words: leagues, cups and money.

For almost a century, the concept of league cricket had divided the country on a north/south axis. Structured leagues had existed in all counties north of Birmingham since the 1890s. In both the industrial heartlands and their rural hinterlands, cricket was intensely competitive and reflective of its immediate communities. Perhaps it never quite attained the status of football in its claim on local loyalties, but in some areas, particularly Yorkshire and Lancashire, this was only a matter of degree.

In the south, until the late 1960s, league cricket was shunned as an alien notion. Perhaps, in some respects, this reflected another facet of Gentlemen v Players, although there were many 'players' in the south and, one assumes, a few 'gentlemen' north of Birmingham. More accurately, it mirrored the winter oval-ball game. Since the historic meeting in the George Hotel, Huddersfield in August 1895, when a group of northern clubs broke away to form their own competition, rugby had developed two cultures that came to inhabit parallel universes. Although cricket never experienced the same cleavage, the cultures of northern and southern cricket unfolded in isolation from each other.

At its highest level, club cricket in the south was dominated by the informal, but highly influential, Club Cricket Conference - the 'MCC of the recreational game'. This organisation bound together 'gentlemen's' cricket, promoting an ethos based on friendly fixtures and a strict amateurism; the similarities with rugby union were unavoidable. Below the elite level, thousands of village and suburban clubs across thirty counties followed this lead, not in any formal or directed way, but because this best reflected 'their' type of cricket.

What happened in the 1960s to change this established pattern is difficult to analyse. Geographical mobility as cricketers moved from a northern league environment, the emergence of league structures in other 'strictly amateur' sports (rugby union and hockey), greater cross-over with football: all may have played some part. Probably, the gradual erosion of the Gentlemen/Players distinction was the main underlying influence.

Whatever the explanation, there is no doubt that league cricket mushroomed in southern England. In the mid 1960s, there were few league structures while, by 1980, they dominated Saturday cricket to the extent that those clubs who resisted the change were finding it difficult to fill their fixture lists. Sunday friendlies were retained, but these were increasingly seen as less prestigious matches.

Saturday cricket in Norfolk developed along these lines. There had been some 'minor' leagues in the inter-war era - indeed South Walsham's inter-war cricket had been dominated by membership of the Freethorpe and District League - but this was a localised grouping and marked out competing clubs as inferior in terms of cricketing status. Like the Mid-Norfolk League, the Norwich and District League and the Beck Flegg League, it may have carried some prestige in terms of parochial bragging rights, but serious cricket - at least 'Gentlemen's' cricket - did not take place within a league structure.

The first breach in Norfolk was the work of an unlikely pioneer. Peter Powell - Norwich Wanderers, Ingham and former Norfolk captain: the archetypal gentleman cricketer - must have needed an outlet for his statistical urges; one suspects that had he known where his initiative might lead, he might not have taken the first, albeit limited, step by creating a 'merit table'. The concept was almost certainly borrowed from rugby union, whose senior clubs had reluctantly accepted this form of measurement - devised initially by the national press - to assess their relative performance.

At one level, Powell's initiative, known as the 'Little League', was probably an attempt to preserve the status quo which was encapsulated in the prestige of a group of a dozen elite clubs; he seems to have decided whose results against whom would be worthy of inclusion. The level of attention that merit table position was given by clubs and their players cannot be accurately assessed at a distance of almost fifty years, but the local press was lukewarm in its interest, both the EDP and EEN publishing the merit table irregularly and showing scant attention to its end of season outcome.

Yet the 'Little League' was the precursor for the creation in the late 1960s of the Norfolk Alliance. Powell's self-perpetuating group of elite clubs were the founder members, but their assumed superiority quickly came under challenge. The 'players' were at the gate; cricketing meritocracy was bursting for expression and the breach had been made. Cromer, late entrants to the 'Little League' and Bradfield, never admitted to its ranks, stormed to the top of the local cricketing pecking order, while, over the next few years, Norwich Wanderers - Powell's citadel - the club that provided the bulk of the county side in the 1950s slumped to find their level among the hoi-polloi.

Where the senior clubs led, the next echelon of Norfolk clubs quickly followed. In 1972, a 'Federation' of the second tier - Acle, Thetford, Horsford, Brooke, Fakenham, Hunstanton and others - created their own merit table. This lasted a mere two years before it became the Norfolk League. Starting in 1974 with three divisions of eight teams, by 1981 there were six divisions of ten teams. Both competitions - Alliance and Norfolk League - formed additional divisions for their clubs' 'A' teams, while the West Norfolk League was formed to create a competition for clubs west of Swaffham. Village clubs with ambition - Swardeston, Great Witchingham, Topcroft, Old Buckenham - flocked to the newly-established structures; league membership became the sought-after badge of status.

Within a decade, club cricket in Norfolk had undergone a revolution. Saturdays now meant league cricket, but what of Sundays? Since reforming after the Second World War, South Walsham had opted to play their cricket on the Sabbath. In the 1950s and 1960s this had allowed a set of regular fixtures to be arranged against prestige clubs, even if it did mean a couple of annual trips into Suffolk in order to 'maintain standards'. In the early 1970s, under Peter Fisher's stewardship, as many as possible of these traditional contests were clung to, despite Walsham's weakening talent pool.

However, from 1975, the club's fixture list started to change quite significantly. This was partly a consequence of a belated acknowledgement of the club's lower status, but of equal impact was the emergence of two interlinked changes: the introduction of competitive cup cricket and the shift in player perception of non-competition cricket. Cup cricket was not new; innumerable local, mainly midweek, trophies had been available from the 1930s and competition for the Norfolk Junior Cup had begun as early as 1891. But what happened in the 1970s was different.

Many of Walsham's traditional opponents were eager to enter the 60-over Carter Cup, which quickly established itself as the county's premier Sunday competition. A few years later, the entrepreneurial Stan 'Jimmy' Biss offered an additional Sunday cup, with the added incentive of financial awards in its latter stages. Clubs a little lower down the food chain still had the Norfolk Junior Cup which, under pressure from league competitions switched from Saturday to Sunday, while the CTS - with its unlikely sponsor, the City Tyre Service - added to the opportunities for pot-hunting. All of these cup competitions had their subsidiary 'plate' events. In addition, for the really ambitious clubs, there was the National Village Cup.

South Walsham dabbled with two of these competitions, but one win in the National Village against Loddon in 1972 was the only success. Three defeats - in the second round of the national competition, the Carter Cup and its plate event - were sufficient for the club to withdraw from this form of the game. Cup cricket was expanding in the years when Walsham were at a low ebb; perhaps, if playing standards had been higher, the incentive to continue might have been greater.

As a consequence, Walsham's fixture planning became problematic and a new range of opponents appeared. Not all clubs turned to Sunday pot-hunting, but the days of playing oppositions stocked with county players was over. Where the 'bigger' clubs were still played, this would be at 'A' team standard at best. Such was the hold that competition cricket - league and cup - began to exercise on the minds of many club cricketers, particularly at senior level, that the quality Sunday friendly slipped quietly into cricket's traditions rather than forming a vibrant element in its present. This established the context of South Walsham's cricket from the mid 1970s.

The third element of cricketing change in this era was money. The financial dimension of the game was changing at all levels. Internationally, the landscape was being transformed by one man: Kerry Packer, the Australian TV mogul and owner of Channel 9. His battle with the ACB, his national cricket board, over televising Test cricket spilled over to other nations as their professionals left the 'official' game to participate in 'Packer's circus' of 'exhibition' games. Their eagerness was understandable; cricketers had always been at the lower end of the wage scale for professional sportsman.

When the dust finally settled on the five-year conflict, there was considerably more money in the game, not all of which found its way into the pockets of the international superstars. County professionals became better paid and, with an increasingly business-based approach, their employers began to seek alternative forms of revenue, mainly through sponsorship. The realisation that money could make a difference and bring success was not lost on ambitious clubs. Kerry Packer may have had no interest in Norfolk club cricket but, indirectly, his approach infiltrated the thinking of one man who brought a new dimension to the game in the county. That man was Stan 'Jimmy' Biss.

The highly successful Yarmouth caravan site owner, obsessive pigeon fancier but rather less renowned Acle cricketer examined the Packer model and decided that it was transferable to a more modest setting. In 1972 he had set up a new club - initially named Vauxhall - on the plot of land in Brundall on which he had already built himself a large house. For a few years Biss, who had played a few games for South Walsham in the late 1960s, was content to invite friends to enjoy a low key game of cricket against clubs with no pretensions to league status or Carter Cup ambitions. However, the Packer revolution fired his imagination. Within a few years, he showed what could be done with an injection of money: new players arrived - accompanied by rumours of 'boot money'; a sumptuous two-tier pavilion was constructed; a new Sunday cup competition, unsurprisingly eponymously titled, was launched.

Having established the foundations, an amalgamation with established Norwich side Mallards - one of the 1960s 'Little League' elite - enabled the newly-styled Vauxhall Mallards to leapfrog rivals into the upper echelons of Norfolk cricket in the early 1980s. Thirty years later, despite the death of the club's founder, they remain one of the four top clubs in the county. The intervening years have been studded with success in league and cup competitions and, in 1999, they became founder members of the East Anglian Premier League. Their employment of overseas professionals, several of whom had played Test cricket, set a trend which other ambitious clubs felt obliged to follow.

As the Biss revolution began at the end of the 1970s, few could have forecast the scope of the changes that his wealth - albeit only a small proportion of it - injected into a cricket club would have over the next three decades. In their early years, Vauxhall played South Walsham as a regular fixture. From 1980 onwards, the gap between the two clubs became so wide that the five-mile distance between the grounds in no way represented the cricketing chasm that separated them. Money had transformed many areas of the game, but it was to the huge credit of Walsham and a hundred other Norfolk clubs that not only had they survived, but that the true spirit of cricket burned as brightly, arguably more brightly, on the village playing field as it did in the palatial surroundings of Biss acres.

CHAPTER TWENTY TWO *A Bit Of A Dip*
1979-1981

The key change in 1979 was the retirement of Ken Kerry. Although he had only played regularly for Walsham for a few seasons, as captain Ken had been an excellent steadying influence on some of the young players who could occasionally get a little excited. He had a less successful season in 1978 and perhaps that suggested that it was time for him to call it a day, although he did serve a few years as the club's President. There were four debutants: Keith Denton, the third member of the clan, Steve Munday, Tony Kinsley and club legend number three - Garth Futter

Beginning as a raw teenager, by the end of the 2012 season Garth was homing in on Peter Edrich's South Walsham record of 729 wickets. His tally of 706 suggests that, if he stays fit he should get there in 2013. As a youngster, he started off with a longish run, but he does think a fair bit about his bowling and, as the years have passed, his run-up has gradually become shorter and he produces his impetus from the shoulder. In his early days he was once called for throwing, against Essex tourists, Margaretting. Shock was expressed, particularly as he had just uprooted a batsman's middle stump! As he matured, he also developed into a hard-hitting middle-order batsman, with nineteen half centuries, although a century has always eluded him. However, he has won many games, not only with his bowling but with his cameo batting performances. Now approaching fifty years of age he has passed the 6000 run mark in just short of 600 appearances.

Garth Futter

Of the three other newcomers, the one who made the greatest long-term impact was Keith Denton. He started playing as a youngster and quickly became a very good player who, in 1982, opted to test himself at a higher standard, but returned in 1997 for another five seasons. The only Denton to score a century - a brilliant 122 against Great Oakley on the Northamptonshire tour in 1990 - he continues to play on an irregular basis, when his work commitments allow, and his 200+ games have yielded over 4,000 runs.

Both of the other debutants also made a significant contribution. Steve Munday was a very useful slow bowler, who could always put it on the spot; he very rarely got hit around, although he barely turned the ball, He always thought he was a better bat than his figures showed and he could be a little difficult to handle at times, but his bowling speaks for itself. He took 183 wickets in a thousand overs at 18 runs per wicket and played for nine seasons before moving on. Tony Kinsley was a classy batsman who played over fifty games in four seasons, scoring over 700 runs at an average of just under 20.

Following three seasons where more games were won than lost, 1979 was very disappointing. Starting with two defeats and four draws in the first six matches, the struggle for runs was surprising as the line-up was not particularly different to the three previous years. The seventh game of the season, the occasion of Keith Denton's debut, was typical. Chasing 172-5 against Bradfield, at 29-7 only Vaughan stood firm with 33 not out, although, amazingly, his resistance enabled a draw to be secured at 60-8. Those 60 runs came from 41 overs, although Bradfield only used three bowlers. Maybe if they had tossed it up a bit more, they might have got the final two wickets.

The results during 1979 seemed to take the club back to the early 1970s when wins were few and far between. The main reason, almost certainly, was the loss of the main strike bowler Trevor Johnson. In the previous eight seasons he had always bowled over 200 overs. Indeed, in 1977 he bowled 298; no one has ever come near that number again. He was coming towards the end of his career and was only able to bowl 72 overs during 1979, taking sixteen wickets at an average of 10. He missed several games and, despite the improvement of Colin Denton, oppositions were no longer being knocked over so regularly. Conrad could only bat, as he was nursing an injury, and Kim Futter was still making his way in the game.

The first win of the season didn't arrive until the middle of August in the game when Steve Munday made his debut. Hoveton and Wroxham were beaten by 5 wickets. Chasing 139 after Malcolm Hill had taken his best figures (5-38), runs from Vaughan and Watkins finally broke the lose or draw sequence. With morale raised, Old Buckenham were beaten the following week, Johnson taking 4-23 off 16 overs as Buckenham were dismissed for 104. Despite a fine effort from their opening bowler, Andy Emms, who took 3-9 off 16 overs, Colin Denton and Watkins saw Walsham home by six wickets. The game was also notable for the debut of Garth Futter.

Runs from Conrad and Watkins led to the third and final win of the season by 55 runs against Kirkley A. Conrad made 107 not out, the first Walsham centurion since 1967 but the season was disappointing: just three successes from twenty two completed games. The usual batsmen still scored the runs: Conrad (724), set a record high aggregate, Vaughan was just short of 500, while Colin Denton scored 371. In the bowling department it was much more of a struggle, only Colin Denton with 26 and Kim Futter 20 gaining any reasonable return.

At the end of the season Mike Conrad decided that he wanted to play a higher grade of cricket and moved to Wanderers, although he still remained a friend of the club and played in some touring games. He was very competitive and it did make sense for him to try to prove himself at a higher level but, after a season of limited success, his loss made it all the more difficult to return to the years of regular victories.

In 1980, Steve Munday became a regular, as did Tony Kinsley, while the Futter brothers continued to improve. However, Trevor Johnson played just a few games and slowly drifted from the scene when he moved to Cambridgeshire. No one of significance made their debut, and it looked as though it would be a real struggle without Conrad and Johnson.

The season started badly against Lowestoft, who scored 230-3 declared, to which the Walsham response was 66-8 off 51 overs. All their players bowled; it was a real low - Walsham were embarrassingly bad! Doug Mattocks, the Norfolk wicket keeper at the time, took a real liking to the bowling and smashed a quick 124. In the next match Watkins baled out the team; chasing 154 against Coltishall, the innings was soon in trouble at 17-4, but his 73 not out pulled it round to 122-4 in a drawn game. Another draw against UEA saw Vaughan come desperately close to his first century. Always a team player, he went for a big hit on 97 and was stumped. However, he struck a good vein of form, making 51 not out in the win against Hoveton and Wroxham and then, finally, reached three figures with a 101 not out against Eaton in a score of 156-6. It was a marvellous innings and a great day for him and the team, who were delighted to see such a popular player score a century. John Chilvers, the Eaton captain, also remembers the day:

'A winning draw for Eaton, as I recall. What made the match so memorable was that John Vaughan scored his maiden hundred. The obvious joy, albeit quietly expressed, that this gave John - a fine cricketer and a gentleman of the first rank - places this recollection at the top of my list of memories of games against South Walsham.'

Wins against Bradfield and Margaretting kept Walsham on the up and Keith Denton started to score significant runs, top-scoring in a drawn match against Earlham Lodge. There was an incredible game against Coltishall. Walsham were fielding a strong side, but collapsed to 40-8. Kim Futter and Alex Evans came together and inched the innings to 87-8, but Evans' dismissal, followed by a duck for Ray Lusted, closed the innings at 87 off 41 overs. In reply Coltishall found the going equally difficult and they finished on 78-8, also off 41 overs. Colin Denton took 2-13 from 12 overs, while Vaughan took 2-7 off 8 overs. It had been a fine bowling and fielding performance.

After a defeat at Riddlesworth and a win against Eaton, there was another exciting game against old friends from Stamford Bridge, who were bowled out for 141, Doug Palmer taking 5-7 from 9 overs. In reply, Walsham finished on 136-9 with Palmer also top-scoring. Good innings from Vaughan against Loddon and Dereham A led to two emphatic victories, while Colin Denton played his part taking 4-16 and 5-38 in these two matches. In the Dereham game, Vaughan and Kinsley added 142 for the first wicket - a record at the time.

After the hilarities of the famous 1980 York tour (covered in Chapter 20), Walsham returned to Norfolk and, following a draw against Hoveton and Wroxham, there was a one wicket defeat against Old Buckenham. However, this game was not without its significance: Kim Futter, who was now becoming quite a force, picked up his first five wicket haul.

The next match was another one of those days that will always be remembered by those involved although, sadly, not for positive reasons. Travelling to Wisbech to play the Old Grammarians, an early departure from Norwich gave the opportunity for 'refuelling' on the way, not unheard of for Walsham! Fielding first, one or two of the players seemed to be suffering a bit, and a poor performance - 'fielded like idiots' is probably the apt phrase - Wisbech reached 180-3 at tea off 51 overs. Not a hammering, but it did produce some critical comment. Ray Lusted piped up and said he thought he had done well and was told that 'he should never have been fielding in the covers'. (The author admits responsibility for this indiscreet and unnecessary remark). Ray took offence and immediately started changing. David Watkins, who was the skipper that day, told Ray that if he was required to bat, he would bat. Ray was not happy and said he was off home, possibly forgetting he hadn't brought his car and was 60 miles away from Norwich!

The game finished in a draw, Walsham falling only 30 runs short of victory with six wickets down. There was certainly tension in the changing room and Ray said he would not be playing again and he kept to his word. This was extremely sad, as he had played a major part in keeping the club going in the early 1970s, spending hundreds of hours tending the wicket. But he was a very proud man and didn't feel able to change his mind. After an interval of many years, he came to watch a game and was as pleasant as ever. Those who had known him wondered if he had ever regretted his decision to leave Walsham after a decade of dedication.

The rest of the season was winless and, when it was analysed, could be described as 'the season of the draw'. Many of the draws had seen Walsham hanging on to avoid defeat. The key players had been John Vaughan and Colin Denton. Vaughan had a brilliant season scoring 806 runs at 42, while Denton and Kinsley both scored over 300. Denton had been the star bowler taking 57 wickets in 250 overs at an average of 13. Palmer and Kim Futter both took over 20 wickets, while Denton (15 catches) and Kinsley (14) excelled in the field. At the end of the season, like Mike Conrad before him, Colin Denton decided to try his hand at a higher level of cricket with Norwich Wanderers, but still played for Walsham when his commitments allowed.

The 1981 season saw Walsham struggle a little for players, Doug Palmer played mainly for Norwich Etceteras, Conrad and Denton were both now playing for Wanderers and Malcolm Hill had decided to call it a day as had Trevor Johnson. On the plus side, John Westgarth returned to the fold and the club welcomed a new bowler, Derek Gorrod. 'Del', as he was always known, played over 360 games for Walsham over the next 20 years. He was always looked upon as a slow medium left arm trundler, but he took over 300 wickets and was rarely 'tonked' by the opposition's batting.

In the first five matches of the season there were three draws and two losses and the side were second-best in these games. Runs came mainly from Vaughan and Kinsley and the wickets from Munday and the Futter brothers. The first win came in rather strange circumstances against Trevor Johnson's new club, a strong Cambridgeshire village side called Thriplow. An all-day game had been organised and Walsham were strengthened by the presence of both 'Wanderers', Conrad and Denton. It was a good wicket, but after about an hour's batting the scoreboard read: South Walsham 43-6. By lunch the total had edged up to 90-6, with John Westgarth 20 not out.

After lunch, Westgarth fell early to make it 95-7. Colin Denton came in and, with the bowlers tiring, hit a quick fifty. Meanwhile, Alex Evans who had never previously batted for much over an hour continued in a placid role, finally being dismissed for 39 in about three hours. Ironically, he was caught by Trevor Johnson at silly mid on, the same spot where he had fielded for Johnson's bowling over the previous eight years. Walsham declared on 172-9 off 62 overs. Thriplow seemed to be mentally shattered by this experience and they were bowled for 77 in 25 overs. All six Walsham bowlers took wickets and victory was achieved with more than an hour to spare.

A fortnight later, in an excellent game against local rivals Acle, Walsham finished a dozen runs short of the target of 156 with two wickets in hand. This included a recovery from 29-5 as Westgarth (63) and Evans (36) again produced a major partnership for the sixth wicket - 97 on this occasion. Many games were drawn in 1981, although there was a second win against Hoveton and Wroxham. Once again Westgarth (61) was among the runs in a total of 151-6. Hoveton were dismissed for just 66, Kim Futter taking 4-22 from 10 overs. More draws and a couple of defeats followed.

The end of the season record was: three wins, five defeats and the rest draws - a rather disappointing campaign. Only Westgarth and Vaughan managed 300 runs, while Futter (32) and Munday (28) were the only two bowlers to make a significant mark in the wickets column, Derek Gorrod (11) being the only other bowler to reach double figures.

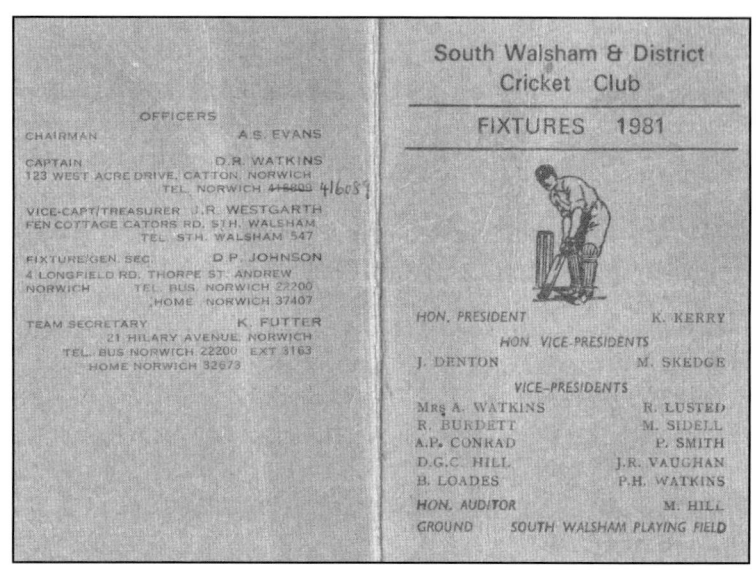

Fixture Card 1981

CHAPTER TWENTY THREE *Regrouping*
1982/83

There were no new faces as the 1982 season started, although results began to improve. The first game was an encouraging seven wicket win over Coltishall with Colin Denton taking 3-1 and Westgarth scoring 50 not out. This was followed by a 16 run win against UEA, when Westgarth scored his only century for the club (108 not out) in a total of 167-7 declared. Despite this success, all seemed lost when UEA were cruising at 117-1, with plenty of time to go. Enter bowler Mike Sidell, who took 5-26 in 5 overs as UEA slipped to 151 all out - 'a win out of the jaws of defeat' as the cliché-writers like to say! In the next match, Sidell was at it again taking 4-29 off 9 overs as Hoveton and Wroxham were bowled out for 62 in reply to Walsham's 145-3, most of the runs coming from Kinsley and Keith Denton.

There was a bad spell after those two wins - three draws and a heavy defeat against Bradfield - but a good draw was obtained against Thriplow chasing a total of 216 in 39 overs. This was followed by another excellent game against Coltishall. On a wicket where run-scoring was difficult, Coltishall were restricted to 110 off 51 overs, Munday starring with 5-30 from 12 overs while Vaughan 2-9 from 8 overs and Garth Futter 1-8 from 8 overs also pinned down the opposition. After tea, Walsham found batting just as difficult, except for John Vaughan who scored 52 before being run out. That was the difference between winning and drawing as Walsham finished three runs short with just one wicket left. Quite a game, despite only 218 runs being scored from 93 overs.

This tight finish was followed by another close draw with Gothic in which Watkins top-scored with 42. Gothic held on 15 runs short of victory with 2 wickets left. Following a disappointing defeat against Eaton, it was back to winning ways against Dereham. A Sidell and Westgarth helped Walsham to 138-9 declared before the Futter brothers saw off the Dereham batsmen. Kim took 4-24 and Garth 2-8 off 7 overs, before Munday with 3-9 raced through the tail as Dereham slipped to 89 all out.

Stamford Bridge visited Norfolk again, but Walsham were on the wrong end of the draw after the visitors had been bowled out for 179. The modest reply (124-9) saw Gorrod top-scoring with 23 not out; hitting double figures was a rare event for Gorrod! Hoveton and Wroxham were beaten despite a poor batting performance by Walsham (98 all out), the bowlers compensating by dismissing the opposition for 71, Colin Denton taking 4-19 and Sidell 3-18. An unusual feature of this match was that two players - Garth Futter and Alex Evans - both held on to four catches in the same innings. That particular statistic can't have happened on many occasions in any class of cricket.

After this match, the squad departed for a tour of Worcester which is detailed in Chapter 27. On returning to Norfolk, Walsham received what can only be described as a 9 wicket 'hiding' from Gothic, after making only 94 of which Keith Denton scored 44. The next win came against Cringleford, despite old friend and tour-mate Derek Holyman picking up five wickets. Westgarth's 72 not out led the way to a total of 162-8, and Cringleford were bowled out for 100, with five wickets for Colin Denton and four for Munday.

This game was also Mike Sidell's last before he and his wife Liz were tragically killed on holiday in America. It was somehow appropriate that his final game should be on the Cringleford playing field, which was very near to his surgery.. He was a very well-educated man, but he also knew how to enjoy himself. Although well into his forties, he was still a leader in the singing and the 'games-playing'. More of a batsman than a bowler, he would occasionally have a trundle and usually do quite well. He played 97 games for the club and his death came as a major shock to all. He was extremely popular and was badly missed not only by South Walsham cricketers but by all who knew him.

The statistics for the season were seven wins and five loses, the rest being drawn or abandoned. The top run scorer was Westgarth (440) followed by Vaughan (313) while Watkins and both Dentons scored over 250. In the bowling, Munday did well to take 37 wickets at 14.7 apiece, while Colin Denton (26) and Kim Futter (24) and Sidell (19 from just 60 overs) also made impressive contributions.

Family commitments meant John Westgarth didn't play in 1983. Neither did Colin Denton or Tony Kinsley and, with the tragic loss of Mike Sidell, the squad was suddenly four players light from the previous season. In addition, Garth Futter was struggling with football-related injuries. However, three players joined the club and made a significant impact: Terry Ogden, Fred Leak and Steve Belton. Between them, over the next twenty years, they were to play over 920 games, score over 9,000 runs and take over 700 wickets: they were very three valuable additions.

Terry Ogden made his debut against Mattishall as a batsman, scoring 26 at number five, but it was as a bowler that he will be best remembered - together with his 'lively' behaviour after he had enjoyed a few drinks! He played regularly up to 2002, taking 473 wickets in 2700 overs. A fine off-spinner whose quicker ball was more rapid than some of the so-called 'medium pacers'; he would quite often catch out the wicket keeper when standing up to the stumps. He almost certainly could have played at a much higher standard; he had done so in his youth, but hadn't played for about twenty years until he joined Walsham. He was also a magnificent singer with a very wide range of songs, drank in the same class as the Futter brothers and was

Terry Ogden

an all-round good club man, even though sometimes you wanted to hide when he was set on enjoying a good evening. Beneath the veneer of the respectable primary school headteacher was a wild man!

Steve Belton was a youngster who lived in the village. He had potential as a batsman which he came to fulfil as he moved into his twenties and, latterly, he also became a good slow left arm bowler and a brilliant catcher fielding close to the wicket. This 'quiet village lad' was soon led astray by the drinkers in the squad and, in his early days, Westgarth and Evans took responsibility for his 'education', once dropping him off at his parent's house at about 4.30am after a midweek game. He moved to Cambridge in 2000 and, unfortunately, has gradually played less and less, but his record of over 5600 runs, over 200 wickets and 115 catches is impressive and he still has power to add.

Although he was not in the Ogden class, he enjoyed a drink and a song and it was never too quiet when he was around.

The third new regular was Fred Leak, who played for about ten seasons, mainly as a steady batsman, who scored just under 2000 runs in 140 games. He was a great theorist of the game, which used to amuse his team-mates but he enjoyed his cricket. His son Marcus made his debut for Walsham in 2009 and Leak (snr) has returned to the club in an umpiring capacity.

Steve Belton

The first game of 1983 was against Kirkley. In a low scoring match Walsham were delighted to bowl out the opposition for 101 and, at 57-3, all looked well. However, a collapse to 74 all out, with only Watkins (32) making an impact produced a disappointing defeat. This was followed by a tense match against Eaton. Walsham managed 107, with Watkins (58) again in the runs and Eaton finished on 102-8. Denis Ellis, yet another 'Etcetera' who played occasionally, took 3-31 off 25 overs as Eaton failed to reach their target from 51 overs.

John Vaughan scored 50 against Gateway - a touring side from Surrey - but, frustratingly, the game was lost by one wicket. Draws and defeats followed; it wasn't until July that the first win of the season was achieved, by three wickets, against Coltishall. The opposition were held to 131-7 which was knocked off thanks to Vaughan and Watkins. More draws and defeats followed, until a second win was achieved, against Hoveton and Wroxham.

They scored an impressive 186 with Kim Futter (5-51), but Vaughan (75) and Munday added 98 for the first wicket, and when Watkins hit a quick 33 not out Walsham were home in just 33 overs. In the latter stages of the season, run-scoring increased. Against Acle, Hodds (83) and Vaughan (40) led the way to a good total (197-6), but a strong Acle side won easily by six wickets.

Gothic's total of 198 and the capture of early wickets left Walsham in trouble at 97-7. However, Alex Evans joined Keith Hodds and took a watching brief as the powerful 'regular guest' almost won the game in a single-handed assault on the Gothic bowling. In one over he hit five boundaries before wandering down the pitch at the end of the over to observe that *'the only one I middled was the one that got fielded at mid on.'* That was typical Hodds: never got excited about anything much, but a good player to have on your side. He went on to score 104 not out but, despite Evans supporting with 24, Walsham finished thirty short with two wickets left. The final game of the season saw a win against Cringleford by seven wickets, with runs from Vaughan and wickets from Gorrod. To end a disappointing season, the final two fixtures were rained off.

It had been a less-than-successful year: three wins, five losses and lots of draws. Only Vaughan (494) and Watkins (394) scored runs with any regularity, while Kim Futter (28) was the only bowler to pass the twenty mark. The club had spent two years re-grouping, but needed some impetus to bring back the good times.

CHAPTER TWENTY FOUR *Consolidation*
1984/85

Things ticked along quite well in 1984: David Watkins was in his fourth year as captain as well as being chairman, while Ken Kerry remained President for a fourth year. In addition, the club welcomed: Fred Leak, playing on a more full time basis, Joe Abbott, a handy all round sportsman who was particularly good in the field, Gary Lewis, a useful bits and pieces player and Ben Key, a local youngster who showed some promise. These four were the additions to the hard core of Watkins, Ogden, Vaughan, Belton, Gorrod, Garth Futter and Evans. However, a serious loss to the squad was Kim Futter who had quit Norwich Union to work in a bar in the Greek Islands. He obviously missed some aspects of life in Norfolk as, on many occasions, he would ring up on a Saturday night to find out how Norwich City had got on. It was three years before he returned in 1988 to pick up the opening bowler mantle.

The season started with an excellent win over Kirkley. Walsham made 159, Watkins top-scoring with 43 and Kim Futter, playing his penultimate game before his move, hit a quick 25 and Evans chipped in with 22. Kirkley had fielded a strong team and Walsham were delighted to bowl them out for 143, Futter picking up 3-33. In stark contrast, the next match resulted in a 148 run defeat by Aldborough, although the team returned to winning ways with a nine wicket win over UEA, thanks mainly due to 75 not out from David Watkins. This became three wins out of four after a fine performance against Hoveton and Wroxham who collapsed from 81-0 before declaring on 163-9. Ogden, beginning to show what a very useful bowler he was, took 3-27 and Denis Ellis 3-34. In reply, Vaughan (77) and Leak (55) saw Walsham home in just 36 overs.

The wins kept coming: Gateway - a team from Surrey - bowled out Walsham for 120, only Watkins and Leak passing twenty, but with Colin Denton temporarily back in the ranks taking 4-4 and Ogden 3-0 they were knocked over for just 61. Thriplow were beaten by 27 runs: Walsham scored 173-9, but the opposition collapsed from 101-4 to 146 all out, Vaughan and Ogden doing the damage. A one-wicket defeat to Wisbech Old Grammarians followed, despite an excellent 63 from Vaughan. Ogden continued to pick up wickets - another two in this match - while Steve Belton's slow left arm spin was starting to become another option for skipper Watkins. It was back to winning ways with a successful chase of 172-5 against Dereham. Belton had excelled himself with 2-17 off 10 overs while Greg Savill, who played a few games that season, scored 74 and Leak 48.

A four-wicket defeat against a competitive Anglians side was followed by a run of five draws. Rollesby were held when chasing 183-3, Walsham slipped to 91-7, but Belton hung on with 33 not out in a total of 148-8. There was a close finish at Acle where Evans had to hit a six off the last ball of the game to win - a major challenge for somebody who had never hit a six in his career. He missed - and the match was drawn!

After the run of draws, Kirkley got their revenge with a five-wicket win, despite steady bowling from Ogden and Lewis. This was followed by a very heavy defeat against Shipdham - chasing 222 Walsham only managed to score 45 to lose by 177 runs; Shipdham were a strong side in the 1980s as they moved up the divisions in the Norfolk League. Only Belton managed double figures in what was, on paper, a reasonably strong Walsham side. However, bouncing back in the final game of the season, Walsham finished 13 runs short of victory with 4 wickets left when chasing Dereham's 195-5, which included a whirlwind innings of 67 from N Walter who scored his runs in about 5 overs. Belton, ably supported by Vaughan and Watkins, led the reply with 66.

The Chairman's game was rained off after what had been a mixed season: six wins, five defeats and seven draws in the eighteen games completed. The bowling was limited: Munday hadn't played as much as had been hoped and Garth Futter was struggling with injuries. Consequently, Ogden was the only bowler to pass the 20 wicket mark. The batting was more successful: Watkins (447) led from the front while Vaughan (359), Leak and Belton passed the 250 mark.

The 1985 season saw Keith Hodds play more regularly, a return to fitness of Garth Futter and more regular appearances from Steve Munday. The only change in the management of the club was that Terry Ogden became Chairman, a role he held for twenty years until his retirement in 2005.

The first game of the season was a tight draw against Kirkley. Vaughan (70) started with a bang, but Walsham collapsed to 140-9 only Joe Abbott (23) significantly troubling the scorers. However, the game was memorable for the contribution of Garth Futter who had arrived late - a little worse for wear - following a celebration from a Sunday morning football final. In later years Garth has always been someone who could still perform quite well with a few beers inside him, but on this occasion, after the team had apologised to Kirkley for his state, he batted at number eleven and proceeded to hit 26 not out in three overs before Gary Lewis was run out in a reasonable score of 173. Kirkley finished on 167-8 in an entertaining game, Munday taking 3-29 and, remarkably, Futter managing a respectable five overs.

The next match against Rollesby was even closer. After struggling to raise a team - finally turning up with ten men, including Joe Abbott's ten year old son Mark - at 76-2 when chasing Rollesby's total of 102, Walsham were bowled out for 101. However, it was back to winning ways in the next match, a seven-wicket win over UEA with Munday taking four wickets and Hodds and Vaughan among the runs.

A bad wicket at Wentworth Green saw Norwich Postal bowled out for 98, of which former Walsham player, Steve Royal top-scored with 23. After slumping to 36-5, Vaughan (39) took charge to scrape to a two-wicket win. In a rain-affected 20-over match against Hoveton and Wroxham, a Walsham total of 96 was just enough to squeeze home as the opposition could only manage 89-7. In a good performance against Acle, Hodds hit the highest individual score (93 not out) in a total of 179-4 when chasing 193.

Two draws followed, firstly against Shipdham when Walsham's 124 was met with a reply of 89-7, Garth Futter taking 4-43. This was reversed in the next match against Wisbech Old Grammarians, who scored 155-8 while Walsham managed only 68-6 off 41 overs in reply, Leak top-scoring with 21.

The next month saw a mixture of results. A comfortable win against a touring side called Riverside, with Garth Futter claiming a five- wicket haul and Vaughan and Belton knocking off the runs, was followed by defeat against Great Melton after they were set 156 to win. Coltishall chased a similar total (174), but knocked them off easily for the loss of only two wickets. A draw against Rollesby was achieved as Walsham finished 28 runs short with two wickets left, Ogden top-scoring with 43.

Returning to Norfolk after an 'eventful' tour (the subject of Chapter 27) the match against Acle resulted in a 32-run defeat, despite good bowling from Futter and Munday and 40 from Leak. The following game produced an unusual result - an equal score draw with Gothic. Walsham made 149, both Leak and Futter passing 30. In reply, Gothic made a slow start adding 93 for the first wicket, but a battling Walsham fielding performance with three run outs, culminated in one run being needed off the last ball. The batsman missed and Evans triumphantly claimed another stumping. This thriller was in marked contrast to a low scoring draw at Gunton Park against Kirkley. They made 136-7, with Gorrod picking up early wickets, but a Walsham slump to 43-8 was retrieved by Watkins and Evans adding 36 for the ninth wicket to save the game in a lowly total of 79-8.

The season finished on a high with three victories. Revenge was achieved over Shipdham in a 107 run victory, Vaughan leading the way with 53. They fell away badly totalling only 69, in which former Walsham player Tony Kinsley was one of only two players to reach double figures, Munday (3-8), Futter (2-4) and Belton (2-6) claiming most of the wickets. Dereham A turned up with only 10 players and, despite another hard hitting innings from N Walter, only managed 95, with 4 wickets for Futter. Things looked a little uneasy at 83-7, but Futter came in and quickly won the game with a six. The Chairman's game saw more runs for Vaughan and Hodds in a total of 223-3, to which the Chairman's XI managed 176 in reply.

The season's account: eight wins and four defeats with the other games either drawn or abandoned. Taking into account that Walsham were now regularly playing without two class players - Denton and Conrad - it had been a good season with eleven players scoring at least 100 runs. Vaughan led the way with 570 at 27.14, although Hodds had the best average with 45.92 from 551 runs scored. Watkins and Munday both passed the 200 mark. In the bowling, Munday had an excellent season taking 35 wickets while Garth Futter picked up 30 and Vaughan 22.

CHAPTER TWENTY FIVE *A Slump In Fortunes 1986/87*

Following the success of the previous season, 1986 was rather disappointing. David Watkins stood aside and Derek Gorrod took over the captaincy, a role he fulfilled for three seasons. After the first few games Joe Abbott moved away from Norfolk, but the club recruited the very useful Mike Key, who was to play on an occasional basis for the next fifteen seasons, making 99 appearances and scoring just over 2000 runs with a top score of 127 not out in the first game of the season against Gothic. He also proved to be a useful wicket keeper and slow bowler. However, it was his ability to hit a cricket ball a long way for which he will be remembered. On his day, very few bowlers could stop him. Against Gothic, Vaughan (43) added 110 with Key for the second wicket, but no one else made double figures in a total of 212-7. Gothic responded in excellent fashion; going for the win, they finished 18 runs short with three wickets left, Munday taking 5-67 from 18 overs.

Despite 53 from Watkins, Walsham were hammered by Kirkley but then finished in control of a drawn match against Gt Melton. UEA's final pair held out for a draw despite a brilliant bowling performance from Vaughan (6-27) but there was a sad defeat against old rivals Eaton. Walsham managed 122, Munday top-scoring, but they knocked them off for the loss of only three wickets. In another low scoring game against touring side Willowherbs, Walsham went down by three wickets, Gorrod bowled a marathon spell of 4-40 from 19 overs. Only Hodds and Key made any runs as Walsham were on the wrong end of a draw with Acle and then went down by three wickets to Shipdham, despite good bowling from Munday (4-32). Gt Melton finished just 10 runs short of victory with three wickets left, in a match which saw Leak top-scoring. In another drawn game, Walsham held Margaretting from Essex to 156-9 declared and replied with 145-5, Hodds (89*) and Watkins (45) bringing the first victory of the season closer.

After being well beaten by Dereham - Walsham managing only 103 on a good track with Garth Futter hitting 29 - a draw followed against Norwich Etceteras. Another defeat against Eaton by 43 runs, with Futter, whose batting was steadily improving, top-scoring with 39, preceded three more draws against Coltishall, Rollesby and Acle, the highlights being Belton's 40 against Coltishall, Munday's 4 wickets against Rollesby and Vaughan's 6 wickets, Evans' 5 dismissals and Leak's 59 against Acle.

Only in the middle of August did the first win of the season finally arrive. Gothic turned up with nine players and were bowled out for 109, Walsham replying with 110-5, Hodds (66*) leading the way. Evans was having a purple patch behind the timbers with 13 victims in 4 games. After only making 89 against Halvergate, Walsham were well in the game as the local rivals slumped to 35-6, but Jimmy Forder hit 34 to see Halvergate home. In an excellent game against Dereham A, they made 181-5 and Walsham were looking good at 156-5, but collapsed to 172 to lose by nine runs. Key hit 46 and Leak was left high and dry on 41 not out.

The 1986 season saw the first President's match although it was a very tame affair. The President's side made 161 while Walsham replied with 124-6 off 34 overs. In recent years the game has been played rather more positively!

After the successes of 1985 this had been a very disappointing season: one win from 26 games and that against a side with just 9 players. Hodds (362) scored the most runs and topped the averages, while Leak, Vaughan and Watkins all passed the 200 mark. Munday (40 wickets) was once again the most successful bowler, Vaughan claiming 34 and Gorrod 22. Evans had his most successful season behind the stumps with 35 victims.

Unfortunately, 1987 was not much better. The squad was the broadly the same as the previous season, although Keith Hodds didn't play much and this was a big loss. There was one new recruit, Neil Johnson from Halvergate, a hard-hitting batsman and useful medium-pace bowler. Although it was obvious that Neil could be a very destructive batsman, in his first five seasons he failed to average above sixteen which was frustrating for him and for the rest of the team who knew he could do much better. In his early days he had a habit of getting out in various strange ways and always saw a fielder on the long-off boundary as a challenge that should be taken on. Lots of times he cleared the ropes but sometimes he didn't! Over his Walsham career, as well as fifty half-centuries, Neil has hit fourteen centuries - although it took him five seasons to score his first. After this breakthrough, he became a very valuable player winning several games almost single-handedly. He has withdrawn for the present, but if he played for a couple more years he would reach the magic 10,000 runs. He can also be a useful part of the attack, but back injuries have limited his bowling to a few overs a spell.

The season started with a close game against Coltishall, who managed 123-9 to which Walsham replied with 110-9, Vaughan, Watkins and Belton all passing twenty. Two defeats followed, both by two wickets, against Kirkley and Great Melton. In the Kirkley match, Garth Futter hit a rapid 44 from the tricky position of 69-7 to raise the total to 140, but it was not enough. Similarly, after scoring 186-9 against Gt Melton, they eased home in the 39th over. The next match was abandoned when UEA were well placed. Watkins and Vaughan had added 74 for the first wicket, but a collapse to 113-9, was followed by a 10th wicket stand of 30 to finish on a respectable 143-9. UEA were 49-1 when the rain came.

Neil Johnson

A narrow 11 run defeat against Eaton followed; they scored 180-2, and Walsham went for them in typical style with Munday hitting 64 before a spirited ninth wicket stand of 48 between Johnson and Gorrod brought victory close. John Reynolds, a regular Walsham tourist, bowled all the way through the innings taking 4-79 from 26 overs. The first win of the season was finally achieved by two wickets against Acle. Vaughan (3-20) helped to restrict Acle to 137-9 off 45 overs, then he and Key led the reply taking the score to 104-3. Although another five wickets were lost in getting the remaining 34 runs, Johnson came in at number ten to hit the winning runs.

In a poor performance against Hoveton and Wroxham, Walsham collapsed to 96 all out despite 46 from Vaughan. The opposition also slumped to 60-6, but Keith Knell hit 32 not out in 4 overs to win the game for them. A rare event occurred in the next game as Walsham passed the 200 mark against Gt Melton, Lewis top scoring with 58. Melton slipped to 112-7, but an eighth wicket partnership of 73 prevented the win, although Ogden had a good day picking up four wickets. A typical game against Eaton saw a game fizzle out into a draw after Walsham had scored 198-7 with runs from Vaughan, Johnson and Belton. Eaton replied rather defensively finishing on 129-4. Following some good scores there was a six-run defeat against Dereham A who were bowled out for 99, the last five wickets falling at the same score. At 58-3 Walsham were in charge, but Andy Luckhurst took 6-11 to bowl Dereham to a narrow win.

Derek Gorrod had the best figures of his Walsham career against Rollesby (8-3-9-4). A good set of figures, but what was more remarkable was that 'Del' never took 5 wickets in an innings in the 367 games he played for the club. Rollesby still scored 180-7 but, after a good start at 81-1, Walsham collapsed to 114 all out, Watkins top-scoring with 53. Results got worse: a 17 run loss to Cringleford , despite four wickets each from Munday and Vaughan, and then a massive 154 run defeat against Coltishall. For the author the match only lasted three balls: Richard Pipes, a rather wild young bowler, fired the third ball of the innings very wide down the leg side and a dramatic dive with left hand outstretched only resulted in a collision between elbow and ground, a dislocation, the casualty department and the end of wicket keeping for the season. Greater discretion would have resulted in five wides - assuming the umpire was watching! The match was an equal disaster: Coltishall scored 212-8, with Vaughan taking 6-56; Walsham managed 58

Two more heavy defeats followed: against Rollesby, despite 5-8 from Vaughan, and against Wanderers with Gorrod taking 4-42. However, against all the odds, a win was achieved against Acle. They scored 191-6 and, thanks to Vaughan (71) and Lewis (52), these were knocked off for 5 wickets in just 39 overs. Unfortunately Vaughan, Watkins and Leak were unavailable when Drayton provided strong opposition. They cleared out Walsham for 53 and knocked them off for the loss of only one wicket. Kirkley also won easily although there was an improved performance against Gothic, who made 176-5 to Walsham's 156-9, with Hodds (33) top scoring and Leak playing out the final over. The season closed with an enjoyable draw with the Chairman's team who scored 236-8, Walsham replying with 201-9.

It had been a disappointing year with only two wins, both against Acle. Insufficient runs, although Vaughan and Watkins both passed the 400 run mark, while Leak, Futter, Lewis and Johnson passed 200. The bowling also lacked a cutting edge, only Vaughan (24) passed 20 wickets, but at this time he was expected to score the runs and take the wickets. He was always up for it but he needed support. The hope was that the 1988 season would produce some much-needed improvement.

Fixture Card 1986

CHAPTER TWENTY SIX *On The Up Again*
1988/89

The 1988 season saw a major change in Walsham's fortunes. Two new players - Andy Scales and Richard Whiteside - arrived, while Kim Futter returned following his time on the Greek Islands. Andy Scales has proved to be a fine batsman as his record shows. Currently, he has scored nearly 15,000 runs averaging over 35 from over 470 innings and there are many more years left in him yet. He is the fourth 'legend' of the club, having passed the magic figure of 10,000 runs. Richard Whiteside also strengthened the batting and has passed 6,500 runs. An excellent fielder, particularly close in, he has also picked up just short of 100 wickets with his slow bowling. Both have been stalwarts for more than twenty years.

Richard Whiteside   *Andy Scales*

The first match of the season - a warm up game against Norwich Etceteras - was not a great success, as they scored 227-7 in 40 overs. Indeed, it could have been worse as they were 172-2, but 4-10 from Neil Johnson brought about a bit of respectability. Steve Belton (32) and David Watkins (24) were the only Walsham batsmen to score any significant runs as the innings closed on 93-8 from 40 overs. Out of practice, but things were to improve.

The next match was against Kettering Old Colonials - a two innings affair played on a Saturday - the only time since the 1930s that Walsham had played either on a Saturday or in a two innings contest. The game was won easily, with Terry Ogden the star man with a match total of 7-84. After the customary draw with Eaton - Walsham's total of 166-9 being too challenging for the opposition who closed on 129-6 after being 16-4 - Walsham hit a good spell of three wins. Thetford A were beaten by nine wickets with Watkins and Leak among the runs, Acle were defeated by five wickets when chasing down a total of 174, Leak hitting 50, and Hoveton and Wroxham were overwhelmed by nine wickets, Walsham chasing down a modest total of 100 after Kim Futter, on his way back to his best, claimed 5-34. However, things went wrong in the next match against a strong Coltishall side, who were bowled for 131, Garth Futter taking 3-21, but no batsman managed 20 as Walsham slipped to 81 all out.

This was followed by a very strange game against Saxlingham, Odd situations sometimes occur in friendly cricket that probably wouldn't happen in any other sport. The game started quite normally when David Watkins and John Vaughan added 21 for the first wicket, but things went dreadfully wrong when nine

South Walsham Squad 1989

wickets were lost for just 10 runs, the total slumping to 31-9. Saxlingham 'tried to make a game of it' by tossing the ball up, but the batsmen just kept getting out. However, the 10th wicket pair of Gorrod and Evans held out and added 40 for the last wicket, Evans top-scoring with 22 not out. As tea approached, Walsham were finally dismissed for 71 off 42 overs. Shortly after the interval, Saxlingham also found themselves struggling as Walsham battled to defend the meagre total with Kim and Garth Futter - in the mood to put on the pressure - both bowling economical spells. Kim finally took 5-29 as Saxlingham were bowled out for 60 off 38 overs. Walsham had won a game that Saxlingham had really gifted with their generous bowling, but to have a match when only 131 runs were scored from 80 overs was, in itself, quite amazing.

Returning to more 'normal' cricket, seven draws followed. The first was entertaining as David Watkins (38) top-scored in a total of 141-9 against Dereham A, who replied with 117-8, Kim Futter taking 4-36. Against

Cringleford, Walsham finished 22 runs short with two wickets left, Mike Key having top-scored with 37. In the return game against Dereham A, they scored 153-9 declared as Walsham finished on a strange, and rather embarrassing, total of 134-3. Most of the batsmen couldn't hit the ball - although Steve Belton made 82 not out - and Dereham couldn't take any wickets. This game was Andy Scales' debut. He made just a single and must have wondered what sort of cricket was being played, particularly as on the following Sunday - against Eaton - Walsham scored only 105 in 51 overs, Belton top-scoring with 32. This was possibly a unique occasion as Walsham, who had scored only 85 at tea, batted on into the second session. The innings had been interrupted by rain, but it was felt that at least a hundred should be set. However, this rather backfired as, after another rain break, Futter and Terry Ogden bowled unchanged as Eaton finished on 41-9 from 31 overs. Kim Futter took 6-10 in 16 overs as former tourist John Reynolds blocked out at the end.

The next game saw another close draw, as Wanderers scored 109-5 declared and Walsham slipped to 77-7, but held on at 100-9. Scales scored his first half-century for the club against Acle and, with Watkins hitting 85, Walsham passed 200 with only three wickets down. Acle were never really in it as they reached 137-8. Rory Ringer, who played several games in 1988, and also proved to be a very useful tourist, took 4-44. Richard Whiteside made his debut in this match and scored 16 not out.

After these seven consecutive draws, Walsham gained an emphatic victory over Saxlingham by 105 runs, scoring 179-8 with runs from Vaughan and Hodds. Ogden (5-20) and Kim Futter (3-8) made light work of Saxlingham after tea. The final game before the tour was against Kirkley. Walsham scored 143-8 declared, while Kirkley managed 122-7 with Ogden and Futter again among the wickets, but neither team could force a win.

Returning to Norfolk after another successful tour (see Chapter 27), Walsham played St Catherines, a touring side. This was a really bad-tempered affair as they played it more like a football match - and a local derby at that. John Vaughan scored a splendid 53 out of 111 pulling Walsham out of trouble from 42-3, but the bowlers fought back to dismiss them for 80, with Richard Pipes - an occasional player - taking 4-8 and Kim Futter 3-19. Kirkley were beaten by 48 runs as they slipped from 81-2 to 111 all out, with more wickets for Pipes and Ogden. Walsham also had the better of a draw against Halvergate, making 178-7 declared with Leak among the runs. The 'Hares' slipped from 70-2 to 131-7 and settled for the draw. The final game of the season was against a Chairman's team, which consisted of seventeen players! Despite this, they were bowled out for 165, Walsham knocking these off for the loss of only two wickets, Watkins and Johnson adding 107 for the third wicket to win the game with ease.

The 1988 season was one to relish. Walsham were on the up, winning nine and losing just four with the rest drawn. Watkins (651 runs and averaging 32) topped the run-scoring, while Belton (404), Vaughan (300) and Leak (267) did well. However, it was Kim Futter's return which had made the difference as he took 41 wickets in just 160 overs at 9 runs apiece. He was well supported by Terry Ogden with 36 wickets at an average of 17, while Derek Gorrod picked up 21 wickets. Evans equalled his 1986 tally behind the stumps with 35 victims, while Watkins and Belton both reached double figures in the catching department.

1989 was the first full season for Andy Scales. A new left arm slow bowler - David Kurley - was also welcomed. He just turned up one day at a home game and asked to play, as he did for three seasons. Otherwise, the squad was unchanged although Garth Futter took over the captaincy from Derek Gorrod for his first of three years in charge.

The season didn't start very brightly with a six-wicket defeat against a useful Fakenham side. Leak and Belton scored a few runs in a mediocre total of 110 and Kim Futter took three wickets in reply, but Walsham were never really in the game. A draw against Lowestoft Railway followed in a game that might have been lost. They scored 161-5 and Walsham finished on 77-8 after 48 overs. The first win of the season was against Eaton who struggled to 104-8 in 49 overs, Kim Futter taking 5-20 from 10 overs. Walsham knocked off the runs losing just one wicket with Mike Key (46 not out) top-scoring.

The following match - against Thetford - nearly produced a milestone for one of the club's stalwarts, although it must be said that the opposition were not at their strongest that day. However, a century is a memorable achievement and Walsham went from 1982 to 1989 without a regular player scoring one. Unsurprisingly, David Watkins was, in true sporting cliché, 'absolutely gutted' when he was caught behind for 99. He couldn't believe he had got himself out in such an innocuous fashion. To the whole team, the result of the game seemed secondary, although in reply to 203-5 declared Thetford were dismissed for 79. Ironically, in the next match - a draw against Acle - Mike Key showed how to do it with 102 not out. John Vaughan also batted well with 75 not out, as they added 168 for the second wicket while Watkins waited patiently with his pads on. Acle slumped to 11-4, but held on at 157-9 with Garth Futter, back in the groove, taking 4-27.

A dishonourable draw followed against Bexley Hospital, although there was a reason for the Walsham approach. Good bowling from the Futter brothers had the opposition at 33-6 but, as the pressure was taken off, they reached 175. When Walsham collapsed to 53-8, Bexley went for the win, but Ogden and Evans dug in and finished on 63-8 from 39 overs. However, the next match saw an improvement in form with a 31 run win over Kirkley. Walsham scored 155, with Vaughan hitting a half-century, but it was Ogden (6-49) who was man of the match. Against Datchworth, a touring side from Hertfordshire, David Kurley marked his debut with three wickets as they scored 173-4. In reply, after a bad start, Watkins and Johnson got the scoreboard moving and Kim Futter hit a six off the fifth ball of the last over to see Walsham home by three wickets.

Andy Scales scored his first century for the club - 116 against Saxlingham in a Walsham total of 203-3 - in a game that Walsham controlled as the opposition were bowled out for 168. A fourth consecutive win was achieved against touring side Elsenham, the club that ex-Walsham player, Gary Lewis, had joined when he changed jobs. Walsham bowled them out for 97 and, with a half century from Mike Key, won easily by six wickets. The winning run came to an end in an entertaining game, Walsham scoring 176-8 while Dereham finished eleven runs short of victory with five wickets left.

The next game was the annual all-day affair at Ingham. Commonsense demanded that Walsham fielded first as one of the county's top sides opened up with Carl Rogers, who was to make his debut for Norfolk the following season, and Paul Wilkinson a prolific scorer of runs in local cricket and, like Rogers, a former member of the MCC groundstaff at Lords. Garth Futter was very pleased to bowl Rogers for 28, while Derek Gorrod dismissed Wilkinson for the same score. However, John Burton hit a century and Ingham were able to declare on 238-8 from 57 overs. Walsham collapsed to 77-5, only John Vaughan (86) really getting to the grips with the bowling in a total of 167.

The next game was a 'bore draw', Cringleford responding to Walsham's 170-4 (Belton 61), by struggling to 134-6 against the very occasional deliveries of Fred Leak. The tone had been set early in their innings as Kim Futter had started with seven consecutive maidens. However, the match, against Dereham, provided a welcome contrast as Walsham scored 187-5 with a half-century from Scales. The Dereham opener, Mark Stokes, had to rush away before the end of the game and swung the bat from ball one hitting a quick 70. This had kept Dereham up with the run rate and they kept going, getting home in the final over by two wickets. Another draw was fought out with Eaton as Neil Johnson hit 79 out of 196-6 and the opposition finished on 149-7, Garth Futter taking 5-36. Three defeats followed: against a good Wanderers side, against Hales who chased down a total of 147 to win in the last over by three wickets, despite Kim Futter taking 4-43, and against Saxlingham by six wickets.

However, there were great celebrations in the next match, against Loddon, as John Vaughan hit 101 not out in a total of 193-3 declared. The opposition showed very good spirit as they made every effort to win the game finishing on 182-5. Vaughan continued his purple patch with 82 against Cringleford but, chasing a target of 164, they struggled and finished on 123-7. Vaughan (81) again led the way in a total of 171-5 against Kirkley, but they collapsed to 64 all out in the face of excellent bowling from Terry Ogden (5-17). The penultimate game of the season was an interesting affair against Thetford. Walsham slipped to 55-7 only for Garth Futter (39) to help to lift the score to 133. Thetford innings also collapsed to 39-6, but they recovered to 115-8, as the game ended in a draw. In the final game against the Chairman's XI, they reached 196-5 with Keith Denton hitting 51. Walsham were well on the way to victory at 95-2 when the rain came. Both teams adjourned to the bar!

The headline statistics of the season were seven wins and six defeats with the rest drawn. John Vaughan (668 runs at 39.2) topped the run-scoring with six other players passing the 250 mark. Heavy reliance on the Futter brothers in the bowling department was evident as Garth (40) and Kim (35) were followed by Terry Ogden (22). Two quite successful years ended a decade which had been very mixed for the club, but there was a sense of anticipation that another really strong period was approaching, A fourth 'golden age', perhaps?

CHAPTER TWENTY SEVEN *The 1980's Tours*

In 1982, the club tour - by now a regular, although never annual, event - pitched up in Worcester. Arranged by David Watkins, who originated from the area, it was the usual squad plus Andy Milbourne and Kevin Wilson, useful cricketers who played for Gothic, and Paul Munnings, a lively bowler from Beccles. The first match was a 20-over affair against Newland Swan. Walsham were clearly the better side, but still managed to lose by one run in the dark. However, the most memorable part of the day was in the pub after the game. As was - and remains - part of the ritual of South Walsham tours, thirst drove the squad straight to the bar for 'a few drinks' on the first night. Vaughan nipped behind the bar to help with the service and the singing started. The locals protested but, after a little persuasion, they relented and a brilliant night was had by all.

South Walsham Tour Squad 1982

However, when Steve Munday - whose reputation as a 'handful' was, by now, well-established - returned to the hotel, he and his nameless roommate started to make quite a racket in their room at about 2.30 am, just as others were ready to turn in. This was not unusual on the first night of a South Walsham tour but, in the adjacent room, a brooding John Westgarth was determined on revenge and the next night he produced his master plan. At about 1.00 am, with everything quiet, he rang reception to complain about the noise in the next room. The night porter was very polite and said he would sort it out. Westgarth, who was roomsharing with the author, heard the phone ring and Munday was awakened from his slumbers. A minor argument ensued, then all went quiet. Half an hour later, just as Munday had got back to sleep,

Westgarth rang the night porter again, this time very insistent about the noise next door. After a couple of minutes, the night porter was knocking on the Munday door again, disturbing the sleeping duo. Finally, Westgarth went down to the reception desk in just a towel - not a pretty sight - to complain for a third time. The night porter suddenly realised that he had been 'had' and the semi-naked Westgarth was told to go back to his room and behave himself. But he had enjoyed his revenge!

The second match was against Old Vigornians a Worcester club made up of former pupils from David Watkins' old school. Bravely, Walsham opted to bat first against a very strong side, which included Brian Brain the former Gloucestershire and Worcestershire bowler, who performed in a slower style until Watkins hit him for six, whereupon he decided to show that he could still bowl rather sharply and uprooted Watkins' middle stump. What made the day particularly memorable was that the game was played on a pitch which adjoined the Worcestershire County ground and, while Watkins was batting on one pitch, David Gower was batting on the other. Not much difference in style and technique - except Gower was left-handed - *'as Watkins was wont to claim!'* However, after being 149-5, a final total of 156 all out was disappointing. The 'old pro', Brian Brain - the only known example of an 'anagrammatic' cricketer - claimed 4-17, probably not the most important spell of his career, but at least several of Walsham's band of cricketing enthusiasts could claim to have been dismissed by an ex-professional bowler. Old Vigornians had no trouble in reaching the target and won by eight wickets.

After the game, the squad had a meal in Worcester and went on to a night club, where a few of the visiting Leicestershire players were frequenting a venue that would probably be frowned upon in the modern era of professional cricket. On the way back to the hotel, Messrs Gorrod, Wilson, Evans and Futter (K) were walking past the Worcestershire County Cricket Ground when they spied, just behind the gates, an impressive 'Players and Officials only' sign. In their drunken state, it was agreed that this item would look perfect outside the Walsham cricket 'pavilion' (or 'shed', as it was then). Over the gate they bounded - the sign was acquired and the booty-hunters made to return to the hotel. Unfortunately, however, the heroic quartet suddenly realised that they were being watched by two men in an 'unmarked' car. At this point Evans and Futter (K) made good their escape, leaving the hapless duo of Gorrod and Wilson holding the sign. For police officers, the watchers from the car were unusually forgiving; they could see the funny side, but insisted that the sign was taken back. Moreover, the miscreants were warned that if anything similar went missing during the rest of the week - they would be back!

This escapade was not ideal preparation for a match against Old Elizabethans, who enjoyed a 'strong side' reputation. Walsham batted first and, despite runs from Watkins and Hodds, the chastened tourists were well beaten by seven wickets. However, the final game of the week provided a surprise. Chaddesley Corbett was to be the toughest fixture and, initially, they treated their now relatively sober opponents rather like country cousins. From 29-3, quality batting from Hodds (52) and Wilson (77) lifted the score, enabling skipper of the day, Kim Futter, to declare on 182-5 just before tea. Chaddesley Corbett - which sounded like the name of a retired major - thought that he had declared too early, so it was a superb feeling to bowl them out for 71, with Paul Munnings taking 5-14.

The champagne moment was when their star man named Bond - not James, as far as we were aware - hit the ball like the proverbial rocket and it disappeared into Westgarth's, admittedly ample, stomach. He clung on and Mr Bond was gone for six - shaken and stirred, one assumes! It was one of those days that cricket occasionally provides, when David slays Goliath. Unsurprisingly, Kim Futter was hugely delighted with his debut as skipper and, despite their pretentious name, Chaddesley Corbett took it in good part and consumed copious quantities of beer with the exultant Walsham squad. Worcester had been a good tour!

1985 saw the Walsham touring caravan coming to rest in Gloucestershire. Despite the fixtures being rained off on the Monday and Friday, the three midweek matches remain deep in the club's collective memory, although perhaps not for the right reasons. Terry Ogden had arranged the tour, as he did many others, and Walsham were strengthened by: Alan Warnes, a very handy batsman from Bradfield, John Reynolds from Eaton, a mature slow left-arm bowler with a considerable capacity for mild beer and Bill Griffin from Halvergate. The first game was against Poulton, who were a useful side but, with Warnes hitting exactly 100, a tea-time total of 193-8 was pleasing. However, despite bowling 49 overs with (using the term loosely) 'spinners' Reynolds and Munday bowling 29 between them, Poulton finished on 172-8 and the match was drawn. The 'non-spin twins' returned combined figures of 6-88 as their batsmen struggled, but the lower order could not be shifted to force the win.

Team HQ was a pub called the Golden Farm in Cirencester - an interesting establishment - where the landlord seemed quite happy to serve at any time and the merry tourists were quite happy to drink at any time. It was the 'tour of the straw trilby'; one belonging to the author ended up over the front door of the pub stuck on the horns of a ram. It was also the tour of the trumpet: Terry Ogden, who never needed much prompting to play, was an accomplished performer, but reveille in the morning and the last post when he went to bed, was regarded - not unreasonably, on reflection - as somewhat offensive by the neighbours. The major problem was that in getting to bed about 4.00 am and up again at 7.00 am, there weren't many quiet hours!

South Walsham Touring Party 1986

The following two days will always be remembered for matters which only had a vague connection to cricket. Arriving to play Cirencester Town, the heavens opened. There seemed to be absolutely no chance of a game, although the weather forecast did give some hope for the evening. The opposition were very accommodating and seemed as keen as the touring band to try and get some sort of match played. Some of the squad started to have a few beers........and then more beers......the singing started........then the games started. Steve Belton was probably in the worst state, and he was going home in the evening to take his driving test the next day. At one point, he not only lost his watch but was in a state of undress, which amused many who were present, though goodness knows why. Belton in a state of undress is a far from pretty sight!

Late in the afternoon, the rain stopped and the captains agreed to play a 25-over match with no-one bowling more than five overs. The first task for the Walsham skipper was to find eleven players who could stand up! Belton was in no state to play and, rather cleverly, Terry Ogden was 'loaned' to the opposition. Walsham batted first and, on a very wet pitch and sodden outfield, managed 100-7. Leak scored 21, Hodds and Evans 15 apiece; they were three of only five players who knew what was going on and could be relied upon to remain upright. Alan Warnes looked on with detached amusement, although he must have 'enjoyed' similar riotous times when touring with Bradfield. Obviously, the total was inadequate, but then there was a transformation: everyone seemed to sober up and battle as hard as they could and Cirencester were bowled out for 94. It was back into the clubhouse for a few more pints, then back to the 'open all hours' pub for another lengthy session. Belton was left to find his way home back to Norfolk for his driving test. He failed!

If that day had been incredible, the next day was even more so. Terry Ogden had arranged the tour and it seemed to be appropriate that he should have the honour of captaining against Bradleys, who were being skippered by an old friend of his. This turned out to be an error of major proportions! Bradleys were a strong side and batted first. Ogden was fairly well oiled, but could still talk normally and, on the face of it, seemed to be OK. He decided that Garth Futter should open the bowling with the wind behind him and Steve Munday should open the bowling against the wind: so far, so good. However, after four overs he came to the conclusion that both bowlers were on at the wrong ends, so he brought on John Reynolds for one over to change the bowlers round. John was very much a bowler who enjoyed a spell of 15 overs and wasn't best pleased to be taken off after one over. This was rather revolutionary, but neither bowler had taken an early wicket, so why not? He then told Fred Leak where to stand as the wicket-keeper; the experienced keeper started to fume. The alcohol-boosted skipper then began to change the field until everyone was on the leg side except John Reynolds, who at the time was in his mid-fifties; Reynolds was designated to patrol the whole of the off side on his own and, quite reasonably, started to protest. At the same time, Leak threw his gloves down in frustration and, shortly afterwards, Ogden dropped a simple catch - or, to be more accurate, the ball just missed hitting him straight on the top of his head. He never saw it coming.

Something had to be done and David Watkins - the headmaster (although so was Ogden in his saner guise) - took control. The disconsolate, and far from sober, Ogden wandered off to the pavilion, protesting that if the team weren't going to obey him he wasn't playing anymore, presumably in what he construed as an adult version of 'taking his bat home'. He was a lovely chap, but asking him to be skipper had been a big mistake!

However, matters went from bad to worse, as the game moved on with Bradleys declaring at 235-4 off 39 overs. Coming off the field, Ogden was discovered by his mutinous team-mates lying asleep in the corner of the pavilion. Recognising that he was unlikely to be able to bat, the Bradleys skipper agreed that one of our players could bat twice - a kind gesture, which was appreciated. Initially, the Walsham reply went well as Keith Hodds and John Vaughan added 107 for the first wicket, but the innings collapsed to 167-9, despite a valiant 23 from Evans.

By this time the drizzle, which had been falling for most of the Walsham innings, was becoming heavier. Enter Keith Hodds: for a second time as the last man, with John Reynolds at the other end. If there are two batsmen in Norfolk cricket who never give their wickets away, it was, and still is, these two. They defiantly played down the line, blocking each delivery as the drizzle turned to steady rain, and as the Bradleys players became more and more annoyed. After all, it was a friendly and they had bent the laws of cricket in allowing Hodds to bat twice. The draw was achieved although, for once, most would have preferred to lose. As the opposition trooped off - soaking wet - we could sense that they were pretty fed up with South Walsham CC. Unusually, sheer embarrassment meant that we didn't stay long in the bar, 1988 saw the touring squad - the usuals plus Rory Ringer and Bill Griffin from Halvergate - in Shropshire. The first game, against Broseley, was a mis-match; they were a quality side and Walsham were soon in trouble. Despite releasing

South Walsham Touring Party to Shropshire 1988

the pressure, a total of 150-9 declared was insufficient and, although Rory Ringer took 3-61 from 19 overs, they won by seven wickets. The problem with the 1988 squad was that Walsham had just three front-line bowlers - Ringer, Derek Gorrod and Terry Ogden - plus a few overs from Gary Lewis, as neither John Vaughan nor Kim Futter had opted for the tour.

On the first evening a few of the usual games were played and, as always, it was the new tourists who suffered. Rory Ringer was caught by the 'broom game' and, although the squad gathered round him to make sure he didn't hurt himself, he avoided everybody and head-butted a table! His eye swelled up and closed, putting him in doubt for the next game against Welshpool. He was firmly told that he had to play - he was the top bowler, and, as this was the first time that South Walsham were leaving England to play cricket, it constituted an international match! The Welsh opposition proved to be quite tough, but Walsham managed 157-8 declared, Watkins scoring 49. In reply, Ringer, who more-or-less passed his fitness test, bowled 11 overs for a respectable 46 runs, with Gorrod (4-73) and Ogden bowling the remaining 23 overs. Walsham almost won their first - and only - 'overseas' (or at least cross-border) fixture as

Welshpool reached 156-9, but the last man hit his first ball over the pavilion for six to win the game by one wicket. Played one, lost one remains the club's record outside England. After the game there was an 'interesting' time in the bar and, consequently, four of the squad made a lengthy taxi journey back to Shrewsbury in the early hours.

The next match was against Madeley. On arrival, the rain was coming down, but the host club were very accommodating and play got under way at about 3.15 pm. They were a useful side and quickly knocked up 181-5 from 36 overs. The Walsham reply was uninspiring to say the least. Madeley were clearly a superior side, but were prepared to keep the game open at 89-6. They tossed the ball up, and the Walsham tail really should have kept going for the runs. However, the seventh and eighth wicket partnerships were not prepared to give their wickets away. Madeley bowled everybody as Walsham 'crabbed out' to 120-8. Few friends were made with the opposition, and it was hard work in the bar to bring them round

The game against Condover was played on an extremely cold August day and they were held to 161-3 off 41 overs. Their side contained two Australian professionals, although few other players of note, but Walsham slumped to 80-7 before Keith Hodds (39 not out) and Rory Ringer (26 not out) lifted the score to 155-7 just seven runs short of victory. Throughout this tour, there was a feeling that the oppositions felt they were doing a favour to the Norfolk intruders by playing them. It was hard to be impressed.

The piece de resistance on this tour was the accommodation: a Shrewsbury hotel, whose proprietor had helped to arrange the fixtures but, from his domestic arrangements, made it clear that, from his perspective, this was very much a money-making exercise. The best example of this was his use of double rooms which contained four single beds. In addition, his humour was not quite on the Walsham wavelength and swords were regularly crossed. His promised highlight was the 'tour dinner' which Walsham were to share with East Grinstead, another set of cricket tourists who were also staying at the hotel. On the appointed evening, both groups assembled in the restaurant. Although this had all the appearances of another money-making exercise by the proprietor, everyone dutifully sat down to enjoy the meal. However, Walsham were a loud bunch of lads having a good time, while East Grinstead were a mixed group which included wives and girlfriends. They protested about the Walsham noise, but what did anyone expect of South Walsham tourists?

Then the fun started: one of the East Grinstead party threw a bread roll in the general direction of the rural rowdies - a very big mistake! Retaliation was immediate, as suburban Surrey - and the posh bit, to boot - was met with the full force of strong-arm Norfolk 'yobbos'. (OK - two were headteachers, but they were on their summer holidays). A barrage of bread rolls knocked over glasses of the best wine that the stockbroker belt could find in deepest Shropshire. This was followed by outraged protests that some wine had stained the ladies' dresses (and what posh frocks, they were!). In the traditional schoolboy fashion the Walsham defence was that 'they had started it'.

Gloatingly, however, Norfolk honour was upheld - Walsham had finished it! Both teams had probably felt rather frustrated by the hotel; Walsham never returned, and it's questionable whether the proprietor, however mercenary his motives, would have welcomed this. Like a lot of tours at this time, it had been organised by Terry Ogden in his sober winter months. It was certainly no reflection on him, but 1988 was probably one of the club's less successful ventures, despite its international dimension.

CHAPTER TWENTY EIGHT *Cricket In The 1980's*
The Oppositions

By the 1980s local cricket had settled into the pattern that would be recognisable to those playing in the second decade of the twenty-first century: almost exclusively league-based on Saturdays with cups and friendly games on Sundays. There were two small Sunday leagues - in mid-Norfolk and north Norfolk - and a looser federation of clubs who competed for the Burgess Shield. These three competitions were eventually to merge into a much larger mid-Norfolk league, but its evangelisation of league cricket on Sundays did not begin until the late 1990s.

South Walsham held resolutely to their tradition of competitive friendlies; the main contrast within this format between the 1980s and the 2010s was the number of potential opponents. Thirty years ago, most senior clubs ran two regular sides on Sundays and, although the stronger team focused on cup competitions, the 'A' teams could provide a stern test. Alongside these was a group of junior clubs who either played friendlies when they did not have cup fixtures or who, rejecting 'pot-hunting', retained the traditional Sunday format. Walsham's fixture list in the 1980s provided an eclectic mix of matches against clubs from all levels of the Norfolk cricket pyramid.

Partly for reasons of tradition, Walsham enjoyed regular fixtures against some of the leading clubs in the area: Lowestoft, Kirkley, Bradfield, Dereham and Norwich Wanderers. These usually turned out with 'A' strength sides, although it could never be anticipated whether an established Norfolk player might be available. The great advantage of fixtures against senior clubs - as Peter Fisher had realised in the dark days of the 1970s when he had fought so tenaciously to retain them - was that a good wicket could be guaranteed. In addition, these games, particularly at Barton Turf - the idyllic setting for Norwich Wanderers - and Denes Oval, Lowestoft gave a sense of occasion to the day. The latter always attracted more than a sprinkling of spectators; it felt like a major venue, as indeed it was having hosted several Suffolk v Norfolk games in the 1960s.

But the 'jewel in the crown' was Ingham: the club, the ground, the hospitality, the occasion. Ingham were part of the fabric of Norfolk cricket. In the 1970s - the early years of the Norfolk Alliance and the Carter Cup - they had been unchallenged as the strongest side in the county. Their first team usually contained at least eight players who had represented Norfolk, including the legendary Tracey Moore who, with over 400 wickets, was the second-highest wicket-taker in Norfolk's history. Billy Rose, Paul Borrett, 'Fred' Handley, Gerald Goodley: the names were a roll-call of cricketing talent. And there was a link with South Walsham, unsurprisingly through the Edrich family. On his retirement from first-class cricket, W J 'Bill' Edrich - whose many relations had steered Walsham through the two decades after the Second World War - returned to Norfolk to play for Ingham.

In the 1960s, the ground had provided the venue for a series of Edrich XI against Lords' Taverners charity matches. Although these were 'fun' games in which large crowds could enjoy watching the cricketing prowess of showbiz stars like Brian Rix, Nicholas Parsons, Leslie Crowther and Richard 'Mr Pastry' Hearne, these occasions also brought Peter May, Basil d'Oliveira and the incomparable Gary Sobers to Ingham. Sobers certainly remembered Ingham, although not exclusively for the cricket. He has maintained that he was offered a lift back from Norfolk to London's West End by Graham Hill, the cricketing Formula 1 driver, and the journey was completed in 1 hour 55 minutes!

Ingham, an obscure village three miles from the NE Norfolk coast, became a cricketing mecca and presiding over the club was the genial figure of 'Jack' Borrett, the man who shaped the ethos and recruited the talent. He set the tone that made visits to the ground so memorable: the three course lunch - for Ingham, Sunday friendlies were all-day affairs - cricket played in the true spirit of the game and a highly sociable post-match evening. Jack was always the first to the bar to buy the opposing captain a drink. Inevitably, this was an act of consolation, as Ingham defeats were virtually unknown during their halcyon years. The Ingham fixture was the high-point of the season for Walsham and for many other local clubs who were welcomed to their near-perfect rural setting.

Other rural grounds, although lacking the prestige of Ingham, had their individual attractions. Gasthorpe Rec. may sound like a grim municipal outpost in the South Yorkshire coalfield but it was, in fact, a rather pleasant cricket ground fifty yards from the Suffolk border. It was home to Riddlesworth, another of Walsham's regular opponents of this era. The two adjoining hamlets of Gasthorpe and Riddlesworth barely contained sufficient souls to raise a cricket team between them and a lack of players finally led to the club's demise in the 1990s. In some respects they paralleled 1950s/60s South Walsham in being dominated by one family - the Savages - an array of fathers, sons, uncles and cousins who found it increasingly difficult to recruit newcomers to their remote but well-maintained ground. Riddlesworth were a sad loss to the local cricket circuit.

Similarly, now lost - almost certainly for ever - is the 'ground for John and young Henry': the home of Hoveton and Wroxham. Set within the parkland of Hoveton House, the ground was created by the father of John - JRC Blofeld, QC and High Court judge - and his younger brother, HC Blofeld, the incomparable 'Blowers'. In many respects, the cricketing ethos here was semi-feudal, the squire's sons playing for the club in their school holidays, after the Eton v Harrow match at Lords in which both represented the former, and university vacations (although Henry never completed his degree). Fortified by other farming families who provided the batsmen, the 'peasants' did the bowling duties, although there was one notable exception to the 'natural' order. This was Neville Yellop, the taciturn but technically proficient opening batsman, who provided the anchor for most Hoveton and Wroxham performances.

Such was the respect in which he was held that quite recently, in the middle of a *Test Match Special* commentary, 'Blowers' veered away from learned discourse on red buses and errant pigeons and started to recall Neville Yellop, the yeoman opener. Unavoidably patrician in tone, but steering just clear of being patronising, 'Blowers' recalled with affection and respect, a man who may have played for the squire, but was highly regarded for his cricketing ability. As the scions of the house of Blofeld established their reputations on the national stage - in their respective careers, passing judgment on criminals and cricketers - and as the rest of the team retired from the game, the club dissolved after a brief attempt to link with neighbouring Ashmanhaugh. Although a legacy of the 1950s, Hoveton and Wroxham were another loss to the local cricketing community.

Thankfully, other regular opponents of the 1980s have survived although some have succumbed to mergers. Several, including Old Buckenham, Acle, Saxlingham and Great Melton have risen in status. Old Buckenham's magnificent ground, on which the 1921 Australians were entertained by the eccentric millionaire Lionel Robinson, has provided the platform for an ascent to the higher reaches of the Norfolk Alliance where, not far behind them, are the other three. Great Melton have developed a quite superb new ground at Melton Park, far removed from Wymondham Rec and Eaton Park, where they played their home games in the 1980s.

Aldborough continue to flourish on their wonderful village green, undoubtedly the best ground of this kind in the county, as do Rollesby who, at the time of writing, are probably the strongest village side outside the Norfolk Alliance. Coltishall, Cringleford and Loddon have survived by virtue of amalgamations with Norwich Wanderers, Earlham Lodge and Hales respectively, although Gothic's merger with CEYMS only delayed their demise. Walsham's long-established fixture against Eaton, which began in 1977, has survived the cycles of success and downturn that have beset both clubs over thirty-five years as the Norwich-based club have graduated from Eaton Park to the rather more scenic City of Norwich School ground.

Fixtures against other more distant opponents - Wisbech Old Grammarians and Thriplow - have fallen by the wayside, while UEA students no longer play against local clubs. As for touring sides, Walsham have maintained their tradition of entertaining several every season, not the same sides as in the 1980s but these games continue to provide an opportunity to meet at least some new opposition every season, particularly in non-tour years. It takes two sides to make a good game of cricket and, although many opponents have changed over the past thirty years, only rarely have fixtures been lost due to any ill-feeling between clubs. That, in itself, is evidence that Walsham have continued to play cricket within the true spirit of the game.

CHAPTER TWENTY NINE *Up and Down Again 1990/91*

The 1990 season was particularly enjoyable and successful. In exceptionally good weather, twenty eight out of thirty games were completed: fourteen were won, seven lost and six drawn with one tied. Andy Scales scored 969 runs - a record which still remains intact - while John Vaughan (828) was not far behind. Watkins also scored over 500 while Belton, Johnson and Garth Futter hit over 300. Kim Futter picked up 51 wickets from around 210 overs, while Terry Ogden bowled over 250 overs in taking 43 wickets.

Two new players - Chris Gould and Neville London - were welcomed. The former played over 100 games in seven seasons and, having returned in 2009, has now passed the 100 wicket mark. Although no great shakes with the bat, he has always been a keen bowler and an excellent and extremely enthusiastic fielder. Neville London played for five seasons, but became ill and, sadly, died in 1996. He had played at a higher level for Wanderers, but thoroughly enjoyed his five years with Walsham. He had retired from playing quite a few years before joining, and came back to the game that he had missed with a wish to play for his local village. He was useful with both bat and ball and played around forty games.

The season started very successfully when Kirkley were defeated by 55 runs. Neil Johnson (41) led the way in a total of 139, while David Kurley (6-22) soon saw off the opposition who were dismissed for 84. This was followed by a winning draw against Bradfield A, with half centuries from Vaughan and Scales. The same two batsmen were at it again in the next match, adding an unbeaten 105 as Walsham beat Rollesby by ten wickets. However, only Vaughan and Belton made double figures against Eaton and a total of 107 was never enough, in a game that was lost by five wickets.

In the next match Keith Denton - who had moved to Norwich Barleycorns - was among the opposition that was bowled out for 159, Kim Futter taking 5-48. Scales led the way with 84 not out in an eight-wicket victory. Then the batsmen chased down 189 against Thetford to win by two wickets; Kim Futter took five wickets, while Scales was again in form with 79.

Unfortunately, skipper Garth Futter made a tactical error against Old Buckenham declaring on 193-7, after he had reached his fifty. Buckenham, with Mike Gibbins hitting an aggressive 122 not out, soon reached the total. However, another five-wicket haul for Kim Futter set up a comfortable victory over Saxlingham as Vaughan and Watkins hit half centuries.

Scales' form continued as he hit 112 not out against Elsenham who crabbed out for a draw, while Vaughan hit 93 against Dereham A in a high-scoring draw. Two very exciting victories followed. David Kurley took 4-54 as Margaretting (Essex) knocked up 190-8, but 99 from guest John Buttifant and 47 not out from Garth Futter saw the target reached in only 37 overs. The next

Keith Denton, left, and Chris Gould enjoying a pint in their early Walsham games - still playing 20 years on

match saw a rare win against Ingham A, by the narrow margin of one wicket. Chasing 199, all was going well at 137-1, but a dramatic collapse to 196-9 with one ball left made for a dramatic finale. Cometh the hour, cometh the man: Ogden arrived at the crease and promptly hit the ball to the boundary.

A win followed against Cringleford, then a 98-run defeat against Dereham A. Scales hit a ton against Eaton and, with Kim Futter and Ogden among the wickets, this game was won easily. However, Norwich Wanderers proved tougher opposition, easily passing the Walsham total of 181. The squad then departed for a vintage tour in Northamptonshire which is detailed in Chapter 32.

The first game back in Norfolk - at Overstrand - continued the tour atmosphere. Walsham batted well to reach 218-3, with another 50 from Scales, but shortly after tea the heavens opened and the pitch was rapidly flooded. The entertainment started: one of the Overstrand players had a guitar and lots of fun was had by all. It was a very late night home.

A defeat at Deopham - on their notoriously 'dodgy' pitch - was followed by two draws with Bradfield and Old Buckenham. The highlight of the Bradfield game was Ogden (7-51) taking Walsham career-best figures, while in the Buckenham game, despite Leak top-scoring with 36 not out, Walsham were very much second best. The President's game saw Scales hit 130 not out as the President's target of 243 was easily surpassed, but the season finished on a losing note, by five wickets against old friends from Halvergate.

South Walsham Squad 1990

After the highs of 1990, the following season wasn't so successful, with just five wins out of 23 matches played. However, three players of note made their debuts: Ben Watkins - son of David - the often-injured Norfolk 100 metres champion, but also talented cricketer; John Pennington, an extremely useful sharp medium-paced bowler who took 99 wickets over a period of about 10 years; and Stewart Mallett, an occasional player up to 2009, since when he has become a regular performer, entertaining all and sundry with his weekly rants on a wide range of topics.

Garth Futter continued to lead the side which started with a one-wicket loss to Kirkley. Walsham managed only 110, Whiteside scoring 56, but Kirkley made heavy weather of chasing a small target before they scraped home. A Watkins half-century was not good enough to stave off defeat by five wickets against Acle A, but the first win came against Bradfield A, who were beaten by 35 runs when set 169.

However, amazingly, interest in the next match catapulted South Walsham into the media spotlight. This was triggered when Christine Futter - wife of Kim - wrote to the Yarmouth Mercury, complaining about ladies not being allowed to be members of the MCC. Her 'distaff concordat' decreed that South Walsham ladies would not be helping with the cricket teas the following week. The EDP and national press ran features on the story. Anglia Television even suggested coming along to the game to film the deserted males making the sandwiches - a suggestion which was politely declined. The match turned out to be a total anti-climax, as Walsham quickly dismissed Eaton for 43, with Neil Johnson who was 'guesting', as they were a man short, scoring almost half their total. There was plenty of time to prepare the teas! Ironically, it was Kim Futter that hurried the game along with 5-6 in six overs. The runs were knocked off for the loss of four wickets.

1990 President's Day - President's XI

After a heavy defeat against Overstrand, one of the highlights of the season came at Thetford. The home side scored a creditable 205-7 by tea and, with Walsham slipping to 103-7 - Johnson making 66 of those - all seemed lost. However, Ogden and Kim Futter came together and turned the game around, adding 105 for the eighth wicket to produce a two-wicket win. It had been a brilliant effort by the two bowlers, Ogden (66 not out) making his highest score for the club.

The next two matches - against Bexley Hospital and Old Buckenham - were drawn, but revenge was gained for the previous season's tour defeat at Great Oakley, when the Northamptonshire side were hammered by 93 runs, after half-centuries from Scales and Whiteside. A winning draw against Saxlingham was followed by a heavy defeat against Dereham A. The annual visit to Ingham was a disappointment: after they were contained to 217-9, with Neville London taking 4 wickets, Walsham - with a strong side - mustered only 44.

Irthlingborough's hospitality on the 1990 tour was repaid as they arrived in a coach with about fifty people for an all-day game. They had a couple of players who had played for Northants seconds and scored freely, declaring on 351-6 off just 57 overs. Walsham were never in with a chance of repeating the heroics of the previous season's tour match and were bowled out for 183, Garth Futter top-scoring with 42. In an exciting game against Dereham A, Walsham made 199-6 (Watkins 92) and they finished a few runs short with seven wickets down. It was also close against Eaton, who chased 184 and were only eight runs short of victory with nine wickets down.

Another highlight of the season was a three-wicket victory against Norwich Wanderers who declared on 204-4. Walsham looked out of it at 131-6, but quick runs from Kim Futter (43 not out) and a solid half century from Whiteside secured the win. The only down-side to this game was when Derek Gorrod fell over while umpiring, injuring his hand. This freak incident was to keep him out of the side for several weeks.

Walsham passed 180 in the next two matches - against Acle A and Barleycorns - but neither score was good enough as both games were lost, by four wickets and three wickets respectively. There was a half-century for Scales in the Acle game, while Key and Garth Futter did likewise against Barleycorns. However, it was six defeats in a row to end the season, as Walsham came second best to Halvergate (by 95 runs), to Old Buckenham (by five wickets), and even to the Presidents XI (by 31 runs).

In a disappointing season, Richard Whiteside (480) scored the most runs and finished top of the batting averages, while Scales, Watkins and Vaughan all passed the 300 mark. The main wicket-takers were Terry Ogden (37), Kim Futter (36) and Garth Futter (25). The 'fourth golden age' was proving to be elusive.

Press Cuttings 1991

Why cricket ladies took the strike

By Richard Batson

NORFOLK cricketing maidens bowled a googly at the MCC — when they downed tools as a protest over a "no women" rule.

The loyal "tea ladies" drew stumps at South Walsham and left the men to fend for themselves with the cups and saucers, urn and sandwiches.

Their action followed the call by former England women's cricket captain Rachel Heyhoe-Flint to withdraw traditional pavilion duties over the MCC's vote to keep women out of their club.

Bowler's wife Mrs Christine Futter said most of the South Walsham men supported the idea of women in cricket and thought the MCC decision was chauvinistic.

She added: "Many women are very much involved with cricket at local and national level.

"The game should not be the exclusive preserve of men. It is enjoyed by both sexes, and a section of the viewing public should not be excluded from a pavilion by virtue of their sex.

"In this day and age of equal opportunities it is simply outrageous."

Mrs Futter is making her views known to the MCC in a letter.

Husband Kim said most of the team were in favour of the women's action, although one or two did think it was rather unreasonable of them.

He said catering could have been a problem except that the team had won their match against Eaton easily — allowing plenty of time for the lads to butter the bread.

"It was just incentive we needed. Perhaps they should strike every week," he joked.

"We were right about the guys being reduced to pathetic, jibbering wrecks without our strength invigorating cuppas, girls....."

Cricket storm brewing

I READ with amusement the letter from Michael Cheetham, the captain of Rollesby Cricket Club (Great Yarmouth Mercury, May 24). That is, I assume it to be "tongue-in-cheek."

It read similar to a letter I would accredit to Mr Pooter from the wonderful "Diary of a Nobody", an upstanding character in the Victorian heyday: "A man endeavouring always in his clumsy and self-conscious way, to act according to his lights."

It certainly needs a letter like this to remind us how ridiculous the MCC really is.

Men who treat women as fragile beauties whose main aim in life is to be domestically adept fail to understand that this is an image of their own creation. Something that was completely shattered by women during wartime when they undertook "men's work", undermining the argument that they were unsuitable or incapable of doing physical and manual work.

It is true men allowed us the role; they also passed us the Equal Pay Act 1970 and the Sex Discrimination Act 1975 — laws that set out that there should be equality and no discrimination.

Radical feminism no, just plain common sense in a democratic society. I'm sure Mr Cheetham recognises these lawful rights in his own place of work!

Well, if the letter wasn't tongue-in-cheek, then I'm sure I could consider an alternative sandwich filling from egg and cress so he could eat his own words.

(Mrs) C. FUTTER,
South Walsham Cricket Club,
Brook Street,
Buxton.

THE SUN, Saturday, May 18, 1991

Cricket crumpet strike

A VILLAGE cricket team was caught out when wives and girlfriends went on strike.

They refused to make the match-day tea and crumpets in protest at the MCC's vote to stay a men-only club.

Bowler's wife Christine Futter, strike leader at South Walsham, Norfolk, said: "The vote was outrageous chauvanism."

Most of the team agreed — but had the last laugh. They bowled out the opposition in 90 minutes

---

EASTERN Evening News

OPINION

MOST cricketers have been hit i worse places than their stomachs s the impact of campaigners like th South Walsham "tea ladies" i withdrawing their usual refreshme service is difficult to assess.

The women are quite right! angered by MCC's decision to kee women out of their club at Lords.

Most of South Walsham's me sportingly accepted that they coul not expect their bread buttered o both sides. But whether the rumble of protest reach Lords is a differer matter.

CHAPTER THIRTY *Improving but...*
1992/93

Results took a turn for the better in 1992; out of 26 games played, eleven were won and the same number lost with the rest drawn. Perhaps the biggest changes during these two years were off the field, as new facilities made a dramatic improvement in the club's cricketing environment.

It was not before time. When the playing field had opened in 1948, two wooden buildings had been erected, one as the village hall and the other one as changing rooms for the various sports played on the field. These had continued to be used, although gradually looking more and more dingy, until 1974 when Ray Lusted, who was very active in the club's cause at this time, decided that the 'pavilion' was overdue some smartening up. After the redecoration with cheap paint - sahara orange and army green - it looked dreadful, but probably held the building together for a few more years.

There is no doubt that if any of today's environmental health officers saw where the club prepared the teas, the building would have been condemned immediately. There were no known cases of food poisoning emanating from South Walsham's catering although, on one occasion, a mouse watched those washing up with keen interest. By 1991 both the changing room and the village hall were, to put it mildly, becoming 'tired' and, although showers had been installed in the changing rooms, even these were getting very tatty.

The club benefited enormously when the new village hall was built and, for the start of the 1992 season, the brand new accommodation included decent toilets, a kitchen and the use of the village hall for the teas. In addition, there was a new wooden pavilion by the pitch which was also used as a store. For those of nostalgic inclination, the old wooden buildings can still be seen at Holly Farm - but their loss was not mourned!.

1992 was a typical season, with Walsham trying to win games rather than settle for draws. No new players joined the club, but Kim Futter took over from his brother Garth as captain. The six-game losing streak from the end of 1991 was extended to seven as Walsham went down by four wickets to

Kirkley, but was finally ended in a draw with Eaton. Batting first, Walsham made 180-4, mainly thanks to fifties from Whiteside and Scales and Eaton replied with 141-5, Garth Futter taking all 5 wickets. The long-awaited win finally arrived after Bradfield A had scored 145. Walsham struggled to 45-5, before London and Garth Futter added 79 for the sixth wicket to help Walsham over the line, finally by three wickets. Insufficient runs (145) against Thetford led to defeat, although Acle A were held to a draw. They scored 160-7, with Gorrod picking up four wickets. Walsham slipped to 87-6, until the Futter brothers added 56 for the 7th wicket to give the side a respectable draw.

Two victories followed. London (53 not out) hit his highest Walsham score in a six-wicket win over Happisburgh, while Kim Futter (5-18) blew away the Cromer top order in a game that was won by 71 runs. This was followed by defeat in a low-scoring game against Old Buckenham, and a crushing defeat by Saxlingham. They recovered from 45-6 to 176-9, to which Walsham's reply was a mere 90 runs. Another half-century from Vaughan couldn't prevent another defeat against Dereham A by five wickets, but this was compensated by a comfortable victory over East Harling by 95 runs, Watkins top-scoring with 74.

This began a winning streak. A total of 227-6 against Margaretting (Essex) resulted in a 61 run win, while Happisburgh were beaten by 73 runs, with a Scales half-century and four wickets from Ogden being the highlights. The next game is one that lives on in the memories of all who played - Steve Belton's finest hour. Having struggled against Dereham A to reach 160-7, skipper Futter used his 'trump card' - Belton's left-arm spin. He steadily went through almost the whole side taking 9-58 from 16 overs. It was a remarkable performance with a dramatic finale. The last wicket fell on the last delivery of the final over, the ball slowly rolling on to the stumps after hitting the batsman's pads to give Walsham a narrow win. It was the best set of bowling figures since 'young George's' all ten against St Barnabas in 1955 and has not been bettered in the last twenty seasons.

A winning draw against Eaton was followed by a five-wicket defeat to Wanderers and another loss - to Dean, a touring side - by two wickets. A high scoring draw against Acle produced another exciting finish. They hit 223-5 and all was going well for Walsham at 153-1, with Vaughan and Whiteside in charge. However, after trying to go for the win, the game ended with the last pair hanging on precariously on 194-9. There was another terrific game against Ingham A, who declared on 264-4. Walsham battled back from 97-6 to 234 all out. At one point, a victory looked possible as runs from Johnson, Ogden and Evans gave Ingham a real fright before their 30-run victory. A pre-tour boost was welcome as Halvergate were beaten by six wickets.

On return from the tour to the New Forest, Johnson scored a magnificent century (135 not out) at Cromer, striking several sixes on a ground which gives every encouragement to the big hitter. However, the game will also be remembered for Steve Belton throwing a big 'wobbler' when he had been run out for 0; it took until after tea to calm him down! Walsham scored 246-6 and won by 90 runs. However, indifferent weather badly affected the end of the 1992 season, and the final game saw Walsham slip to a disappointing six-wicket defeat to East Harling, despite 75 from Scales who ended the season as leading run-scorer.

Scales (720) was followed by Vaughan who passed 500 and Whiteside with over 400. The wickets were shared around: Kim Futter (34), Belton (32) Garth Futter (23) and Ogden (22). John Chilvers remembers the Futter brothers at their peak *'I still recall an over I faced from Garth on Eaton Park which was the most hostile I have ever survived. A really good bloke, but he was amazingly aggressive on that occasion.'* He also remembers Terry Ogden: 'in the words of David Trett, 'Flat Jack', or, more frequently, 'bloody Flat Jack'.

The 1993 season saw average performances on the pitch: seven wins, seven draws and seven defeats but, as always, the spirit remained high. Kim Futter continued to captain the side and there were no new players of note. The season started with a very close game at Kirkley. They scored 216-9 with Belton and Ogden among the wickets, and Walsham looked home and dry at 191-2 - Vaughan and Scales both hit half-centuries - before seven wickets were lost for just five runs and the final pair ended up hanging on for the draw. The next match, against Eaton, was just as close. Walsham could only muster 103-9 off 53 overs, but Eaton found it just as difficult, finishing on 98-9 with Kim Futter and Ogden among the wickets. John Chilvers, the Eaton captain, remembers the game: *'about 100 overs for about 200 runs: real Test match stuff.'* Bradfield chased down 183 to record a six-wicket win while, in the next game, Belton led the way with a half-century as Walsham posted

181-4 against Halvergate. The opposition couldn't quite reach the target, finishing just short on 176-6.

The first win of the season arrived against Acle. They made a good score of 194-4, but Walsham replied with 196-5, good contributions being made by Whiteside, Belton and Watkins. Four defeats followed. The first two were to Happisburgh by four wickets and Cromer (21 runs). In the next game, despite Walsham making 184-2, Thetford chased down the runs to finish on 186-8, despite five wickets from Kim Futter. In the fourth game of the sequence, Ingham proved a little too strong after reaching 219-8. Walsham were going well at 147-5, with Garth Futter hitting 70, but there was a collapse to 160 all out.

The second win of the season came at Cromer where Scales (74) and Whiteside (55*) were the main contributors in a total of 223-7. The bowlers then steadily worked their way through the Cromer batting to bowl them out for 172. Walsham again topped the 200 mark against Dereham A, Johnson hitting 86 and London 50 in a total of 208-5. Dereham went for the runs, but finished just short with seven wickets down. Revenge for a previous defeat was gained when Happisbugh were beaten by eight wickets, while Garth Futter (5-35) helped the cruise to a big win in the return fixture against Dereham.

Halvergate were clear winners by five wickets but, in the next match, Old Buckenham were narrowly defeated - by five runs - in a rain-affected game, Garth Futter (56*) was again the star. Two more wins followed against touring sides: narrowly, by two wickets, against Buxted Park, thanks to Garth Futter again taking five wickets, and a little more convincingly against Wellow Exiles by 40 runs. At 91-8, Walsham had been in trouble in this match, but Kim Futter's only half-century for the club raised the total to 155-8. Belton (5-44) then played a major role in bowling out the visitors.

The side were very much out of sorts when losing to Somerleyton by five wickets, but played better against Norwich Wanderers. In this game, the home side scored 170-5 and Walsham made a good effort to chase the runs, finishing on 162-9. Johnson hit the club's only century of the season - 102 out of a total of 226-5 - against Thetford, but the opposition were never likely to win finishing on 156-8. The final game of the season was against John Westgarth's Presidents XI. This ended in a close draw in which the

President's side made 246-7, while Walsham finished on 243-9.

When the season was analysed, Vaughan (432 runs) finished top of the batting averages, while Johnson and Scales also passed 400 runs, Watkins and Belton falling just short of this mark. Belton (28) finished as leading wicket-taker while the Futter brothers and Ogden also passed the 20 mark. It had been another enjoyable but, in terms of results, an average season. There was a lot of talent in the side – could it come together to produce another vintage season – or even an era?

Press Cuttings 1992

The hat-trick

South Walsham recorded their third win on the trot when they beat Happisburgh by 73 runs.

Walsham's John Vaughan (28) and Andy Scales (50) started the innings well, with only a run out mix up separating them. Richard Whiteside (32) played well, while Garth Futter and David Watkins with 12 each both fell as they tried to increase the run rate.

Happisburgh's reply started badly losing the openers in the first two overs. Walsham were particularly pleased to see Ritchie go caught by Chris Gould, one of four catches he took, he dropped a fifth chance which would have created a new club record.

Happisburgh hit back to take the score to 53 before Landamore (15) and Ivan Andrews (33) fell to Gould and Ogden.

Terry Ogden (four for 11) and Steve Belton (two for 11) quickly wrapped up the innings as Happisburgh collapsed to 80 all out.

Walsham recover

South Walsham drew with Eaton, after batting first and struggling to start with, needing 75 for 4 off the first 28 overs.

John Vaughan (18), Neil Johnson (23) and David Wathers (19) all contributed to the score but it was a 97 run partnership between Andy Scales (86 not out) and Garth Futter (28) which really started the scoreboard moving.

They lifted the score to 168 with their partnership lasting just 18 overs. Andy Scales batted superbly on a difficult wicket to reach his highest score of the season as Walsham reached a respectable total of 194 for 6 dec.

In reply it always looked whether the Walsham bowlers would get the Eaton batsmen out rather than whether they would reach their target.

Eaton adopted a rather negative approach rarely hitting the ball off the square. Kim Futter made an early breakthrough with 2 for 14 but N Dunmore held firm scoring 29 off 40 overs. Walsham did not help themselves dropping five catches but the game petered out to a disappointing draw with Eaton just making the 100 off 50 overs.

Honours go to the home side

South Walsham went down to Ingham A by 30 runs in an enjoyable game at Ingham on Sunday.

Ingham batted first on a good batting track and fast outfield, and the Walsham bowlers found it difficult to stem the flow of runs as the Ingham batsmen enjoyed themselves.

After 50 overs Ingham declared on 264 for four leaving Walsham about 60 overs to chase victory. The most successful bowlers were Steve Belton with two for 70 and Evan Gitsham 2-36.

In reply Walsham struggled early on against tight bowling from Roper and Rossi. David Watkins (31) and Mike Key (20) took the score past 50 following the early loss of Richard Whiteside.

Garth Futter and Evan Gitsham (27) kept Neil Johnson (55) kept Walsham in with a faint chance with some typical hard hitting.

All seemed lost when Johnson went leaving Walsham on 147 for seven but Terry Ogden (49) and Alex Evans (34) put together an entertaining stand of 71 to bring the score up to 218 for eight. Kim Futter made one or two lusty blows as Walsham still went for victory.

The last wicket fell on 234 after a gallant display from the Walsham tailenders.

The bowlers Gus Roper (two for 60) off 24 overs and B Rossi (6-92) off 28 over both bowled well for Ingham.

Cup time

The annual fixture between South Walsham and Halvergate for the Graham London Memorial Trophy resulted in a win for South Walsham by six wickets.

Tight bowling especially D Gorrod (9-2-26-3) and exceptional catches by G Futter and D Watkins restricted Halvergate to 136. S Mallett jnr scored a very solid 43 with a fine array of shots around the wicket.

South Walsham's reply was solid if not spectacular at the beginning. N Johnson batted soundly and respectively for a match winning 40 with A Scales supporting with 23.

Steve's got 'em in a spin

South Walsham beat Dereham A by 41 runs on Sunday at South Walsham in a friendly.

The star of the day was Steve Belton whose left arm variety of spin got the Dereham batsmen in a real tangle.

With some good fielding, backing up Belton's bowling, Dereham never looked in with a chance of victory.

As the last over approached Dereham were battling out for a draw, a missed stumping from Alex Evans' seemed to mean Walsham would have to settle for a draw.

But Belton managed to squeeze the sixth ball of the last over through the defences of Russell. The ball rolled towards the stumps and was just rolling hard enough to knock off one bail, much to the relief of Evans and the other Walsham players.

Earlier Walsham had batted well against steady bowling with John Vaughan continuing his good run with 51 ably supported by Andy Scoles (23) David Watkins (25) Fred Leak (14) and Garth Futter (16) plus a good knock by newcomer Matthew Holmes (25 no) to reach 169 for seven.

Dereham managed just 118 as the last word was left to Steve Belton with a club record of 16-2-58-90.

Well done Steve, the celebrations after the game gave him a headache on Monday morning.

Second victory

South Walsham gained their second win of the season when they defeated Happisburgh by six wickets at Happisburgh on Sunday.

Happisburgh elected to bat on a dry fast pitch and were soon in trouble as opening bowlers Ken Futter and Neville London both took a wicket in their first over. Ian Ritchie brought about a recovery with 43 and Steven Andrews hitting 38 not out as Happisburgh reached 146-9 at tea.

Walsham got off to a steady start with Steve Belton (14) and John Vaughan (38) scoring well. Geoff Winter playing only his second game for Walsham took control with a fine 52 not out. Winter and Garth Futter, taking some cheeky singles at the end saw South Walsham home on 147 for four with just nine balls to spare.

Much better as Walsham get a draw

South Walsham turned in a much better performance this week when they played out an exciting draw with Norwich Wanderers at Barton Turf.

With both Futter brothers struggling with injuries Derek Gorrod and Neil Johnson opened the bowling for Walsham.

Gorrod gained an early success dismissing Halford for 22 but it was fine bowling from Terry Ogden (2-38 off 14 overs) and Neville London (2-47 off 15) which slowed the progress of the Wanderers batting.

South Walsham were content in holding the Wanderers side to 170 for 5 by tea.

David Watkins and Whiteside went early to the useful Latarche, but John Vaughan (42) and Terry Ogden (39) dug in with a useful 51 partnership.

Ogden in particular was in sparkling form only brought to a halt by a ball which kept low trapping him lbw.

Useful contributions from Steve Belton (13) Neville London (12) Alex London (12) Alex Evans (15) and Kim Futter (17 not out) brought Walsham close to victory as they made every effort to win the game.

Needing 15 to win off the last over No 11 batsman Derek Gorrod hit a superb four but bowler Halford held his nerve and Walsham finished on 162-8 just nine runs short of victory.

Press Cuttings 1993

Regular changes spell success for Walsham

South Walsham scored a very comfortable victory on Sunday when they beat Happisbugh by eight wickets.

Happisburgh struggled from the start against some particularly aggressive bowling by Garth Futter (2-17 off seven).

Happisburgh never recovered from a poor start with only R Moore (38) coming to terms with the bowling.

Skipper Steve Belton changed his bowlers regularly and every bowler gained at least one success.

Matthew Holmes (3-12) had the best figures in his first game following a long injury.

Geoff Winter was also making his first appearance this season and he took 2-13 off two overs.

With the wides column adding 18 runs to the total, happisburgh reached a disappointing score of 97.

South Walsham quickly got off the mark in their replay scoring 27 in the first four overs before Andy Scales went for 15.

Neil Johnson hit a quick 13 as South Walsham slipped to 41-2.

There were no more problems for the Walsham batsmen as John Vaughan (42 not out) and Richard Whteside (21 not out) batted steadily to give Walsham an eight wicket victory.

Vaughan, Scales star

South Walsham Cricket Club started their 1993 season with an exciting home game against Kirkley.

Kirkley batted first on a good track and made quick progress against some early season bowling from Walsham.

Kim Fitter showed his usual control with 1-21 off 8 overs but the other medium pacers revealed a lack of net practise.

Kirkley continued to score at five an over and it was not until the last hour that Walsham started to pick up wickets. Spinners Terry Ogden 3 for 60 and Steve Belton 4 for 37 prevented Kirkley from scoring an even bigger total, although 212 was an excellent score so early in the season. Scott (34), George (23), Cowling (51) and Bishop (44) all showed good form for Kirkley.

John Vaughan and Andy Scales started steadily in reply with a target of 213 off about 36 overs a tough total, but once they had seen off the opening attack Vaughan and Scales started hitting the ball to all parts of the ground as Kirkley sportingly opened the game out.

Scales was first to go after a splendid 74 following a record first wicket partnership of 158. Vaughan followed shortly after just failing to make his ground, going for another quick single John Vaughan was applauded back to the pavilion after a wonderful 87.

With four overs left and Walsham standing at 191 for 3 victory was in sight but Kirkley bowler Roderick picked up five wickets in two overs and Terry Ogden had to play out the last over to draw the match.

A superb game played in tremendous spirit.

First win of year

South Walsham won their first game of the season when they beat Acle A by five wickets on Sunday.

Acle A batted first and despite a slow start batted well to score 194 for four declared.

Andy Sims dominated the innings with a fine 110 not out, despite being missed twice it was a splendid innings with some good clean hitting.

Colin Tovell batted well for 16 as did Jack Bull for 21 not out. Youngster Ben Watkins took two wickets while Garth Futter was the pick of the bowlers with one of 42 off 15 overs.

South Walsham despite losing John Vaughan early on scored runs steadily with David Watkins (36) showing good form.

The game seemed to be heading for a draw, when Acle skipper Kevin Gilbert sportingly opened the game up to buy wickets, Richard Whiteside (51) and Steve Belton (47 not out) took full advantage and started to hit the ball all round the ground, when the opening bowlers returned Walsham had brought the run rate required down to three runs an over.

Garth Futter hit the winning runs with just 10 balls to spare.

An enjoyable game played in a super spirit.

Walsham away day win

South Walsham gained a good away win against Cromer A after getting off to a brisk start thanks to openers John Vaughan and Andy Scales who added 56 for the first wicket before Vaughan fell for 22.

Neil Johnson upped the tempo with a lovely 20 and Scales went shortly after for an impressive 74.

Although South Walsham became a little becalmed, Richard Whiteside then played some splendid shots in the middle order and with Ben Watkins (19) and Neville London (13), South Walsham pushed the total to 223-6 with Whiteside 55 not out.

When Cromer batted, South Walsham were quickly amongst the wickets with Derek Garrod bagging early wickets.

South Walsham were always on top but R Copus and A Lawes gave Cromer some hope, both just falling short of deserved 50s.

Steve Belton was the most successful bowler, polishing off the Cromer tail with two overs to spare and ending with 3-26, but it was a good bowling performance by all six Walsham bowlers.

CHAPTER THIRTY ONE *Moving In The Right Direction 1994-96*

In a more successful season in 1994, new skipper Steve Belton presided over eleven wins and only six defeats in the twenty-three games completed. This was achieved despite John Vaughan being injured. The season started quietly with a draw against Eaton, who finished on 105-7 when chasing Walsham's 151-6. The next match - against Bradfield - was memorable, particularly for Scales and Watkins as they added an unbeaten 228 for the first wicket. Strangely, both players finished on 100 not out, with 28 extras, when the declaration came. It was a terrific effort much celebrated in the bar afterwards, but it wasn't quite enough to win as Bradfield finished on 190-9. Against Dereham A, the opposition were

Record Partnership - 228 v Bradfield

12-3, chasing 154, when the rain intervened. Two defeats followed: away at Cromer A, by one wicket and by four wickets at home against the same opposition as they chased 179 fairly easily. The all-day game at Ingham ended in a 50-run defeat, but the next match saw the first win of the season, a 53-run success over Bradenham A. Runs for Scales and London and 3-30 from Belton eased the way to victory.

A match was played against Halvergate in memory of Graham London, Neville's son, who had tragically died during an asthma attack. Graham had played a few games for Halvergate, as had his father, and it seemed appropriate that, as Neville was now a Walsham player, the game should be between the two sides. Halvergate always had the 40-over match under control and won comfortably, despite 54 from Kelvin London, Graham's uncle, who was guesting for Walsham. Against tourists Downsiders, Walsham cruised to victory by nine wickets as Scales and Key added 178 for the first wicket before Johnson came in and hit his first ball for four to win the game. The better end of a draw against Thetford A was achieved after setting 210-9, (Belton 50); Thetford finished on 154-6.

A strange game at Happisburgh, when 99% of Norfolk was bathed in warm sunshine, had to be abandoned due to sea mist after Walsham had scored 241-6 with a tremendous 132 from Neil Johnson. Happisburgh's reply was going well on 95-1 when it became impossible to continue. Johnson continued his good form in the next match, hitting 95 out of a total of 243-3 against Bradfield, who were bowled out for 193, Ogden (5-67). In the game against touring side Singleton, Johnson was at it again, scoring 91 out of a total of 210-5. They made a good effort to win the game, but finished eight runs short with only four wickets down. However, Walsham were second best by 54 runs against Old Buckenham, despite the efforts of Garth Futter who took 5-34 and scored 58 not out.

South Walsham Squad 1994

The 'Ploughmen' were beaten by four wickets and this was followed by another win, against Felthorpe, with Garth Futter again the star with 43 and 5-18.

After the successful tour to East Sussex, Walsham hit a purple patch winning four games in a row. Dereham A were beaten by four wickets, mainly due to the efforts of Garth Futter and Andy Scales and while Beccles scored 204 in the next match (Garth Futter 6-75) - short work was made of the total as Walsham hit 205-1, Scales making 96 not out. The opener led Walsham to another win, this time against Halvergate, as the hosts made 194-4, but Scales hit 76 not out and Johnson 74 as Walsham won by seven wickets.

Thetford turned up with just nine players and paid the penalty in a 62 run defeat after Scales hit his fifth successive fifty.

The final game of the season saw a draw with John Westgarth's President's XI who scored 152, Walsham finishing three runs short with just one wicket left. It had been another very enjoyable season, Scales top-scoring with 822 runs while Johnson and Watkins both passed the 500 mark. In the bowling, Garth Futter excelled with his highest-ever total of 49 from 203 overs while Kim Futter, Ogden and Belton all passed the 20 wicket mark.

President's XI 1994

After this level of success, the 1995 season was disappointing, mainly because of the wet weather which caused six of the 26 fixtures to be lost. There were no new recruits, although Andy Scales took over from Steve Belton as skipper. The season started with Ogden taking 5-55 against Kirkley who scored 163; Walsham held out for the draw on 119-9. Against Dereham A, Walsham's seemingly poor total of 101-9 almost proved to be enough as Dereham collapsed from 80-0 to 97-6, but they reached the target without further alarm. Beccles gained revenge for the previous season on their excellent track. Walsham batted first and hit 229-2 (David Watkins 86), but it was not enough as Beccles knocked them off to win by five wickets in just 34 overs.

Eaton were the next team to beat Walsham by four wickets, while the first win of the season came against Cromer A by three wickets. They scored 159 and Walsham reached the target, Ben Watkins, David's eldest son, top-scoring with 43. Somerleyton were beaten by a massive margin of 133 runs after being dismissed for only 40. The Graham London Memorial Trophy was retained by Halvergate as they won by 46 runs. David Watkins carried his bat for 63 not out, but no-one could stay with him.

The all-day annual visit to Ingham finished in the usual manner. The home side declared on 263-7 and Walsham were going well at 153-2, but collapsed to 187 all out. The next game, against Kirby - a touring side from Essex - saw Watkins and Whiteside added 208 for the second wicket, one run short of the all-time record for the second wicket. Both players made hundreds, but it was particularly pleasing for Whiteside (103*) who hit his only Walsham century. Kirby finished on 163-7, securing the draw, but great celebrations followed the Whiteside 'ton'. Walsham scored 220-5 against Bradfield with Johnson and Matt Holmes - an occasional player, who lived in the village - both hitting half-centuries, but Bradfield were too strong and cruised to a five-wicket win in 40 overs. On a wet wicket Walsham were second best in a draw against Terrington St Clement who scored 151-5. In reply, Walsham could only muster 84-8 as the West Norfolk side tried and failed to blast out the tail. A good total of 212-7 was reached against touring side Withyham, but they finished on 164-9 to secure the draw.

The next win came against Old Buckenham A by 44 runs. Scales hit 94 not out and, after Johnson had powered to a half century, Ogden (6-51) winkled his way through the Buckenham batting. Walsham scored over 200 for the third game running against a side called Fives Sports from North London. Whiteside led the way with a half-century, but the tourists held on for a draw. Scales hit a century against Somerleyton but, again, the opposition played out time. A tight game saw Walsham go down to Eaton by 21 runs, despite good bowling from Garth Futter and he was in form again in the next game against Halvergate as he took 5-17 in their total of just 74. This game was over before tea as the runs were knocked off for the loss of just two wickets. Scales hit 69 against Cromer A, but a total of 161 on their small ground was not enough as they won by four wickets.

There was a fine victory at Bradfield. After the home side had hit 186-6, a century from Scales and a half-century from Watkins saw the total reached in just 35 overs. A nine-wickets down draw was forced against Dereham A while, in the penultimate game of the season, Walsham were bowled out for a modest 143 by Bradenham only for the rain to cause an abandonment. The season should have finished with the President's game, but that was abandoned because of bad weather. In a year when it had sometimes been a struggle to field a team, there were still several individual successes. Scales and Watkins both passed 600 runs, Whiteside was just short of 450 while Johnson passed the 300 mark. Terry Ogden was top of the bowling averages and took 30 wickets while Garth Futter and Gould both passed the 20 mark.

The 1996 season proved much more successful on the field of play with fourteen wins out of twenty-three completed. However, there was sadness within the club. Neville London, who had been ill for some time and unable to play was elected President at the 1995 AGM but passed away later in the year. His death was a major loss and, to fill the breach, John Westgarth was re-elected as President for his seventh year in the post.

Andy Scales continued as skipper and led the team to an excellent victory in the first match of the season against Dereham A, scoring exactly 100 out of a total of 219-4. The opposition were dismissed for 132, with spinners Ogden and Belton picking up seven wickets between them. Another run-fest took place at Beccles. The home side scored 209-5, but Scales again led the way with a 'ton' to see Walsham home by six wickets. However, after only being able to muster nine players against Eaton the penalty was paid in a six-wicket defeat. Despite a last wicket stand of 58 between Gorrod and Evans against Kirkley, it proved nowhere near enough as they romped home easily in 33 overs.

However, the season was about to turn as, of the next nine games, eight were won and one drawn. The first of these victories was a struggle against a touring side called Akademicals. They scored just 88 but, thanks to Whiteside with 32 not out, Walsham crept home by two wickets. Against another touring outfit, Broomfield Hospital, a 41-run win was set up by Scales again leading the way with 85 not out. Bradfield A were defeated by four wickets with Chris Gould (4-12) the star man. Halvergate were beaten comfortably after they managed just 109, Walsham knocked them off for the loss of just three wickets.

The next game was a classic. Walsham bowled out Kirkley for 228 after they had passed the 200 mark with only four wickets down, Gould (6-18) quickly mopping up the tail. A century partnership between Watkins and Rupert Holmes got Walsham off to a great start and, with some hard hitting from Garth Futter, victory was achieved by three wickets in just 38 overs. Gt Yarmouth and Gorleston were then dismissed for 120 and a Watkins half-century led the way to another victory. Diss A proved a little more difficult.

After Walsham hit 200-8 declared, Diss held on at 169-8, despite four wickets for Belton.

The match against Eaton was another classic. They declared at 196-4 after Keith Halford had completed a century. Walsham only had ten men and had struggled in the field. The reply was going well at 149-3 with Scales on 70 not out, when Halford took a hat-trick. More wickets followed as Walsham slipped to 171-8, leaving just Belton and Evans to battle it out. A few edges and lusty blows later, an unlikely victory was achieved. Rarely can someone have scored a century and taken a hat-trick in the same game and finished on the losing side!

Richard Whiteside (4-48) turned bowler as tourists Verdayne Green were bowled out for 133, Walsham reaching the target for the loss of four wickets. Kelvin London's 'Select XI' scored 165-7 and again these were knocked off with ease. However, the next match was the return game against Eaton and they were 'pumped up' to gain revenge for the defeat of a few weeks earlier. Walsham batted first and quickly collapsed to 16-4, eventually creeping to 91 all out, of which Belton scored 46. Halford - utterly determined to avenge the previous game - took four wickets and bowled very quickly that day. Eaton won by seven wickets.

Bad weather, resulting in an extended break, marked the return from the Somerset tour. Resuming with the annual all-day game at Ingham, the hosts scored a massive total of 293-4. Walsham were 99-4 when the rain returned and both sides adjourned to the bar, Walsham with a sense of relief. The penultimate game was a close affair; Dereham A hit 208 to which Walsham replied with 206-9. The final game of the season saw the President's XI gain a rare victory by 23 runs.

It had been an enjoyable season in which the tour and exciting wins against Kirkley and Eaton had been the highlights. Scales (763 runs) maintained his excellent form while Belton, Whiteside and Garth Futter all passed the 400 mark. Gould starred in the bowling, topping the averages with 39 wickets, while Ogden was the only other bowler to pass the 20-wicket mark.

Press Cuttings 1994

Scales and Key lay a formidable basis

CRICKET: South Walsham played two games this weekend playing touring side Downsiders from Surrey on Friday and Thetford A on Sunday, both played at South Walsham.

Downsiders elected to bat first and were soon in trouble at 7-3 thanks to some lively bowling from Kim and Garth Futter.

A partnership from Davis (28) and Rose (42) lifted the score to 80 before they fell off consecutive balls. Glazer (37) and Issacs (27 no) pushed the score up to 179-9 dec at tea. Steve Belton was the most successful bowler with 3-54 although Garth Futter was the best bowler on show with 2-55.

At the start of the innings the target looked quite a difficult one but Andy Scales (74 not out) and Mike Key (90) quickly got into their stride. The Downsiders skipper regularly changed his bowlers without success until the score reached 178, just two runs short of victory. Neil Johnson then came in to hit the next ball for four.

The remarkable score of 183-1 was reached off under 25 overs.

On Sunday against Thetford the Walsham batsmen did not have it all their own way early on as Andy Scales, David Watkins and Richard Whiteside were all back in the pavilion with only 35 runs on the board.

Neil Johnson (31) then took charge for a while and Rupert Holmes (28) looked a fine prospect with a classy innings. Walsham slipped to 116 for 6. Steve Belton (58) and Kim Futter (25) then added 66 for the seventh wicket. Belton was in aggressive mood hitting three sixees and seven fours.

When the opening bowlers returned the run rate increased with Kim Futter in particular playing some extraordinary shots. The tail added a few more runs as Walsham reached 210-9 dec at tea.

Thetford started well adding 40 for the first wicket. Rupert Holmes bowled well after Kim Futter broke down with injury.

Terry Ogden slowed the run rate and Thetford lost any chance of victory.

The game then reached a position where Thetford were never going to reach their target and Walsham were unlikely to bowl Thetford out.

The game therefore fizzled out to a draw with Steve Belton taking 2-20 and Andy Scales picking up a rare wicket.

Thetford were slightly flattered by a score of 154-6.

A memorial played in a fine spirit

SOUTH Walsham went down to Halvergate by 35 runs at South Walsham in the annual meeting for the Graham London Memorial Trophy.

Halvergate lost Mike Key in the second over but took charge against generally steady bowling.

Strike bowler Kim Futter seemed out of sorts and it was left to Neville London (2-31) and Kelvin London (0-24) to slow Halvergate's progress.

Steve Cooke (51), Evan Gitsham (35) added 94 for the second wicket while Stephen Mallett 26 no and Brian Brister 23 no brought Halvergate up to 185-4.

South Walsham got off to the worst possible start losing Terry Ogden in the second over. David Watkins (23) and Kelvin London (54) then took charge adding 63 for the second wicket when Watkins fell to a superb catch by Andrew Key.

Garth Cutter with a quick fire 25 kept Walsham in the hunt but with K London and G Cutter both falling to good catches in the deep Walsham lost their way and finished on 150-9 in their 45 overs to lose by 35 runs.

An excellent game played in a super spirit.

Easy wickets for Walsham

SOUTH Walsham beat Somerleyton by 133 runs at Somerleyton on Sunday.

It is not often South Walsham actually outclass an opposition, but they did on this occasion. On a slow wicket Walsham started slowly and both John Vaughan (28) and David Watkins (13) struggled to get going. Richard Whiteside then took charge, scoring an excellent 63 not out. Andy Scales (13) and newcomer Steven Giles (13 not out) lifted the score to 173-4 after the allotted 40 overs. With a slow outfield, Walsham were confident of holding the opposition when they went in for tea.

Somerleyton then batted and moved to 25 for two off eight overs. It was a spirited start but Somerleyton collapsed, losing their last eight wickets in 13 overs for just 15 runs. The wickets were well spread with Derek Gorrod taking two for eight and Chris Gould two for three. Steven Belton finished off the tail with three for six. Although Walsham were happy to win it was a little disappointing not to face a stronger test.

And then there were three

SOUTH Walsham recorded their third win of the season when they beat Bradfield A by 50 runs.

South Walsham batted first with Andy Scales (55) and David Watkins (31) getting the home side off to a steady start.

They added 66 for the first wicket before Watkins was dismissed. With Richard Whiteside (42 not out) playing a secondary role, Scales then hit out to score a deserved half century.

When Scales was dismissed Neil Johnson then took complete charge for the second week running. Neil hit a superb 95 before being stumped going for another big hit.

His score included 10 sixes and five fours and it is interesting to note he was only at the wicket for 14 overs. Walsham were able to declare at 242 for three off only 37 overs.

Bradfield started steadily in reply before Terry Ogden struck in the sixth over to dismiss Harmer for 16. Loades and Rice continued the good work against generally steady bowling.

With Bradfield reaching 86 for two it looked odds on a draw but with Ogden picking up five for 67, Bradfield then slipped to 105 for seven.

Sadler and Christmas then hit out to score half centuries and lifted Bradfield to 193 they both fell at the same score as South Walsham won by 50 runs.

Val(iant) Singleton

SOUTH Walsham just hung on to the draw against Singleton, a touring side from Sussex.

South Walsham batted first with Richard Whiteside (67 not out) and David Watkins (14) adding 35 for the first wicket.

It was Whiteside who held the innings together as Walsham's batting order looked a little frail.

For the third week running Whiteside then played a secondary role in a partnership with hard-hitting Neil Johnson who scored 91. Although not as fluent as in his previous two innings, he still scored quickly enough to lift the South Walsham total to 210-5 by tea.

When Singleton batted the openers Baker (39) and Smith (34) started slowly against tight bowling from Kim Futter and Derek Garrad but it wasn't until Steve Belton came on that Walsham picked up their first wicket after 76 runs.

Singleton then increased the tempo with Symonds scoring 33 and Standing a hard hit 59. Skipper Belton then had to rely on the nerve of bowlers Kim and Garth Futter to save the match as Singleton finished on 203-4 just eight runs short of victory.

Press Cuttings 1995

Scales posts superb 102

SOUTH Walsham had the better end of a draw against Somerleyton at South Walsham on Sunday.

South Walsham batted first and despite losing Steve Belton early on, David Watkins (41) and Neil Johnson (26) progressed at a good pace adding 47 for the second wicket.

Andy Scales then came to the wicket and took charge with a superb century which included 18 fours. He finished on 102 not out when he declared Walsham's innings on 212-4 off just 40 overs.

Steven Giles scored 15 not out to help Scales add 51 for the fifth wicket.

From past experience Somerleyton were always going to struggle to keep up with the required run rate to win the game, and they found it very difficult to score runs against the Walsham bowlers.

After 23 overs they had crawled to 37-3.

The Walsham bowlers have struggled to bow teams all season and this match was no exception. Kim Futter 1-13 from 10 overs and Terry Ogden 2-10 off 9 overs bowled well but Somerleyton reached their goal by holding on for a draw at 82-5.

London pride in trophy

SOUTH WALSHAM went down to Halvergate in the Graham London Memorial Trophy by 46 runs at Halvergate on Sunday.

The trophy is played between the two teams every season in memory of Graham London, who sadly died at the age of 17. It was a particularly sad occasion for his father Neville, who has now had to retire from cricket through illness.

In his speech after the game, Neville put things in perspective, that the game of cricket was there to be enjoyed and making friends, and the result was only secondary.

This was certainly the case on Sunday with the game played in good spirit and the Walsham players pleased to get back on the pitch after three rain-ruined Sundays.

Halvergate batted first on a slow, low wicket. Mike Key and Steven Cooke got them off to a steady start against good bowling. Key was first to go for 15 which brought in Kelvin London, who batted superbly to 112 not out. Perhaps it was fitting that a member of the London family should play the innings of the day.

With Steve Cooke scoring 46 and Steven Mallett 15, Halvergate reached the very good score of 217 for four off their 45 overs. Part-time bowler John Vaughan was the most successful with two for 13.

With the wicket getting slower and lower, Walsham's target looked a tough one. It was even harder when John Vaughan was out in the third over for just a single. David Watkins and Richard Whiteside added 56 for the second wicket but Walsham were falling behind the required run rate.

Andy Scales and Ned Johnson hit one or two good shots but with the lower order getting themselves out going for attacking shots, Walsham were all out for 171 off the last ball of the 45th over. David Watkins carried his bat with 63 not out. Andrew Key was Halvergate's most successful bowler with three for 41. There was no doubt that the best team won on the day.

Memorable day for two batsmen

SOUTH Walsham were held to a draw by Kirby, a touring side from Essex and while the game petered out rather disappointingly it will be remembered for a long time by two Walsham batsmen.

South Walsham batted first against an excellent opening spell from the Kirby bowlers Wilson and Oram; after the first 13 overs Walsham had managed only 17 runs for the loss of Andy Scales.

It was here the game completely changed. The next 27 overs saw David Watkins (106 not out) and Richard Whiteside (103 not out) put the Kirby bowlers to the sword. Watkins hit 17 fours while Whiteside managed 12.

It was a great day, particularly for Whiteside who scored his first-ever century while Watkins scored his second century.

Their partnership was 208 for the second wicket, a club record and Walsham were able to declare 10 minutes before tea at a score of 216-1.

When Kirby batted the openers started slowly against steady bowling from Chris Gould 0-16 off seven overs and Terry Ogden, (2-28) 12 overs. Skipper Scales juggled his bowlers as Kirby continued their slow progress. It was clear that they were always going to fall short but lack lustre fielding did not help Walsham in their efforts to force a victory.

After 48 overs Kirby reached 163-7 for a somewhat disappointing draw.

It was a day to celebrate with Whiteside and Watkins as the team enjoyed the watering cans of beer in the pub afterwards.

Tail hold on for a result

CRICKET: South Walsham just managed to hold on to a draw at Dereham A on Sunday.

Dereham batted first against rather variable Walsham bowling and it wasn't until the introduction of Garth Futter that Walsham looked like taking a wicket.

Futter eventually took three for 57 off 14 overs, while Terry Ogden chipped in with two wickets as Dereham made 164-5 declared.

In reply, South Walsham started really well adding 53 in quick time David Watkins (25) was first to go and Steve Belton who struggled once Watkins was out, played really well for 34.

Walsham batsmen then became becalmed adding only 14 runs in 11 overs.

Neil Johnson (32) then lifted the tempo, as the required run rate went up to over six runs an over, several wickets were then sacrificed in an effort to score quick runs, but good bowling from Dereham made life very difficult for the Walsham batsmen.

Tailenders Pennington and Evans were left to defend the last three overs to prevent a Dereham victory Walsham finished on 124-9.

Master batting

SOUTH Walsham were well beaten when they went down to Ingham A by 76 runs.

Ingham batted first and had to play carefully for a while against some tight bowling from the Futter brothers before lunch.

R Wagner, the Ingham opener, then cut loose, hitting the ball to all parts of the ground with a super 156 not out.

Again the Walsham fielders put down the odd chance but it was a superb innings well appreciated by all who were watching.

Ingham declared on 263-7, leaving Walsham about 65 overs to reach the target.

Walsham were short on bowling and it was noticeable that while only 120 runs came from Kim Futter (1-64) and Garth Cutter (3-57) in 34 overs, another 125 came from the other 18 overs.

Walsham set off in enterprising fashion with Andy Scales (61) in his best position as opener. David Watkins (25) played second fiddle to Scales in a partnership of 88 for the first wicket.

Richard Whiteside kept the innings going with a knock of 28, but after an excellent start and Walsham on 115-1, wickets started to fall.

Neil Johnson reached double figures with 17 but the remaining batsmen failed and Walsham slipped to 187 all out with 12 overs remaining.

On another day Walsham might have reached the target and it was particularly disappointing to see such a collapse following a super start.

CHAPTER THIRTY TWO *Runs, Runs And More Runs*

The 1997 season saw Richard Whiteside take over the captaincy from Andy Scales, after a couple of successful seasons, but the club's tradition is for the captaincy to be passed around on a regular basis. Whiteside's successful first season - of 25 completed games, 15 were won - was helped by the return to the fold of Keith Denton, who had been playing at a higher level for Barleycorns, but thought it was time to return to his cricketing roots. John Pennington, previously an occasional player, enjoyed a full season which strengthened the attack. Jon Moore made his debut and, although not a prolific run-scorer, became an excellent fielder, thoroughly good clubman, great tourist and served as the club's treasurer through to 2010.

The season opened with a ten-run win over Dereham A in a 40-over contest. Walsham were dismissed for 138, but tight bowling restricted Dereham to 128-6. Vaughan showed he could still turn his arm over when he took 4-24 as Drayton were skittled out for 98, and were comfortably beaten, as were Eaton - by five wickets - after they had set a total of 139-9. Two further comprehensive wins followed: against Winterton by 64 runs and Hardingham by 8 wickets, Watkins and Denton hitting half-centuries in the latter match.

Scales made 77 in another substantial total of 206-5 against tourists Bexley Hospital, but they held on for a draw, finishing on 177-8. It was a similar story against Great Melton as Walsham totalled 225-9, with 82 from Denton, but this had batted them out of the game and they finished 47 runs short with only four wickets down. A third draw on the trot saw Walsham fail to beat Broomfield Hospital in a game in which Evans (49) hit his highest score. Unaware that he was so close to a maiden fifty, sheer tiredness caused him to miss a straight one! Walsham reached 175-7, while the tourists struggled to 142-7.

It was back to winning ways against Ashwellthorpe - by eight wickets - with Whiteside top-scoring on 81 not out and Watkins hitting a half century. The Graham London Memorial Trophy was retained as Halvergate were beaten by five wickets. Pennington led the way with 4-15 as they were restricted to 171-9 and Watkins (74) led the reply as Walsham got home in the final over. The Plough Cricket Club were outclassed, Walsham's 226-7 declared ensuring a 124-run victory. Touring side Betsham were let off the hook after losing five early wickets before recovering to 202-9. Walsham appeared to be well-placed at 155-2, but a dramatic collapse led to the last eight wickets falling for only nine runs.

It was back to form as Bradfield A hit 190-6, but some big hitting from the Futter brothers saw Walsham to a narrow victory by two wickets in what had been a terrific match. Against tourists Old Dunstanians, who were a useful side, Walsham struggled to hold them to 237-9, but runs from Denton, Whiteside and Garth Futter opened up the possibility of victory before the innings closed on 205-5 in a high-scoring draw. Another visit from Verdayne Green produced a 30-run victory; despite Walsham being bowled out for 105, Garth Futter (6-19) saved the day. The first defeat of the season came at Vauxhall Mallards where, despite Johnson hitting 56 out of a total of 133, Walsham lost by 80 runs.

There was a familiar battle when trying to bowl out Eaton. After Walsham had declared on 178-7, the obdurate opposition closed on 124-6. One of the best games of the season came at Bradenham. Denton hit 75 out of a total of 222-7, but Bradenham chased well winning the game by three wickets with just two balls remaining. Whiteside and Denton both hit fifties in a 52-run win over Great Melton and Pennington was really on song against Happisburgh, scoring an important 23 not out in a total of 171-9 and following this up with 6-36 to see Walsham home by just twelve runs.

It was Gould's day against Nacton, as he took 5-45 in a total of 158. Walsham struggled in reply, but 43 not out from Whiteside led to a victory by three wickets. A draw followed against Old Buckenham. They scored 225-7 while Walsham managed 185-9 with Denton hitting another half-century. There was another good win against Halvergate who hit 164, but 80 not out from Scales saw Walsham home by seven wickets. The highest total of the season came at Cromer against their 'A' side. They scored an impressive 259-6 but, on their small ground, Walsham were always in with a chance and, with Denton leading the way with 99 not out, a narrow two-wicket victory was achieved.

The season concluded with a defeat against the Presidents XI. John Westgarth who had retired several years earlier showed that he could still play by making 68 as his XI amassed 258-8. Despite 77 from Scales, Walsham could only reach 221. It had been a terrific season with Denton (743) top-scoring and Whiteside, Scales and Watkins all passing the 450 mark. Garth Futter (39 wickets) topped the bowling charts, while Ogden (31), Kim Futter and Pennington all passed the 20 mark.

There were no new players in the ranks in 1998. Whiteside continued as skipper while John Westgarth was again elected President, in what turned out to be his final year before handing over to the present incumbent, Ray Norman. It was a rather wet year during which seven out of the 29 matches were lost to the weather. Only six games were won, twelve were lost and the rest drawn. John Vaughan was back in the swing of things, but mainly as a batsman.

John Vaughan celebrates his 10,000th run

The season started with a draw on a slow CNS pitch against Eaton, who recovered from 42-7 to make 120. In reply, Walsham stuttered to 117-7 from 46 overs - very 'un-Walshamlike'. The batting was no better in the next game managing only 95 against Acle A and the match was duly lost. Half-centuries from Scales, Vaughan and Denton produced a total of 244-2 against Happisburgh but, despite bowling 50 overs, they couldn't be winkled out. Bradenham won a good run chase when set 205-7, with half centuries from Watkins and Key, but they cruised home in 38 overs with just five wickets down. Bexley Hospital were easily beaten by 96 runs, but Walsham fell short against Lowestoft. Scales hit 57 out of 174-6, but the home side got home by six wickets with three overs to spare. The match against Old Buckenham was drawn as Walsham made 172-9 and they replied with 142-5.

There was then a run of three victories starting against tourists Broomfield Hospital, whose 131 was passed mainly due to a Scales half-century. A 128-run victory was gained against Ashwellthorpe. Walsham totalled 202-5 before the Futter brothers combined to take eight wickets. Kim Futter was again among the wickets against Cromer. Walsham scored 179-7 with an unbeaten 70 from Denton. In reply, after starting well, Cromer collapsed from 100-3 to 161 all out (Futter 6-67).

In a game against touring side Britwell Salome, Walsham paid for releasing the pressure. They were struggling at 123-8, but were given the opportunity to recover to 193-8. Walsham were left just 38 overs to get the runs and, despite a brilliant 88 from Garth Futter, went down by 39 runs. There was a very close draw against Brundall PTE. Walsham scored 195-2 while they finished on 188-8. In a high scoring match against Drayton, Walsham scored 225-6, with 50 from Whiteside, but the Norwich-based side proved tough opposition and hit the winning runs in the final over to secure a three-wicket victory. However, this was followed by a cruise to victory against Eaton, a seven-wicket win being secured by a Scales fifty.

Following a successful tour to Derbyshire, the run-fest continued. Vaughan and Belton led the way in a total of 210-5 against Bradenham, but they fought back to win by two wickets with a couple of overs to spare. The usual all-day affair at Ingham saw the home side hit 303-7, to which Walsham made a modest response and were bowled out for 190, thanks largely to 97 from Scales. Halvergate regained the Graham London Memorial Trophy with a comfortable 58 run win but, in the final game of the season, Walsham beat the President's side by three wickets. Pennington took 5-17 in the President's total of 195 and Denton led the reply with a half-century to secure victory, despite a marathon spell from Kevin Gilbert who bowled 25 overs for John Westgarth's side.

Lots of runs had been scored throughout the season, but Walsham struggled to bowl sides out, possibly because the quality of the pitches - particularly at home - were constantly improving. Scales scored 699 runs, while Denton and Watkins passed 400. Three players passed the 20 wicket mark: the Futter brothers and Pennington.

Press Cuttings 1996/97

Successful weekend for South Walsham

SOUTH Walsham had a very successful weekend when they beat Verdayne Green, a touring side from Surrey, by six wickets on Friday, and Kelvin London's Veterans XI on Sunday by seven wickets.

Against Verdayne Green, Walsham always had the upper hand as the tourists struggled against some tight bowling. They slipped to 65-8 when skipper Scales released the pressure. Murray (42 not out) and Scott (21) took full advantage and lifted the score to 133 all out.

Richard Whiteside took 4-48, while Garth Futter (3-17) and Chris Gould (2-20) also bowled well.

When Walsham batted there were a few early scores as Walsham slipped to 47 for three, but Stuart Mallet (41), Stephen Mallett (20) and an unbeaten partnership of 52 between Andy Scales (39 no out) and Garth Futter (19 not out) saw Walsham home by six wickets.

Against Kelvin London's Veterans XI, the early batsmen struggled against the Walsham bowlers — they slipped to 76-5 until a partnership of 64 between Dave Etheridge (56) and Andy Norman (41 not out) lifted the score to 165-7 after 40 overs. Kevin Byton (3-31) and Derek Gorrod (2-16) were the most successful bowlers, while Kim Futter was again out of luck despite causing the batsmen to hop around with several quick deliveries.

In reply, Andy Scales had a rare failure with 18 while David Watkins scored a steady 32. Garth Futter (43 not out) and Steve Belton (42 not out) added 94 for the fourth wicket to give Walsham victory with six overs to spare.

Scales hits a century

SOUTH Walsham scored a superb six-wicket victory over Beccles on Sunday, Andy Scales hitting an unbeaten century.

Beccles won the toss and batted first on a good track and quick outfield. Walsham's opening bowlers Garth Futter and Chris Gould bowled well without luck and Beccles started to build a big total.

The first wicket fell once Terry Ogden was brought into the attack. As he slowed the run rate, Derek Gorrod and John Watkins both picked up two wickets.

Beccles had a late thrash with Franks looking particularly forceful with a quick 47 not out.

Beccles declared at tea on 209 for five. But Walsham were well pleased with their fielding and bowling and it was a credit to the Beccles batsmen for posting such a useful score.

When Walsham batted, Scales was again in the mood to score a lot of runs.

There was no thought of a draw as Scales started to hit the Beccles attack all round the ground.

Despite the loss of three partners, Scales found support from Garth Futter (45), who hit the dangerous Franks out of the attack.

Once Futter had gone, youngster John Watkins (30 not out) kept up the tempo Walsham reached their target with 14 balls to spare on 213 for four.

Once again it was Scales who was man-of-the-match with 101 not out. It was a brilliant forceful innings with 13 fours.

Beccles played their part in a game played in a tough but good spirit and it was a match enjoyed by all 22 players.

Belton in the wickets

SOUTH Walsham were held to a draw by Diss A at South Walsham on Sunday.

South Walsham batted first and soon lost David Watkins in the fourth over. Andy Scales (29) and Richard Whiteside (20) scored quickly but both got out just as they were getting going. The same happened to Garth Futter (20) and Neil Johnson (25).

Steve Belton produced the best innings with 38 not out. He was ably assisted by Kim Futter (26) and Alex Evans (13 not out) who helped to lift the score to 200-8.

A fiery spell from Kim Futter and steady bowling from Derek Gorrod slowed the Diss progress.

Steve Belton finished with 4-74 off 11 overs. Chris Gould (2-39) also bowled well. Diss made 169-8.

Last pair stage record stand

SOUTH Walsham went down to Kirkley at Gunton Park by six wickets on Sunday.

South Walsham had themselves to blame for not scoring plenty of runs. In-form Andy Scales went first ball and several other batsmen got a start, then got themselves out.

Steve Belton scored 26 and newcomer Kevin Byton had a promising debut with 20.

Walsham reached 103-9 when Alex Evans, scoring seven fours in a quickfire 37 and Derek Gorrod (18 not out) took charge, adding a club record partnership of 58 for

These runs came in 12 overs and showed the batsmen who came and went before them that batting was not that difficult.

Walsham were all out for 161 just before tea. On such a good wicket this score was probably about 50 short of a challenging target and so it proved as opener Snell (26 not out) kept up the tempo and the Walsham bowlers were never really able to stem the run rate.

Steve Belton was Walsham's most successful bowler with 3-37 but Kirkley

Close one!

SOUTH Walsham scored a fine but narrow win against Eaton at the CNS on Sunday.

Eaton won the toss and elected to bat, Keith Halford was soon knocking the ball around in fine style.

The first wicket fell at 70 and Halford was finally out for 111 out of 150, from then on the Eaton innings became becalmed as they only reached 196 for four at tea when a score of 230 seemed likely.

Terry Ogden, with two for 47, was the most successful bowler but Chris Gould and Derek Gorrod also bowled well on a dead pitch.

In reply, openers David Watkins and Andy Scales both set about the bowling from the start, but it wasn't until Garth Futter came in that victory looked possible.

Scales and Futter added 58 in just seven overs, Futter fell to a good catch for a well-struck 35, Scales and Steve Belton lifted the score to 149 for three when disaster struck for Walsham.

Halford bowled Sales for 70 and followed up with two more wickets in the next two balls, dismissing Ben Watkins and Terry Ogden for golden ducks.

Gould and Gorrod hung around with Belton to lift the score to 171 for eight. Alex Evans (14 not out) joined Belton (39 not out) and they were able to add the 29 runs to win, thanks to some careful batting and one or two wayward deliveries from man-of-the-match, Halford.

Another super win and a credit to the fine spirit of the side.

Fifth win in a row for Walsham

SOUTH Walsham scored their fifth win in a row when they beat Kirkley by three wickets at South Walsham on Sunday.

Kirkley batted first on an excellent track and quick outfield and started with a rush, losing their first wicket at 73 off just 10 overs.

Opener Hunt was out for 55 out of 73 but Bishop with a quick 19 kept up the tempo and with Noller scoring 45 Kirkley looked good at 166-3 with 45 minutes to go before tea.

Enter Chris Could who bowled brilliantly to demolish the lower order with six for 16 off five overs, as Kirkley slipped to 228 all out, still quite a demanding total.

Garth Futter also bowled well with 2-49 but the other bowlers were a bit out of touch.

After tea David Watkins (42) and Rupert Holmes (62) quickly put on 104 for the first wicket off just 14 overs.

Holmes, in particular, was in superb form and caused Kirkley skipper Bishop to switch from wicket-keeper to bowler.

He finally dismissed both Watkins and Holmes and a couple more quick wickets fell, but the run rate was maintained with Garth Futter (43) hitting some splendid shots.

Once he was dismissed, Kevin Byton (10) and Terry Ogden (16) continued to hit the bad ball and 14 runs were required for victory off the last over.

With Bishop deciding to bowl medium pace after previously bowling 13 overs of spin, this was food and drink to Kim Futter who hit the first ball for six.

Two were still required off the last ball and Futter hit it high in the air near to the legside boundary.

A difficult catch was dropped and Futter and Chris Gould scampered two runs for victory in a brilliant game.

Walsham delighted

SOUTH Walsham continued their fine run with a convincing eight wicket win over Great Yarmouth, Gorleston and Martham.

Opening bowlers Derek Garrod (3 for 27) and Kim Futter (2 for 31) both bowled very well and Yarmouth were reduced to 61-5.

The second-string continued to keep things tight as Keith Hodds (32 not out) and P Punchard (21) repaired the situation to bring GYGM up to 102-6.

Slow bowlers Andy March and Steve Belton quickly whipped out the final four wickets for a total of 120.

The innings was finished with a hat-trick from Steve Belton as Yarmouth batsman Keith Hodds watched his remaining partners go.

The Yarmouth bowlers gave plenty for Andy Scales (14) and David Watkins (63) to think about.

Good support from Richard Whiteside (21 not out) and Neil Johnson (15 not out) gave Walsham a straight forward victory with overs to spare.

Emphatic victory

SOUTH Walsham continued their good run with a convincing eight wicket victory over Hardingham at South Walsham on Sunday.

Walsham's opening bowlers, Ken and Garth Futter, were in fiery form and the early batsmen were in difficulty against Kim's pace and Garth's accuracy.

When they came off, Hardingham were 74 for five, with Kim taking 2-35 and Garth 3-34. With the pressure off, the remainder of the Hardingham batting order prospered against the second strong bowling and reached a respectable score of 175-8.

The Hardingham bowlers put the Walsham openers under pressure early on but careful batting from David Watkins and Mike Key made sure an early wicket didn't fall.

When they opened out the Hardingham bowlers found it difficult to maintain control. The opening stand was broken at 84 with Key being bowled for 36. Keith Denton came in and started hitting the ball all round the ground. Watkins then fell for a fine 64, while Keith Denton finished with 57 not out as Walsham won the game with five overs to spare.

Upton White Horse Man-of-the-Match: David Watkins.

CHAPTER THIRTY THREE *The 1990's Tours*

By the beginning of the 1990s, the South Walsham tour had become cemented in the calendar as a biennial cricket-fest. This account of the five tours of the decade does contain rather more detail on the cricket that was played, rather than primarily focussing on the alcohol-fuelled off-field antics of previous decades. Perhaps it suggests that the squad most of them at least - had eventually started to mature! However, each tour was not without its memorable post-match moments and the odd bevvy continued to be consumed.

Northampton provided the base for the 1990 adventure. It was the usual Walsham squad, with the addition of the 'veteran' (56 year-old) left armer, John Reynolds from Eaton. The first game was against Isham, a very useful side who quickly reduced the tourists to 59-5, former Kent and Northants left-arm opening bowler John Dye taking 1-6 off eight overs.

South Walsham Touring Party to Northampton 1990

Isham relaxed the bowling, but Walsham could still only struggle to 108. All looked lost as the home side reached 42-1, so much so that one of their players went home! His misjudgement soon became apparent: Isham lost their remaining wickets for 24 runs as Kim Futter, with a 5- wicket haul, ably assisted by John Reynolds who picked up 4 wickets, combined to set up an incredible victory. However, Walsham met their match against Great Oakley. In an all-day game, a total of 227 was dominated by a tremendous 122 from Keith Denton, while Watkins was the only other batsman to pass 20. Great Oakley knocked the runs off easily by eight wickets with 15 overs to spare. However, Walsham did manage to do some damage to the opposition. After the match, the usual games resulted in the host's star guest player managing to fall over and break his collar bone - his main club would not have been impressed when they heard the story of how his injury occurred!

The next match against Stewarts and Lloyds was drawn, after Mike Key had hit 120 out of 195-4. Everybody bowled as the opposition made little effort to go for the runs. The Thursday fixture was against old friends - Kettering Old Colonials - who were comfortably beaten by 86 runs. However, the highlight of the tour was the game against Irthlingborough. Walsham scored 195-7, significant runs coming from Denton and Johnson. Mike Key departed from the game early after losing a couple of teeth - there was blood on the pitch, but it didn't stop play!

John Vaughan and Andy Scales open up at Great Oakley 1990

The former Northants bowler Jim Griffiths - often accorded the title of the 'worst batsman in first-class cricket' - was playing; he didn't try too hard, but soon cleared out Watkins and Belton.

After tea, Irthlingborough always seemed ahead of the game and, at the start of the last over, needed four to win with three wickets left. Vaughan bowled an excellent over picking up three wickets and a tremendous one-run victory was achieved. Again the post-match entertainment included the opposition being introduced to many games, particularly the 'golf game' where you hold the handle of the golf club to your head, run round three times and then try to hit the golf ball from near your feet. Everybody tried: most people fell over, some hit the ball a few yards, except Neil Johnson who just ran round three times and hit the ball about 200 yards. Everyone was amazed but, strangely, whenever he has tried it again he has never repeated the feat. It had been a great tour: three wins, a draw and a defeat, but brilliant fun.

In 1992 it was off to the New Forest based at Brockenhurst: a good hotel, with facilities that included a swimming pool, lots of good pubs, many of which - true to form - were visited by Ogden, Belton and the Futter brothers. The squad was strengthened by Stewart Mallett, son of Stuart who, although only fifteen, was a very useful player. The first match was against Alderholt, where steady batting led to a total of 155-7. Once the first two wickets had been taken, the result was never in doubt as the hosts were bowled out for 108. However, Walsham were outclassed in the Tuesday match against Bramshaw. Totalling only 145, with Scales scoring half the runs, Bramshaw knocked these off to win by five wickets in 40 overs. In the third game, against Exbury, a modest total of 147 was the result of batsmen getting themselves out in many silly ways on a small ground. The home team were going well at 70-3 when Steve Mallett came on to bowl and they collapsed to 99 all out.

Touring Party to New Forest 1992

Keith Denton had arrived to join the squad and that gave a further boost to morale, as did the evening at Exbury which was the highlight of the tour. A round at their social club bar was £15 for a gallon of Guinness and a bottle of port - a bargain as far as the squad was concerned. This offer kept even the hardened drinkers going until the Guinness ran out; they then moved on to Dubonnet until that ran out as well - a great night, although there were a few hangovers the next day. In some ways it was a good thing the fourth game against Beaulieu was rained off as it was unlikely that eleven players would have made it on to the pitch! The final game was against the strangely-named 'Nomansland'. Walsham batted poorly only managing 139 and, despite an inspired bowling spell from Garth Futter (4-8), the game was lost by two wickets.

It had been another excellent tour organised by Terry Ogden, although it nearly resulted in Chris Gould becoming a 'missing person' when he went for a walk in the New Forest one evening after a few beers, and couldn't find his way back to the hotel. He did finally reappear some hours later, looking more than a little worried. Garth Futter also experienced considerable anxiety, as the author vividly recalls:

'I left my wedding ring behind on the first night at Alderholt and Garth Futter picked it up. However, during his next morning's swim he lost it in the pool. Garth was naturally concerned as was I....... initially. What Garth didn't know was that Richard Whiteside had found it, but kept it quiet as Garth continually searched the pool. On the last morning, the attendant finally said to him, 'they haven't told you then?' After three long days, Garth knew that he had been had!'

Drinks after the game at Exbury on the New Forest Tour 1992

The 1994 base was the excellent Norfolk Arms in Arundel, East Sussex. The first game was a very exciting affair against Fittleworth. Walsham declared on 189-9 with guest from Halvergate, Steve Cooke, hitting 62. Fittleworth looked on course for victory as their main man Kitchener hit 101, but a collapse saw them all out for 177, Kim Futter taking the key wickets. It was an interesting track against the amusingly-named Burpham, but Walsham still managed 210-5, with Garth Futter smashing a quick 71 not out. After tea, it was a struggle to bowl out the hosts, although 4-7 from 11 overs from Garth Futter was the highlight. His brother Kim spent most of the match lying fast asleep among the club kit 'resting' after the previous night's festivities which had led to several players feeling a little delicate, and this was almost certainly the reason why a game was drawn that should have been won. Despite a fifty from Watkins, Walsham only managed 166 on a good pitch and small outfield against Steyning Rebels who knocked off the runs for the loss of six wickets. In the final match of the tour Walsham renewed acquaintances with Singleton, who had toured Norfolk some years earlier. Scales led the way with 84 not out in a total of 190-5. The Futter brothers took three wickets apiece as the opposition were bowled out for 168. It had been another great tour enjoyed by the whole squad.

In 1996 it was Somerset that provided the setting for another tour arranged by Terry Ogden. In the opening game, a fifty from Belton helped to produce a respectable total against Crewkerne, but the home side won by four wickets. The Tuesday match was against Ilminster, the base for the tour. Not for the first time, some of the squad had indulged themselves rather too much before taking the field against a strong home side. However, the hosts rather aggressive approach did seem to galvanize Walsham who bowled them out for 171. Uniquely, Watkins took four catches in the outfield while Whiteside, behind the timbers, claimed three. After tea, Whiteside turned in an excellent batting performance hitting 84 not out against a useful attack, and Walsham won by six wickets much to the opposition's disappointment. Even the extortionate bill of £50 for teas didn't spoil the celebrations!

Touring Party to Somerset 1996

The squad were staying within walking distance of the hotel in Illminster and its late night 'honesty bar' was certainly well-used that evening. However, it was downhill the next day, after making 206 all out on a very small ground at Sampford Arundel. The opposition's confidence had been apparent when they gave all ten players a bowl and their skipper was proved right as they cruised home by eight wickets.

In a terrific 40-over game against Curry Rivel, Scales and Watkins hit 144 for the first wicket out of a total of 239-7. The hosts made a really good effort, but lost wickets towards the end of their run chase being bowled out for 191. It was a remarkable game for Terry Ogden who, in keeping with his tour tradition, had enjoyed a drink or two at lunch-time. He bowled an immaculate 8 overs taking 1-26, but when he looked at the scorebook the next day he claimed he didn't remember playing!

The final game saw another win against Broadway and Horton by five wickets. They had a player, called R Kelly, who claimed to hold the record for the number of successive sixes in an innings, somewhere in the region of 13. He hit a few in this game before falling for 33. Gould picked up 5-41 as the home side subsided to 139 all out. Garth Futter was given a rare opportunity to open the batting and he didn't disappoint hitting a quick 41 as Walsham won comfortably. Another great tour, with three wins out of five.

1998 meant that it was tour time again - to Derbyshire - where some very useful opponents were encountered. The first day was rained off which led to quite a drinking session and this probably affected the team's performance on Tuesday at Clifton.

Batting first, Walsham scored 138-9 in 40 overs and the hosts won easily with eight overs to spare. On Wednesday, against Duffield, Walsham again batted first, but were easily dismissed for 103 and the home side had no problems reaching the modest target to win by six wickets.

The squad turned up at Denby for the Thursday match only to find that two other teams were

Touring Party to Derbyshire 1998

already at the ground expecting to play each other. Clearly there had been an error on somebody's part but, as the home club, Denby were very gentlemanly about it and stood aside to allow Walsham to play the 'third' team, Radcliffe-on-Trent. They scored 181-5 and Walsham were still in with a chance at 126-6 with Scales and Garth Futter going well but, once they were out, the innings fell away to 151 all out - a very good game all the same. The final match, against South Wingfield on a very small ground, proved to be the most exciting. In their 40 overs they hit 262-6 with all the bowlers being hit around. Perhaps unwisely, both Garth Futter and Pennington had been rested. Walsham needed a good start and, characteristically, Key and Johnson went off 'like trains' adding 109 for the first wicket. Scales and Watkins both hit thirties, leaving Walsham needing three to win off the final over with two wickets left. Dramatically, Watkins and Kim Futter were dismissed off successive balls and the game was lost by two runs. However, the result was very much secondary; the Wingfield skipper had shown a great enterprise in keeping the game open and encouraging a close finish. It had been a great tour even though Walsham failed to win a game.

As may be evident from these five summaries, although the 1990s tours were becoming rather less 'socially hectic' than those of earlier days, cricket and 'fun' provided a platform for a series of really memorable weeks; they remained the highpoint of alternate seasons. Not only did they strengthen still further the tight bonds that held together this particular squad of players - and there were very few changes in the 1990s - but as each tour added further to the club's tradition, everyone's enthusiasm for touring remained at a high level. The side never went to the same area twice - probably some communities were grateful for this (!) - but touring only in alternate years kept everyone fresh. If the tours had been annual, interest may well have waned. A year's 'rest' between them not only mollified wives and families but increased the anticipation for the next adventure.

CHAPTER THIRTY FOUR *Cricket In The 1990's*

In the final decade of the twentieth century, cricket underwent some fundamental changes in its organisation at national level, which quite quickly filtered down to influence the recreational game. This process can best be described as 'professionalisation' and, from a top-down perspective, has been interpreted as a massive leap forward for the sport. As this chapter will discuss, it is arguable whether these changes were wholly beneficial to the true grass roots of the game as represented by clubs like South Walsham. Some of these changes have materialised in the 2000s, but all had their origins in the 1990s.

Two major influences underlie a host of consequential changes: Sky TV money and the creation of the England and Wales Cricket Board as the sport's national governing body. The influence of TV radically shifted the balance of power in the game as early as the 1970s in the 'Packer revolution'. However, the 'Murdoch revolution' has had an even greater long-term impact on cricket. Although the sport has not fully ransomed its soul in the manner of professional football, there is no doubt that, without the injection of Sky TV money, the game at international level and, in England, at county level would look quite different. Murdoch's 'tribute' extracted from cricket - and this to a man who certainly knows more about phone hacking than he does about cricket - has been an almost total control of TV coverage of Test Matches, ODIs and T20s at both international and county levels. This has expanded the programme of 'Team England' to a commitment to 45 days a year of televised cricket in England. Channel 5 have been graciously permitted to show 60 minutes of highlights shortly after close of play, but that is the extent of 'free to air' TV broadcasting. Thankfully, Newscorp have not recognised the power of radio's *Test Match Special* commentaries. If they had, this national treasure could have been subject to a super-injunction!

TV rights have been 'auctioned' according to accepted commercial practice, but the infinitely greater resources of the Murdoch empire have made this an exercise in futility. Attempts to protect Test matches as one of the sporting 'crown jewels' (as the Grand National, FA Cup Final etc) have failed as the ECB have stood shoulder to shoulder with the true believers in market forces to 'secure the best deal for cricket.' In terms of short-term financial advantage - yes, but at what cost to the long-term health of the game? Sky revenues now not only underpin 'Team England' but provide the county game with its life-blood, while the ECB seek to claim that without this level of finance it could not distribute its largesse to the 38 county-based cricket boards.

This is where the ECB's role as the national governing body became critical. The demand of government - through *Sport England* - that each sport should have an appropriate national body made the creation of the ECB inevitable. By the late twentieth century, the MCC - for two centuries the guardian of the game - was clearly anachronistic; a private club could not be the national governing body of a major sport. However, buoyed by its Sky-wealth and with a sense of mission to 'grow cricket', the ECB sought through financial incentives and pressures to exert its influences at all levels of the game, or at least at all levels that it considered to be relevant to its mission.

However, to an English village club like South Walsham, this perspective had one dangerous flaw - it was unashamedly top-down. Like all NGB's, the ECB had as its primary objective success at national level. In this expectation, it is hard to find fault with its progress. In July 2012 England headed the world rankings in all three formats of the professional game, although this was to be lost in two formats by the end of the calendar year. The creation of the National Cricket Centre in Loughborough, county centres of excellence, academies, England Lions, the emerging players programme, specialist coaches, sports science specialists..........the structure set up to support 'Team England' and its off-shoots is impressive - and expensive. It is the product of the Sky millions.

Recognising the traditions of the first-class county game in England, the ECB continues to underwrite the balance sheets of the 18 financially-dependent major counties. In turn, they have become far more professionalised in terms of administrative and coaching structures than a generation ago. Minor counties, like Norfolk, join the queue for their annual handout of £25,000 - half their revenue.

However, it is the county-based cricket boards who wield the influence and the cash to develop and promote the 'grassroots' game. The key issue is semantic: what is meant by 'grass-roots'? In the 1990s, the ECB took its first steps to influence the previously autonomous world of club cricket.

Inevitably thinking top-down, the outcome was the encouragement - through county boards - of county 'premier leagues'. Senior clubs joining this ECB-sponsored structure would receive annual financial backing provided that they agreed to play all-day games to an agreed format which, interestingly, included the draw (not selling-out to win-lose cricket was one of the new scheme's stronger points). East Anglia - home to three minor counties: Norfolk, Suffolk and Cambridgeshire - was not deemed a strong enough cricketing area to justify county-based premier leagues, so an agreement was made to create the regionally-based East Anglian Premier League. Has it been a success? By funnelling talent into a small number of clubs, it has served its purpose well in terms of the objectives of its creators. Whether it has been equally helpful in strengthening the local club game in its wider context remains an arguable point.

The other area where county-based cricket boards have made a major impact is through their mission to youth cricket, particularly coaching schemes. From the 1990s, albeit slowly in the early years, funding streams to support coaching mainly for promising youngsters began to filter through even to 'minor' counties such as Norfolk. Structured county age-group sides with extended programmes of winter coaching made provision for the elite young cricketer that quite simply had not existed before Sky money and its channelling through ECB priorities made this possible. The emergence of 'quality control' marks - Clubmark and Focus clubs - gave status to 20-30 clubs in the county and legitimised their involvement in youth coaching. Schools' cricket, designated by the ECB as a 'cinderella' area in many state schools, was given a boost through the *Chance to Shine* programme. Coaching courses to develop more coaches abounded.

From the ECB offices at Lords - courtesy, of course, of their landlords, the MCC - it was easy to churn out participation statistics that accentuated the positive: cricket is flourishing and has never been in better health, women's cricket and disability cricket being added to the assiduously promoted message. But could the state of the game be analysed differently if viewed from a different perspective? What was happening at the real grass roots, not as the ECB defined this concept - their premier leagues - but in Norfolk and, to take a readily available example, in South Walsham.

On the surface, little appeared to be changing - 20-30 games a season were still being played and most of the same faces were turning up year-on-year. 'Uncle George's vision' of an elite gentleman's cricket club may have faded, but enthusiasm for the game remained high. But how many of the players were under 30? Where were these products of the coaching programmes who, theoretically, should be demanding a place in the side? What had happened to Gothic, Deopham and Ashwellthorpe - all recent opponents? The first lost their pitch, the other two ran out of players. Why had traditional opponents Eaton left their home - on a park pitch - after 35 years and found refuge on a school ground? Oh yes - they had muttered something about compulsory competitive tendering and the dramatic decline in the quality of the municipal pitches. They were right: the last couple of years Walsham played them on Eaton Park the wicket could, charitably, be described as 'dodgy'.

From a Lord's office, the present was rosy and the future rosier; from the grass-roots of South Walsham playing field, the present was concerning and the future potentially alarming. The 1990s were an interesting decade for cricket, but did they presage a twenty-first century decline or a genuine golden age for the game?

CHAPTER THIRTY FIVE *A New President For A New Millenium*

It was all change at the top in 1999. After nine years as President John Westgarth stood aside in favour of Ray Norman, who has continued in that role ever since. Until his retirement in August 2012, Ray was the landlord of the Upton White Horse, the club's 'spiritual home'. On tours, his quick wit has always made him the 'life and soul of the party'. A 'one-off', it was typical of Ray that, when he heard about a need for a pavilion clock, he presented one on President's Day 2009. He has always been particularly generous with his President's Days, basically funding the whole event.

There are many stories that could be told about the President. On a tour of Essex, he casually wandered around the boundary doing his Jake the Peg - 'with his extra leg' - impression, and then proceeded to have a few beers, donate £65 to the swear box and go to sleep for the afternoon before leading the singing during a karaoke session. The locals didn't know what to make of him! Of the dozens of stories that could be written about Ray, most fall within the principle of 'what happens on tour stays on tour'.

President Ray presents the Pavilion Clock to the Club

As well as a change in the presidency, Keith Denton took over the captaincy from Richard Whiteside. The new skipper always showed great confidence in the squad, particularly encouraging the lesser players, including the author who, quite frequently, would open or bat higher up the order than his ability justified. The only significant debutant was Simon Burns who played 65 games over about four seasons. He was a talented bowler, who took 63 wickets and was improving all the time but, like a lot of youngsters, he was not committed to playing every week and was lost to the game.

The first match of the season saw a high-scoring draw against Garboldisham, who hit 212-7 while Walsham struggled a little to finish on 176-6, with half-centuries from Johnson and Belton. A run of five wins followed, beginning with a cruise past Eaton as a score of 133-9 was chased down to win by six wickets. Half-centuries for Watkins and Denton helped to post a score of 179-8 against Happisburgh, who collapsed from 50-2 to 86 all out with most of the wickets (amazingly) falling to the enticing flight of Watkins who took 5-9 in under five overs. There was a close match with Brundall PTE; Walsham scored 184-9 (Denton 46) and managed to bowl out the opposition for 175, Watkins taking three more wickets. A terrific win against Bradenham followed. Walsham scored 257-6 with fifties from Watkins, Belton and Denton while, in reply, Ogden was in cracking form taking 6-27 out of Bradenham's total of 148. The fifth win came against tourists Wallington Old Foresters, who managed only 111 enabling Walsham to win comfortably by eight wickets. Garth Futter was man of the match with 4-13.

The winning run ended after a total of 220-8 (Johnson 51) had been set against tourists Bexley Hospital, but they held on at 187-9 as skipper Denton used nine bowlers in an effort to winkle out the batsmen. This was followed by a rather strange game against another touring side, Broomfield Hospital. Walsham collapsed to 81-7, only for Whiteside and Garth Futter to add 95 for the eighth wicket to set a reasonable total of 176-7. Broomfield had only turned up with nine players and Walsham won comfortably as the tourists were bowled out for 103. The following game against Saxlingham was drawn. They batted first and hit 210-9, although it could have been more as Belton caused a collapse from 165-1 by taking 7-34 from seven overs. Walsham never looked like winning the game, but Ogden and Gorrod held out on 157-9.

Bradfield were narrowly beaten by seven runs. Having set 178-4, with Whiteside hitting 65, the opposition were bowled out for 171 after collapsing from 114-2. Once again it was Belton (5-50) who did the damage. The return match with Saxlingham could have been a close affair; after Walsham had scored 206-8 from 40 overs, Saxlingham were halfway through their innings on 105-2 when the rain came. The first defeat of the season came against Cromer A. Walsham only made 148-8, despite recovering from 70-7 with Denton hitting 59 not out, but it was never going to be enough as

Cromer won comfortably by five wickets.

It was back to winning ways against Halvergate in the Graham London Memorial Trophy. Half-centuries from Scales and Johnson saw Walsham reach 199-3; Halvergate replied with 151, Ogden taking 4-21. Two more wins followed. In the first, against Rollesby, the opposition were bowled out for 134, Mike Key taking a Walsham best figures of 6-30. At 101-8 the game was in the balance, but Denton came in at number 10 and guided the tail to a two-wicket win. There was a comfortable 71 run win against Eaton. Walsham hit 186-5 with (Watkins 75*), while three wickets each from Burns and Ogden contributed to Eaton subsiding to 115 all out. Scales (70*) top-scored in a total of 167-6 against Brundall PTE who held out on 132-9, despite 4-52 from Belton.

The game against Happisburgh was something of a mismatch. Walsham scored 171-3, with Scales hitting 55. The opposition were never in it as they crawled to 66-8 from 41 overs to secure the draw. The second defeat of the season came against a strong Lowestoft side. Bowled out for 169, they hit back to dismiss Walsham for 143, despite Scales hitting 74. The same player hit 75 in the next match against Halvergate in a total of 188-7. The opposition fought well, but had to settle for the draw as they finished on 174-7. An earlier defeat against

South Walsham President's Squad 1999

Cromer A was avenged when Walsham won by seven wickets chasing 181. Scales (90) again led the way. The final game of the season saw Walsham defeat the President's side by one wicket, Watkins and Gorrod were among the wickets as they made 206-8, but Pennington (68) saw Walsham home.

It had been a highly successful season: twelve wins, six draws and only two defeats in the 20 games completed. Scales (624) finished top of the scoring charts with Denton, Whiteside and Watkins all passing 400 runs. Ogden took 33 wickets with Belton and Gorrod both passing 20.

The 2000 season saw the debut of three players: Kevin Gilbert, Mark Smith and Jimmy Moore. Gilbert played just one game that summer but, played more regularly from 2007 to 2010, he strengthened the squad in those years with his quality bowling and hard-hitting batting. Mark Smith's time at the club developed similarly to Simon Burns - in his 35 games he was very promising, but did not commit to playing regularly. Jimmy Moore, brother of Jon, was a natural sportsman but, once again, was not committed to regular appearances.

The season couldn't have started any worse. Despite having a reasonable side against Lowestoft, Walsham were put in on a damp wicket and, completely outclassed, were bowled out for just 42. Lowestoft won the game by 10 wickets in 12 overs and both sides were down the pub by 5pm! However, this was reversed in the next match as Eaton only managed 74, with four wickets each for Ogden and Belton. Denton led the reply with 41 not out as Walsham won comfortably by seven wickets. In another low-scoring game, Walsham managed 123-9 against Happisburgh, but they could only score 119-6 in 45 overs, Pennington taking 3 wickets. Brundall PTE were beaten by 10 runs in a 40-over game. Walsham hit 168-6 with Watkins top-scoring, but Brundall could only manage 158-9 as they collapsed from 97-2, Johnson picking up three wickets.

Vaughan scored 67 against St Andrews in a total of 198-5, but the game petered out as St Andrews held on at 140-6. The second win of the season came when chasing 174 against Kirkley, Denton leading the way with 52 not out in a four-wicket win. However, the patchy batting continued in a two-wicket defeat against tourists Broomfield Hospital. Having only set 120-6 - Whiteside top-scoring with 46 not out - the opposition got home in 37 overs. Failure to get enough runs led to a further defeat against Happisburgh who dismissed Walsham for 141. Ivan Andrews scored a splendid 75 not out in Happisburgh's reply to see them home by five wickets. However, Walsham followed this up by crushing a weak Bradfield A side, scoring 206-3 - Vaughan and Scales making half-centuries - before bowling out the opposition for 87, Ogden taking 5-12.

This win began a run of four consecutive victories. Another fifty from Vaughan saw a win against Saxlingham by five wickets as Walsham chased down 160. Cromer A were then beaten by 16 runs, Garth Futter taking 5-40 as they fell short of Walsham's188-9, which included half-centuries for

Johnson and Belton. Garboldisham were beaten by three wickets in a low-scoring game, after being bowled out for 123, Whiteside seeing Walsham home with 60 not out. Although it ended the winning run, Walsham enjoyed a cracking game against Coopers, another touring side. They scored 176 all out after being 119-1. After a great effort Walsham fell just eleven runs short, Denton (80) playing the starring role. It was back to winning ways in the next match, however, as the occasional off-spin of Whiteside (5-12) saw St Andrews dismissed for 139. Watkins led the reply with 53 not out as Walsham won by eight wickets. The next match against Eaton finished in a draw. After Walsham had scored 169-6, Eaton looked like winning the game at 96-0, but a collapse saw them hanging on at 140-8. Again it was Whiteside who took the wickets, with 6-44 from 10 overs.

On returning from a tour of the Vale of Belvoir (Leicestershire), the team managed to beat Bradenham by 5 wickets. They scored 157-8, but this total was reached comfortably with Scales hitting 58 and Vaughan 46 not out. Scales (89*) was in the runs again in a draw against Brundall PTE. Chasing 185-6, Brundall held on at 151-8, Ogden taking 3-29. There was a high-scoring game against Happisburgh. Walsham scored 222-3 with Vaughan (110) leading the charge with a career-best innings. Happisburgh chased all the way and finished on 206-6, Burns being the star bowler with 5-46.

Johnson hit a 'ton' in a total of 207-4 in the next match against Cromer A, but it proved insufficient as Cromer cruised home to a five-wicket victory in just 36 overs. Walsham lost possession of the Graham London Memorial Trophy when beaten by five wickets by Halvergate, 163-9 being countered by 166-5. In the penultimate game of the season Scales hit a magnificent 115 out of a total of 178 at Bradfield, but the home side held on to a draw on 155-9 (Ogden 5-38). The season concluded with an exciting President's match. They scored 197, Kevin Gilbert hitting 91, and Walsham replied with 192 (Scales 69). There were great celebrations for the President's team, with 'President Ray' beaming all the way back to the White Horse.

In terms of results the season was not as successful as the previous one: eleven wins, nine defeats and seven draws in the 27 games completed. Ogden took 33 wickets while Garth Futter, Gorrod and Burns all passed the 20 mark. Among the batsmen, Vaughan (644) topped the averages with 42.93, although Scales (762) hit the most runs with Watkins and Denton both being close to the 500 mark. Although he did play a few more games, this was Vaughan's final full season. He said that he was beginning to struggle a little physically, but he remains one of the club's legends with over 11,000 runs and 300 wickets. In his final season he remained as wholehearted as ever and his place in the club's history was assured.

Press Cuttings 1999/2000

Scales in the runs but Walsham draw

SOUTH Walsham drew their latest fixture against Halvergate in an entertaining game at home.

Walsham batted first against the useful attack of Tallowin and Grady. The openers Watkins and Whiteside batted steadily, adding 32 for the first wicket when Watkins went for 12.

Andy Seales then came on and continued his good form by timing the ball very well on a fast track.

Whiteside (22) and Scales then added 63 for the second wicket. Neil Johnson (23) and Keith Denton (27) then chipped in with useful knocks. Scales was finally out for a fine 75 which helped lift the Walsham score to 188-7 at tea.

The Halvergate batsmen started in positive style with Gitsham and Ellingham looking in good touch.

Garth Futter eventually made the breakthrough, bowling Ellingham for 20.

Halvergate slipped to 70-4 when Gitsham was joined by Tallowin. They quickly upped the tempo but as they went for the win Gitsham was run out for 71 while Tallowin was well caught by Futter for 32.

Halvergate then lost their way and from then on did not look as though they were going to reach their target.

A few Walsham fielders had an off day as Halvergate finished on 174-7.

Best bowlers were Garth Futter with 2-30 and the very unlucky Terry Ogden with 1-36 from 11 overs.

Upton White Horse MoM: Andy Scales for his fluent innings of 75.

Vaughan stars in seven-wicket win

CRICKET: South Walsham gained a convincing win over Cromer A by seven wickets on Sunday.

Cromer batted first and got off to a quick start with a few edges quickly reaching the short boundaries.

Denton brilliantly ran out opener Johnson for 17, and Neil Johnson then kept up the pressure by clean bowling three batsmen as Cromer slipped to 40 for four. Booty held the Cromer innings together with a well made 50, but with Gareth Futter also bowling well and picking up three wickets, Cromer were in deep trouble at 110-7.

The tailenders batted extremely well and managed to lift the score to 181 all out.

After tea, Walsham were quickly in trouble as they slipped to 17 for two against some determined bowling.

Opener John Vaughan made his mind up to battle it out and along with Andy Scales staged an excellent recovery.

Scales hit the ball to all parts of the ground while Vaughan played anchor.

When Scales was finally out for 90 the partnership had added 138 putting Walsham completely in charge.

Steve Belton hit a quick 16 not out as Walsham made the required total with overs to spare. Vaughan left on 49 not out, just out on a deserved 50.

On any other day Scales would have been man of the match, but the excellent performance by veteran Vaughan with his big score of the season, saw voted Upton White Horse Man of the Match.

South Walsham start with run-laden draw

SOUTH Walsham opened the 1999 cricket season with a high-scoring draw against Garboldisham.

Missing the Futter brothers and John Pennington, the Walsham bowling attack was a little thin.

With a side averaging just over 40 years of age, Walsham struggled to hold the attacking Garboldisham batsmen, but wickets fell steadily with Scales and Johnson in particular holding on to good catches.

The bowling honours went to Keith Denton (2-37) and John Vaughan (2-42) as Garboldisham declared at 222-8.

Walsham suffered a poor start, losing three wickets for 22.

Neil Johnson (56) and Steve Belton (56 not out) then set about repairing the situation by adding 106 for the fourth wicket.

Despite their great efforts to open up with the run rate, they were always struggling to put Walsham in with a chance of victory.

When Johnson was out, followed by Moore and Key in quick succession Walsham needed nine and an over, which was beyond them.

Walsham finished on 176-6. Upton White Horse man of the match: Neil Johnson.

Watkins such a star

SOUTH Walsham gained a comfortable victory over Old Happisburgh and it was David Watkins who easily won the man of the match award with a well constructed 50 and five wickets, the first time he has ever performed the feat in 35 years of cricket.

Happisburgh inserted Walsham on a damp wicket, which gave the early Walsham batsmen problems and they were reduced to 23-3, a few lusty hits from Steve Belton (24) lifted the score to 58-4.

Keith Denton (61) then joined opener Watkins (53) and gradually got the better of the bowling adding 98 for the fifth wicket. The wicket had proved a little difficult for stroke play and Walsham were satisfied with 179-8 declared at tea.

After tea Happisburgh got off to a poor start against tight bowling from Derek Garrod 2-24 and Neil Johnson.

Happisburgh reached 50-2 and then things really went wrong for them.

John Vaughan 2-10 removed the dangerous Catchpole while Terry Ogden bowled top scorer Moore (44).

It was then skipper Denton brought on occasional off spinner Watkins who mopped up the tail in double quick time taking 5-9 in 4.3 overs.

Happisburgh were all out for 86 with Walsham winning by 93 runs.

Upton White Horse man of the match: David Watkins, a super performance.

Futter back with a bang

SOUTH Walsham cruised to their fifth successive victory when they beat touring side Wallington Old Foresters from Surrey by eight wickets.

The Tourists batted first and put on 38 for the first wicket, but then slipped to 42-5. This was mainly due to good bowling from Garth Futter (4-13) and Terry Ogden (2-20). It was Futter's first bowl of the season following his shoulder injury and his team-mates were pleased to see him back in action. Skipper Denton gave seven bowlers a go as the Tourists limped along to 111 all out.

When Walsham batted, John Vaughan was soon out with only three on the board. David Watkins (38 not out) and Richard Whiteside (32) soon got on top of the bowling and once Whiteside had departed, Andy Scales (31 not out) came in and finished the match off in double quick time.

Upton White Horse man of match: Garth Futter.

Scales hits century

CRICKET: South Walsham drew with Bradfield A on Sunday in an enjoyable match played in an excellent spirit.

Walsham were soon in trouble in humid conditions, losing their first four wickets for 16 runs. Andy Scales stood firm and with Jon Moore added 46 for the fifth wicket. Simon Burns hung around but when Terry Ogden joined Scales the innings turned around.

Scales was finally out for a magnificent 115 out of only 166 runs scored while he was at the wicket. Terry Ogden played his part with 19 not out in a stand of 82 with Scales for the seventh wicket.

Walsham were finally dismissed for 178 with 10 Bradfield players having bowled.

In replay Bradfield soon lost two wickets to the improving Simon Burns. Derek Garrod also picked up a wicket to reduce Bradfield to 28 for three. Bradfield hit back with a fourth wicket stand of 73, as the Walsham fielders struggled to hold on to their catches.

Then catches began to be held and Bradfield tried to keep up with the run rate. Tight bowling from Terry Ogden and Richard Whiteside kept up the pressure as they slipped to 155 for nine with Ogden taking five for 38 from 14 overs.

Bradfield went for the win but a draw was a fair result as they finished 24 runs short of victory with just one wicket left.

Upton White Horse man of the match: Andy Scales.

Fine shots announce Jack's back

ON an overcast day, South Walsham batted first against St Andrews.

Despite the loss of the dependable Watkins early on, they made a solid start with Whiteside making 25.

The innings only accelerated when Jack Denton, in his first game for the club in 25 years, joined John Vaughan. Jack Denton played some magnificent shots making 38 whilst John Vaughan made an excellent 67.

Kevin Denton chipped in a quick-fire 43 not out with South Walsham declaring on 190-5.

The pick of the St Andrews bowlers was Gilmore with two for 31.

St Andrews started steadily against the accuracy of Gorrod and Burns, who both picked up early wickets.

Oxbury with 44 and Clarke with 24 threatened to give St Andrews a chance of victory, but following their demise St Andrews' chances of a win disappeared and they ended with 140-6.

Walsham settle for draw

SOUTH Walsham drew their latest match against Brundall PTE.

Walsham batted first and with Vaughan, Watkins and Whiteside all miss Alex Evans opened up with the in form Andy Scales.

With the bowlers starting well both batsmen started carefully, runs then began to flow as the bowlers tired in the hot sun.

Evans was finally out for 38 with the opening partnership have accumulated 124 in 24 overs, the largest partnership of the season.

Scales continued the good work with Neil Johnson (21) as they added another 37 in quick time.

Scales was finally bowled for an excellent 89, a flurry of wickets went down as Walsham tried to lift the score to 200, but the over-rate had been very pedestrian with only 35 overs in two-and-a-half hours.

Skipper Denton was happy to declare on 185-6.

After tea, Walsham quickly picked up two wickets with an excellent catch by Smith and a splendid bit of fielding from Tony Wright.

Packham (25) and R Martin (50) then batted very well in a stand of 80 and Brundall were in with a chance of victory.

Both fell just past the 100 mark and with it went the chance of victory. Walsham then had to try and winkle out the remaining batsmen.

Thirteen-year-old Mark Smith took his first wicket while Terry Ogden took 3-29 from 14 overs. Brundall held on and finished on 151-8.

Upton White Horse, man of the match: Andy Scales.

Vaughan in solid display

SOUTH Walsham cruised to a five-wicket victory against Saxlingham with three and half overs to spare.

Saxlingham batted first in the 40 over contest and Derek Gorrod quickly dismissed both openers with just 12 runs on the board. Adrian Fisher played some fine shots from 49-2. Saxlingham lost their middle order, slipping to 60-6.

This was due to some slow bowling from David Watkins (3-31) and Andy Scales (1-17). Fisher and Brookes then added 80 runs for the seventh wicket before Brookes went for 34 thanks to a fine catch from John Vaughan off James Moore.

Fisher went shortly afterwards scoring a well made 67. After 40 overs Saxlingham finished on 160-9.

Denton opened up with John Vaughan and Alex Evans, who added 32 off the first 10 overs before Evans went for 10. Andy Scales (34) and Neil Johnson (20) quickly lifted the run rate to put Walsham in charge.

John Vaughan hit a fine 52 and earned himself the Upton White Horse man of the match honours. Keith Denton (29 not out) quickly got into fourth gear, while John Pennington stayed with him to see Walsham home by five wickets.

Halvergate judge trophy reply well

SOUTH Walsham went down to Halvergate by five wickets in the Graham London Memorial Trophy.

In a 40-over contest Walsham batted first and were soon in trouble against tight bowling at 22 for three.

Neil Johnson (37) and John Vaughan (18) then added 55 for the fourth wicket. But just as they were turning things around they got out. Garth Futter (17) and Keith Denton (38) pushed the total to 150 but no batsman was able to play a major innings.

Walsham quickly dismissed Evan Gitsham for two, but from then on the Halvergate batsmen controlled the rest of the game, with Simon Gitsham scoring an excellent 68 and Tallowin (28) and Clarke (39) helping the score along.

Simon Burns was the most successful bowler with two wickets, while Neil Johnson also bowled a tidy spell. Halvergate judged their reply well as they got home with 20 balls to spare on 166 for five.

Upton White Horse man of the match. Neil Johnson — an intelligent innings and a tidy spell of bowling.

CHAPTER THIRTY SIX *Denton Hands The Torch To Johnson* 2001/2

The 2001 season was wet – very wet!

It had been a wet spring and the outfield had been flooded for many weeks. Unfortunately, this also coincided with the time when a local man - Dick Frosdick - retired from cutting the outfield and the parish council employed a private company. Dick had regarded the job as a labour of love, as had Ernie Pollard before him; both had spent hours on the recreation ground keeping everything ship-shape The outfield suffered for a couple of seasons until Neil Johnson and Garth Futter started to give the outfield some extra cuts after the cricket club had purchased the parish council's gang mowers.

With the first three games lost to the weather, the season didn't start until the middle of May and only fourteen games were completed, a record nine games being lost to the weather. After this dismal non-start, the first two matches weren't very satisfactory either. In the first, Sheringham turned up with just eight players, but at least they turned up - credit to them for that - rather than calling off on the morning of the game. Three of their players batted twice, but they weren't very strong and Walsham won by 90 runs, as Watkins hit 92. It was a similar story the following week: St Andrews turned up with nine players, and lost by 94 runs, Watkins hitting 102.

The season - in which Keith Denton carried on as skipper for a third year - really didn't get underway until the third match which was against Halvergate. They scored an impressive 258-2, Simon Brister hitting 131 not out. Walsham replied with a respectable 216-6, Watkins (64) top-scoring for the third consecutive game. In an extremely close match with Bradenham A, Walsham hit 223-6, Watkins and Whiteside both passing the fifty mark. Bradenham hit back strongly, reaching 217-7 off 42 overs. In characteristic fashion, skipper Denton kept the game open by bowling Scales for nine overs and he responded with 4-46.

A poor performance against Saxlingham marked the start of a run of four defeats. In the first, Walsham managed only 110, the home side easily knocking them off with three wickets down. Defeats followed against

Brooke, Lowestoft and Mattishall: a good Brooke side got home by five wickets off 38 overs, after Walsham had set them 174 to win (Vaughan 65); Lowestoft declared at 185-5, and Walsham fell ten runs short; and, despite Scales hitting 70 out of 149 against Mattishall, this total was never going to be enough and the home side scored the required runs with only two wickets down.

It was back to winning ways in strange circumstances in the return fixture at Brooke. Walsham were struggling at 82-6 when the home skipper released the pressure, although a total of only 146 on a small ground meant that defeat looked on the cards at the tea interval. Strolling to 71-1, Brooke had the game under control, but four wickets apiece for Gorrod and Ogden saw them collapse to 130 all out giving Walsham a narrow 16-run victory. It was also the day that Ogden thought that he had passed Kim Futter's record of Walsham wickets and, a few days later, a full colour picture of the triumphant Ogden appeared in the Yarmouth Mercury. At the time, it was not known that Peter Edrich held the club record.

Derek 'Del' Gorrod warming up in his final season

This really seemed to get the season going. The earlier defeat against Saxlingham was avenged by a three-wicket victory, Scales taking four more wickets. A successful chase of Eaton's 188 led to a five-wicket win, Watkins hitting 76. Against Bradenham, in a 40-over game, Walsham had the better of the weather conditions. The opposition struggled to 148-5 but, as the pitch dried out, the required runs were scored off 34 overs for the loss of just two wickets. Another 40-over match against Happisburgh produced a total of 210-6, Johnson hitting 107. Happisburgh failed to keep pace with the run-rate and the game meandered along until they finished on 140-7. After a late call-off, Walsham were indebted to Bacton for offering a fixture in which they made 149 all out before Watkins led the side to a four-wicket victory with 71 not out. It was a powerful batting order that day: Denton, Belton and Vaughan three of the last four in the order. The game against St Andrews was rained off after Walsham had scored a disappointing 156; the home side were well on their way to victory when the rain really belted down and there was no option but to abandon the game.

As was typical of the season, the President's game was rained off halfway through. After the President's side had been bowled out for just 86, it was an early visit to the White Horse! The record of an abbreviated season read: eight wins, two draws and four defeats. Quite impressive, but disappointing that so little cricket was possible. In the individual statistics, Watkins did exceedingly well to score 656 runs in just 13 innings, while Scales was the only other batsman to pass 300. No bowler managed 20 wickets, Scales being top with 18.

Thankfully, 2002 produced better weather and enabled 20 games to be completed. Neil Johnson took over from Keith Denton as skipper and there were three debutants: Jack Belton, the 12-year old son of Steve, Martin Corcoran and Greg Loades. The younger - and slimmer - Belton has slowly become a regular in the squad; his batting has steadily improved although, as yet he has only passed fifty on two occasions. Martin Corcoran really enjoyed his cricket and played over fifty games, but Walsham probably never saw the best of 'Corky'. Greg Loades has played over 100 games and taken 150 wickets with his spin bowling. He has always been a safe catcher and his batting has gradually improved as he has had more opportunities. Greg always had a positive outlook on his cricket and it wasn't long into his Walsham career when he was elected skipper in 2007. It was a great pity for the club that he took a job in Peterborough in 2008, which has meant he only plays occasionally these days.

Neil Johnson's debut as skipper in 2002 started with a heavy defeat. Lowestoft are usually one of the stronger oppositions and playing them in April, when their players are looking for some batting practice, they often have several first teamers in the side. On this occasion, they hit 201-7, Pennington taking three wickets while, in reply, Walsham only managed 117 all out. An abandonment against Eaton came after they had declared at

135-6; Walsham were going well at 87-2 when the rain came. Another overs game at Happisburgh - this time a 30-over game because of the bad weather - saw Walsham post 208-2 (Whiteside 80* and Johnson 79*). As happened in the previous year, in an overs game, there was no pressure to bowl Happisburgh out and they finished on 152-4. Walsham then had the better of a draw against St Andrews, scoring 177-6, the visitors hanging on at 99-9.

The weather played its part again against Great Ellingham in a 35-over game after rain had delayed the start. Unusually, Walsham only had nine players and did well to hold them to 166-4. Replying with 158-4 meant a narrow eight-run defeat. A first fixture against Billingford was won narrowly on a difficult wicket. Walsham managed 132 all out (Watkins 45), but four wickets apiece for Mark Smith and Johnson secured a 22-run victory. The following game against Bradenham was abandoned when the game was evenly poised. Watkins hit 109 not out in a total of 209-2 and Bradenham's reply was going well at 84-3 off 17 overs when the rain arrived. The Graham London Memorial Trophy resulted in a 15-run win over Halvergate. Walsham hit 151-4 in 40 overs, while Halvergate struggled to 136-9, with 84 of their runs coming from old friend Keith Hodds.

The following weekend, two touring sides were played on Friday and Sunday and what terrific games they were! In the first - against West Wittering - Walsham posted 207-2 and the tourists made a super effort as skipper Johnson kept the game open. However, Garth Futter wrapped up the tail as they were bowled out for 203. This excellent game was bettered on Sunday against Woodchurch from Kent. They were well in control scoring 206-5 and Walsham were in trouble at 140-8, but some hard hitting from Johnson (55) and Garth Futter (63 not out) produced a magnificent one-wicket victory. This good form continued against Saxlingham as Walsham scored 200 for the third consecutive game totalling 235-3 (Scales 105). The opposition were bowled out for 166 (Garth Futter 4-18). However, it was more of a struggle against Lowestoft who scored 196-5 before dismissing Walsham for 130 (Garth Futter 57).

Another bad advert for the 40-over format came when Johnson (150 not out) took the Saxlingham attack apart. Walsham totalled 256-1, Scales also hitting 83 not out. Saxlingham's opening bowlers only went for 38 runs in their 16 overs but, once their allocations had been completed, Johnson massacred the second string bowlers. Again not having to bowl the opposition out to win the game, Saxlingham finished on 156-4; fun for batsmen, perhaps, but hardly good for the game. Eaton's score of 171 was successfully chased down in a four-wicket win (Johnson 60 and Garth Futter 56). However, this win was partially due to Eaton's generosity. They had turned up with twelve players when Walsham had only ten. Matthew Guyton - who had only played once for Eaton - was loaned to Walsham and bowled 10 accurate overs, followed by 20 not out. However, his association with the club didn't end there. The game was played on the eve of the 2002 tour and, in the pub afterwards, he was persuaded to join the week's adventure in Wiltshire.

On returning from tour, there was a close match with Old Catton, who scored 157-9. At tea, Walsham were confident of victory, but wickets kept falling and, with the last pair together, seven runs were still needed. Amidst much tension, the win was eventually secured with five overs to spare. The next match - against Happisburgh - was abandoned after Walsham were bowled out for 154, Belton hitting a half-century. A win against St Andrews was achieved after the home side had scored 160-8. Despite struggling to 87-5, Whiteside (62 not out) and Garth Futter (40 not out) added an unbeaten 74 to cross the victory line by five wickets.

The final game of the season saw Walsham beat the President's side by four wickets. For the third time in the season, Garth Futter was loaned to the opposition and he obliged with 50 not out in a total of 222-7. However, Johnson made short work of their score, hitting a magnificent 128 as the target was reached in just 34 overs. He had enjoyed a very successful first season as skipper: twelve wins, seven defeats and one draw in the 20 games completed. In addition, the responsibility seemed to help his batting as he scored 902 runs at an average of over 50. Watkins and Scales also passed the 600 mark. It had been very much a batsman's year; of the bowlers only Garth Futter took over 20 wickets.

CHAPTER THIRTY SEVEN *Johnson At The Helm 2003/4*

2003 was another successful season under the captaincy of Neil Johnson, with over half the games being won. Debut-makers were father and son, Chris and Paul Woods and Chris Pyer. The Woods were excellent acquisitions and have been almost ever-present for the past ten seasons, with Paul playing over 200 games to the end of 2012. From the outset, they have been involved with most facets of the club and Chris' wife Pat now makes the teas every home game, a much appreciated contribution. Chris has taken 240 wickets and scored over 2000 runs while Paul has passed 4500 runs and taken over 150 wickets as well as 120 catches. Paul is an outstanding fielder and rarely drops a catch; indeed his speed around the field means some of his catches have a 'Heineken quality'. He held the captaincy from 2008-11 and led from the front with great enthusiasm. Chris Pyer has played over 50 games in the last ten years; a very useful left arm spin bowler who has taken 70 wickets, it has been unfortunate that he has not been available more regularly.

Chris Woods

The season got off to a slow start with a comprehensive 85-run defeat to Lowestoft, who scored 147-7 from 47 overs. Walsham fell away badly and were dismissed for 62. However, new opponents Cawston were beaten by 32 runs in a 40-over match. After Watkins had scored 78 in a total of 162-5, the opposition were in with a chance at 123-6, but the last four wickets were picked up for six runs. In another close 40-over match against Bradfield, Walsham finished on 163-9, the opposition finishing thirteen runs short of victory. In a high-scoring draw with Great Ellingham who scored 218-4 declared, Walsham hit back with 192-3 (Watkins 83*, Jon Moore 58*). The latter's was his only fifty - to date - for the club). St Andrews were beaten by 81 runs, being dismissed for 122 in reply to Walsham's 203-4 declared, with fifties from Scales and Johnson.

On a difficult wicket at Billingford, Walsham only managed 116-8 in 40 overs; the opposition scored the winning runs in the final over to win by three wickets. The return match at Cawston produced a 22-run win in a 40-over game, the host's 178-8 being their response to Walsham's 200-8. This was followed by an excellent performance against Hatfield - a strong touring side -

Paul Woods

who had won all their previous games on tour. It appeared that they expected their final game to be the easiest of their five, but they came up against two tremendous individual performances. John Pennington took 5-20 in a total of 163 and, in Walsham's reply, Neil Johnson had one of those days when he hit everything for 'miles' as he crashed 109 not out to overhaul the tourists' score in 31 overs to win by five wickets.

Unfortunately, this was followed by a poor performance at Happisburgh. Walsham totalled 103, which the home side easily overcame by six wickets, but it was back to winning ways against West Wittering who made 131 in reply to Walsham's 163. Pennington took 7-50 as he bowled throughout the tourists' innings. There was a cracking game at Swanton Morley where Walsham scored 165 (Steve Belton 86), but the hosts edged home with eight wickets down. In a not untypical game against Eaton, Walsham made 211 (Scales 105), but the traditionally obdurate opposition finished on 109-8. In a similar game against Old Catton, Scales again top-scored with 77 in a total of 206-4, to which they replied with 133-8. However, success against touring sides was maintained against Belhus (Essex), who scored 181-6 but, with Johnson (66) leading the way, Walsham cruised home by four wickets. Unusually, Lowestoft were beaten after being bowled out for 90 (Loades 3-21) in reply to Walsham's186.

Johnson's aggressive 94 in a total of 183-7 against Halvergate set up a close match as they finished on 173-8 (Garth Futter 4-54). Eaton were inserted in the next match and posted a reasonable total of 168-8, but Scales (52) and Paul Woods (37*) played the leading roles in securing a four-wicket win. This was followed by achieving the better side of a draw against Billingford, whose 131-6 was their response to Walsham's165-5 (Watkins 74*). A highest-ever score in a 40-over game - 264-6 against Old Catton - included half-centuries from Johnson and Paul Woods. Despite an explosive start from Catton, wickets fell regularly and they were bowled out for 171 (Garth Futter 3-25).

Another 'ton' from Johnson set up a 96-run win against Happisburgh; Walsham's score of 212-7 proved to be rather too many and the opposition were bowled out for 116 (Pyer 4-24). In an extremely close game against Meridian - a touring side from Nottingham - they scored 205-9, Garth Futter taking four wickets. The game finished in a draw as Walsham totalled 193-8, Johnson and Belton both hitting 42.

However, the 'game of the season' was a high-scoring draw against old friends St Andrews. Walsham scored 215-8 with half-centuries from Chris Woods and Johnson. St Andrews came back hard, finishing on 208-9, with man-of-the-match Chris Woods taking 5-41. In the penultimate game of the season, Bradfield made only 128, Loades and Belton taking three wickets apiece; Johnson top-scored as Walsham cruised home by five wickets.

In the traditional season-ending President's match, Whiteside took 5-9 as the President's side were bowled out for 200 but, after being 168-8, Chris Woods (44*) and Alex Evans put on a ninth wicket stand of over 30 to secure victory by two wickets. It completed a good season: thirteen wins, seven draws and only four defeats. Johnson (826 runs) had another brilliant year, while Watkins passed 600 and Scales 500. In the bowling, Garth Futter (42 wickets) was out on his own, no other bowler passing the 20-wicket mark.

Neil Johnson continued to lead the side in the rather damp season of 2004 when seven games were lost to the weather. The first match was a comfortable win against Rackheath, Johnson top-scoring in a total of 183-7. Against spin bowling throughout their innings, Rackheath replied with 80 (Chris Woods 5-27). Winning ways were continued against Winterton, after a recovery from 51-5 to 161-6 (Steve Belton 68*). Four wickets for Garth Futter saw Walsham home by 36 runs.

Another win came at home to Lowestoft who turned up with only nine players. Walsham posted 193-6 (Paul Woods 67*) and, despite an opening stand of 50, Lowestoft fell away to 117 (Pyer 5-28). It was a mis-match against Martham as Walsham hit 244-5, Watkins top scoring; Martham were dismissed for 84 (Burns 5-14). This was reversed against Caister: Walsham were reduced to 60-7 before Scales (73) and Paul Woods (56) put on 109 for the eighth wicket in a final total of 176. However, Caister won easily, by 10 wickets in 34 overs.

South Walsham Squad 2004

The match against Halvergate was drawn, with Johnson hitting 96 in typical fashion in a total of 208-6; Halvergate finished on 173-7. Defeat followed against St Andrews after Walsham recovered from 96-8 to reach 165-9, last man Evans top-scoring with 37 not out. However, St Andrews made short work of this total winning by six wickets. The annual 40-over match with Happisburgh produced a 45 run win: Walsham hit 208-3 (Watkins 85) and, in reply, Happisburgh scored 162-8 (Whiteside 3-18). In an extraordinary 40-over game at Winterton, Walsham scored 227-4, Watkins and Johnson scoring heavily. It seemed all over at 37-9, with four wickets apiece for Paul Woods and Greg Loades, but the final pair crashed the ball around to good effect adding 93 before Loades took a catch on the boundary.

Walsham scored 161-8 against Bradfield after recovering from 97-8, Loades and Pyer adding 64 for the ninth wicket. Bradfield - whose players didn't seem to grasp the concept of twenty overs in the last hour - finished on 161-7. At an under-strength Overstrand, Pyer took 4-12 in a total of 83 before Steve Belton led the way with 43 not out as Walsham won by six wickets. Eaton were victors by four wickets as they successfully chased 161-9, regular Walsham tourist Jon Fudge hitting 101 not out for the club where he had begun his cricket career. However, all those who batted made a significant score in a total of 245-4 against St Andrews who slumped to 70-8 before recovering to 158-8 to draw the game.

After a very wet tour of Yorkshire, it was back to Norfolk - and improved weather - but defeat at Lowestoft by four wickets. Walsham scored 149-7, but the home side recovered from 40-5 to win the game, despite Loades bowling a terrific spell (3-9 in 8 overs). Happisburgh held on for a draw after Walsham declared on 190-5; Ivan Andrews held their reply together with 72 not out in a total of 125-9.

Old Catton were crushed by 130 runs and the game against tourists Meridian was abandoned. They had set a total of 177 and Walsham were struggling on 95-5 (Belton 52) when the rain came. There was another mis-match with Martham: Walsham made 225-4 and Martham replied with just 28 - four wickets apiece for Scales and Loades. In the final game of the season, the President's team win by five runs after scoring 232-9. Walsham replied with 227 (Watkins 81).

In a wet season, Walsham had won eleven, drawn four and lost five of the twenty games completed. Watkins (691) was the top run-scorer while Johnson was the only other player to pass 500. Loades (32) took the most wickets with Garth Futter, Paul and Chris Woods all passing the 20 mark.

Press Cuttings 2003

CRICKET: Clubs form an alliance in bid to safeguard Sunday friendly matches

Staying friendly

By KEITH PEEL

Seven cricket clubs are going back to the future in a bid to safeguard Sunday friendly fixtures. They've formed the "Friendly Alliance" and are now seeking other sides who want to play friendlies on Sundays.

The founder members are Caister, Eaton, Happisburgh, Lowestoft, South Walsham, St Andrews and Winterton.

South Walsham CC fixture secretary Alex Evans explained: "We are a club which has always played friendly cricket since it was reformed – largely by the Edrich family – just after the last war, and the club wants to continue playing friendly cricket.

"We have absolutely nothing against league cricket, and indeed some of our members play in the leagues for other clubs on a Saturday. What we say, however, is that there should be an option of playing league, cup or friendly cricket on a Sunday.

"To that end, we have formed the 'Friendly Alliance' and what we are looking for now is other clubs to join us, so that we can readily organise a fixture list for our clubs."

He added: "The only rules of the alliance are that the clubs are all affiliated clubs members of the Norfolk Cricket Board, because we want the board to support us, and that the only reason for a late call-off is because of bad weather.

"We believe all cricket should be encouraged, and that there is room in the Norfolk cricket scene for enjoyable friendly matches."

Any other clubs which would like to join the alliance are asked to contact Alex on 01603-891976 – or by letter to 2 Pimpernel Road, Horsford, Norwich NR10 3SQ – by October 31, so arrangements can be put in place for next season.

Record partnership for sixth wicket

HALVERGATE Sunday team had a very enjoyable game with their old friends at South Walsham.

After a game which ebbed and flowed both ways, the teams had to settle for a draw at the close.

Batting first, South Walsham were in all sorts of trouble after a superb spell of bowling by Danny Carter and Tim Crane, reduced them to 47-5 by the 17th over.

However, thanks to a brilliant innings of 94 by Hares Saturday player, Neil Johnson, and supported by Paul Woods (38) they recovered to 179 – adding a record 132 sixth-wicket partnership.

Despite a bad back, Johnson was hitting the ball to all parts of the ground and fell just short of his century when he was caught by Paul Ellingham on the boundary for 94, his innings included six sixes and 11 fours.

When Steve Clarke caught Woods to give Carter his fourth wicket, the total had reached 183-7 at the tea interval.

Carter's final figures were 4-45 from 15 overs of hostile bowling with Crane giving good support as he finished with 3-23.

Halvergate came out with all guns blazing and were well up with the run rate despite losing Ellingham in the first over for six to Garth Futter.

A good partnership of 45 by T Crane (21), and Colin Foreman (21), saw them progress to 51, before Crane was run out in the 11th over and Foreman was then caught on the same total.

A good partnership of 71 by S Willimott and the captain Steve Clarke, saw them take the score on to 122 with 17 overs still remaining and only 61 runs required. Willimott was finally caught after showing a welcome return to form for 30.

With Carter also dismissed, four runs later, South Walsham started to recover and when Clarke was stumped for an excellent 54 with the score now 145-6, the game had swung back their way.

When the Foreman brothers were both dismissed and the total on 172-8, the experienced Keith Hodds (7 not out), and Chris Mills (1 not out) had to play out a nail-biting two overs as the total reached 179.

Upton White Horse Man of the Match: Neil Johnson

Scales hits a Walsham ton

SOUTH Walsham were frustrated against Eaton on Sunday when the Eaton tailenders held out for a draw. The star of the innings, however, was Andy Scales who scored an excellent 105 with 12 fours.

Walsham batted first on a slow wicket and were soon in trouble when they slumped to 55-3 with Watkins, Belton and Johnson quickly back in the pavilion.

Andy Scales however, was going well at the other end and when Richard Whiteside joined him the tempo was lifted. They added 86 for the fourth wicket before Whiteside fell for 22. Matt Holmes hit a quick 27 but the tail struggled to continue the run scoring as Walsham slipped to 211 all out. All credit to bowlers Reynolds and Gray who bowled well to take four wickets each.

After tea, Woods dismissed the dangerous Fudge second ball but Butcher and Best added 35 for the second wicket before Best fell for 14.

It soon became clear that Eaton were not likely to challenge the Walsham score as wickets started to fall regularly to Chris Pyer (2-41) and Garth Futter (3-8) from 11 overs. Both put pressure on the Eaton batsmen but Crowhurst and Chilvers played out the last eight overs to hold on to a draw on 109-8.

Upton White Horse Man of the Match: Andy Scales, a superb century.

Futter's 500th wicket

SOUTH Walsham won by four wickets in a competitive friendly against Eaton on Sunday which saw Garth Futter take his 500th wicket for Walsham.

Eaton were inserted by Walsham and they made a steady start with the father-and-son combination of Simon and Jon Fudge.

It was not until the 23rd over that Walsham had their first success when Simon Fudge was caught on the boundary by Paul Woods off Sanjay Shah.

Wickets then began to fall steadily, although Jon Fudge kept the scoreboard ticking over. Fudge finally fell for a well made 81 but no other Eaton players really got hold of the Walsham bowling.

They declared at 168-8 off a marathon 51 overs. Four of the bowlers took two wickets each, but pride of place went to Futter with his 500th wicket.

Missing Belton, Winterside and Johnson from their batting line-up, Walsham needed a good start from the experienced David Watkins and Andy Scales.

Watkins was first to go for 26 after the openers added 53 for the first wicket.

Scales continued to play well with Jon Moore hitting the loose ball well.

Scales was well caught out for 52 and with Tim Moore out for just a single pressure was building on Walsham.

Paul Woods went on the attack, hitting an excellent 37 not out, while Moore contributed a well-made 34.

Walsham got home by four wickets with eight overs to spare.

White Horse Man of the Match: Andy Scales for an excellent 50 which steadied the Walsham innings.

Futter sparks South Walsham's innings

SOUTH Walsham scored a hard fought victory against Cawston, winning by 29 runs.

The home side insisted on a 35 over match and Walsham chose to bat first on a hard wicket and quick outfield.

David Watkins fell early for five but fellow opener Neil Johnson was quickly in his stride, hitting the ball to all parts.

He went for one shot too many and was very well caught by Slaughter for 48, adding 60 with Richard Whiteside for the second wicket.

Walsham then slipped to 119-5 off 25 overs. Steve Belton who had been batting steadily was joined by Garth Futter who took the bowling apart with good shots and some fine running between the wickets.

The more well-built Belton struggled to keep up, but a few more big shots saw him to 55 before being caught on the boundary.

Futter was then run out for 32 and Walsham finished on 200-8 off their 35 overs.

After tea Cawston struggled against the accurate attack of Futter and Holmes, after 10 overs they were just 25-0.

As they started to hit out wickets began to fall, the fielding of the Moore brothers was excellent with Jim Moore holding on to two exceptional catches.

Jim also picked up two wickets as did Richard Whiteside, but Cawston were never quite able to keep up with the run rate and the game petered out in the last few overs as Cawston finished 30 runs short of victory.

It was a good fielding performance on a difficult outfield.

Upon White Horse MoM: Garth Futter with an innings which set the Walsham innings alight and a very tidy bowling spell which put Cawston on the back foot.

Johnson ton boosts Walsham

SOUTH Walsham scored an excellent 96-run victory over a strong Happisburgh side.

South Walsham batted first and faced some sharp bowling from Catchpole and Beames. Although Scales fell early, both David Watkins and century-maker Neil Johnson played extremely well against some quick bowling on a hard track.

Johnson then went on the attack, and despite offering the occasional chance, he blew the attack away to score his second century of the season.

With Watkins playing the anchor role, they added 162 for the second wicket. Johnson fell for 109, quickly followed by Watkins for 43. Richard Whiteside scored a quick 21 but the innings fell away a little on 212-7 off just 39 overs.

After tea, much to the Walsham players surprise, the Happisburgh batsmen played some poor shots against enthusiastic bowling and were soon in trouble at 15-4. Wayne Catchpole and J Beames went on the counterattack, but when they were both caught it was only a matter of time before Happisburgh were bowled out.

All the bowlers were on form, with Chris Pyer starring with 4-34, ably assisted by Paul Woods 3-33 and Greg Loades 2-20.

Upon White Horse man of the match: Neil Johnson, another excellent knock which set up a comfortable victory.

Double delight

SOUTH Walsham had a successful weekend, beating touring side Belhus by four wickets and Lowestoft by 94 runs.

Against Belhus, the tourists batted first and struck out from the start in a 35-over match. Only Greg Loades managed a maiden as Belhus posted a very respectable score of 181-6.

After tea, Walsham batted similarly, despite early losses of Scoles and Watkins.

Neil Johnson with an excellent 66 moved Walsham well above the run rate. The Moore brothers then added 46 for the fifth wicket with Jon scoring 34 and Jim 15. Garth Futter hit the winning runs with seven ball to spare.

Walsham rarely do well at Lowestoft and when they slipped to 136-8 the usual result looked likely. The only players to score were Steve Belton (33), Andy Scales (25) and David Watkins (26). Paul Woods (36) and Alex Evans (19) came together to add 54 for the ninth wicket and Walsham were able to post a reasonable score of 186.

Futter quickly removed Jenner and D Mann and Greg Loads took advantage of a deteriorating wicket with 3-21. Neil Johnson removed the dangerous Sims (34) and Garrod (11).

With Jim Moore picking up two wickets at the end Walsham won well by 96 runs.

Woods makes big impression for Walsham

SOUTH Walsham cruised to a comfortable win by 93 runs against Ol Catton.

The Walsham players were relieved when skipper Johnson won the toss and batted on a very hot afternoon.

The Catton wicket had been watered and despite a good start from Watkins (23) and Scales (29) it was a difficult pitch to play forceful shots. Both openers fell trying to force the pace.

Neil Johnson then played a typical innings after a slow start and scored 75 with 11 fours and two sixes. At the 32-over point, Walsham were looking comfortable at 184-5.

Paul Woods and Garth Futter then came together and absolutely blew the Catton bowling away.

Woods hit the ball all round the ground hitting 55 not out, his first 50 for the club. Ably supported by some excellent running from Futter, they added 80 in the last eight overs to give Walsham an almost unbeatable total of 264-5 off their 40 overs.

To Catton's credit they came out blazing after tea, in particular opener Knowles who scored a splendid 50 in the first 10 overs. Unfortunately nothing was coming from the other end and although Richards tried to force the pace, wickets began to fall as Catton fell further and further behind the run rate.

Greg Loades, Chris Woods and Garth Futter all bowled tidily and by the time the father and son combination of Richard and Joe Whiteside came on, the game had already been won.

Praise for young Joe Whiteside who picked up two wickets, one an excellent catch by father Richard. Futter picked up three wickets with Paul Woods and Richard Whiteside picking up two each.

Upon White Horse Man of the Match: Paul Woods, a cracking 50 in his enthusiastic bowling and fielding display.

CHAPTER THIRTY EIGHT *The Moore Years 2005/06*

After three excellent seasons from Neil Johnson, the captaincy was taken on by Jon Moore in 2005. The only new player of note to join the club was Kieran Robinson who played nearly 60 games in the following five seasons. While his enthusiasm could not be faulted, he struggled to make an impact with bat or ball.

In the first match of the season Moore's men were second best in a draw against Halvergate. The visitors hit 216-7, Walsham replying with 166-7 (Scales 72). In an exciting four-wicket defeat against St Andrews, Walsham scored 207-4 in 40 overs, Watkins and Scales hitting half-centuries but, with Keith Hunt hitting 105 not out, the Saints got home with just two balls to spare. There was a third defeat in a row against Eaton as they declared on 188-5 off 56 overs. Typically, Walsham went for the win, but were bowled out for 183 in the final over, despite 94 from Scales.

Jon Moore

The first win of the season came against Winterton after Walsham declared at 242-4, Scales hitting a career-best 153 not out. Winterton were never in it and were dismissed for 146 (Loades 5-31). Another win followed in a 45-over match against Billingford. Walsham scored 165-5 (Watkins 76) and Johnson (5-25) had an excellent day as Billingford finished on 144-7. He was in form again in the next match, top-scoring with 72 out of a total of 234-8 against Happisburgh. The visitors made a good effort in reply, hitting 200-5 in a drawn game.

There was another high-scoring game against St Andrews, as Scales and Johnson both hit half-centuries in a total of 240-3. St Andrews were not far behind as they finished on 233-7, Johnson picking up four wickets. In a terrific match against Lowestoft, the visitors made 235-7 and Walsham were still in with a chance at 200-5 - including a sparkling fifty from Paul Woods - but the attacking approach of the tail led to a collapse to 214 all out. However, it was back to winning ways against Old Catton as Walsham hit 223-8 (Scales 59*). The wickets were spread around as Catton were dismissed for 139.

The season was becoming a real run-fest. Walsham passed the 200 mark six times in eight games, including a season's best 244-5 (Johnson 125) against Rackheath. The opposition had their own big hitters and made a game of it, but slipped from 193-5 to 217 all out to give Walsham victory by 27 runs. Touring side Belhus hit 238-6, which Walsham could not match, finishing on 165-8 in a drawn game. A Garth Futter half-century helped Walsham to 219-7 at Billingford in a 40-over match in which Billingford struggled to 142-8.

In a terrific game against Bradenham, Walsham scored 178-9 and managed to bowl out the visitors for 176, with three wickets for Johnson. The game was on a knife-edge all the way, Bradenham looking comfortable at 138-5, before they collapsed to 151-9 only for the last pair to add 25 before Johnson clean bowled the number 11 batsman to produce a three-run victory. After the match with Eaton had been abandoned, Walsham easily beat Viscounts, a touring side from London, who made only 91 (four wickets for Garth Futter) in response to Walsham's 181-6. Struggling to field a side against Lowestoft, Walsham paid the penalty scoring only 118 (Johnson 41) and Lowestoft cruised to victory by six wickets.

Three of the next four games were against touring sides. Bromley Common were strong and knocked off Walsham's 185-6 with four wickets down in only 28 overs. In contrast, in a very light-hearted game against Stamford, the tourists were bowled out for 222 and Walsham should have won but finished on 220-9. In the third game, Salfords won by 48 runs, after being dismissed for 171. Walsham batted poorly and were bowled out for just 123. The highlight of the day was a very lively evening at the White Horse; the pub was packed and 'President Ray' was rushed off his feet dealing with multiple fish and chip orders.

Between these touring fixtures was a draw against Old Catton, who responded to Walsham's 194-4 with 170-8. Defeat followed against

Halvergate, as Walsham collapsed from 98-0 to 185-7 on a very good track. Chris Woods took three wickets in their reply, but they eased home by four wickets. As the season came to a close Walsham had the better of a draw against Bradenham scoring 180-7 including fifty from guest Graham Yallop. Bradenham replied with 152-8 (four wickets for Loades). The season ended with the usual President's game. Ray Norman's side scored 225, but Walsham crept home with 226-8 with forties from Scales and Whiteside.

It had been an average year for results: eight wins and seven defeats out of the 22 completed matches. Run-scoring was high with totals of over 200 in ten matches. It was a record season for Andy Scales who hit 957 runs from 21 innings with an average of 50.37 and the highest individual score of 153 not out. Johnson hit 647 runs while Paul Woods and Watkins passed the 400 mark. In the bowling, Loades took 31 wickets with Garth Futter, Chris Woods and Johnson passing the 20 mark.

Jon Moore continued to captain the side to a reasonably successful season in 2006. In the usual opener, against Halvergate, the visitors proved a bit strong for a rusty Walsham side. Halvergate hit 219-3 and Walsham were never in it finishing on 94-8, only Scales passing 20. However, this was reversed with a 100-run win against St Andrews, when fifties from Paul Woods and Johnson in a total of 231-5 was followed by Loades (5-33) making short work of the Saints batting. Not for the first time, Walsham failed to winkle out the Eaton batting after scoring 176-9 (Johnson 67). Despite an excellent start, Eaton collapsed from 72-0 to 140-8 to hold on for a draw, Loades taking another four wickets. However, Rackheath were well-beaten as Johnson maintained his form with 117 out of a score of 227-2. A 'fifer' for Loades saw Rackheath dismissed for 106.

On a wet wicket against Happisburgh, Walsham really struggled against their opening attack. After 29 overs the scoreboard read 33-4, but some late innings hitting from Chris and Paul Woods and Garth Futter did manage to lift the score to 132. It was not plain sailing for Happisburgh as they reached 92-7, but Cousins hit a quick 25 not out to see them home with no further loss of wickets. The game against Broomfield didn't last long as after 22 overs - and the tourists struggling at 46-6 - the conditions became too wet and both sides adjourned to the pub. In a very enjoyable game against Swanton Morley, Walsham chased down 191 (Watkins 86) to win the game by five wickets, although this was assisted by the opposition appearing to use the game as practice for their fringe players, everyone enjoying a spell of bowling. In another big score (229-2) against St Andrews, Scales hit 98 and Whiteside 83 not out. In reply, the Saints were never in the game, but held out on 129-7 off 46 overs. Walsham then outclassed their next opponents scoring 214-3 against the Kings Arms from Norwich who responded with just 87.

A visit to Aylsham St Giles on a day when England were playing in the football World Cup finals saw Walsham quickly dispose of the home side for just 72, with three wickets from Paul Woods. A quick 60 not out from Watkins led Walsham to victory in just 18 overs which meant both sets of players could watch the game in the pub! Paul Woods produced the innings of the season against Lowestoft, hitting 117 not out in a total of 247-5. Despite an opening stand of 103, Lowestoft lost their way and finished on 174-7 which gave Walsham a comfortable victory in an overs-based match. One of the highlights of the season was the excellent two-wicket victory over regular Essex tourists, Belhus. They made a very good score of 256-5, but some excellent batting from Scales, Johnson and Garth Futter and a bit of wayward bowling saw Walsham home. Futter's 50 with two sixes and eight fours was the star turn.

In another struggle on the Billingford track, which is very different to the Walsham pitch, and with only four regular bowlers, Billingford scored 229-6 in a 40-over match and, despite valiant efforts from Watkins and Johnson, Walsham fell fourteen runs short of victory. However, compensation came in the form of an excellent win over Bradenham with Paul Woods (54) leading the way in a total of 216-9. It was David Loades, Greg's father, who was the star of the day with 6-32, as he helped to reduce Bradenham to 144-9. A last wicket stand of 41 made the Walsham fielders a little nervous until Chris Woods bowled their last man to secure victory by 31 runs.

Walsham then went down to Eaton in a high-scoring game. After declaring on 218-5, with half-centuries from Scales and Johnson, Walsham's bowlers failed to hold the Eaton batting as they won comfortably by five wickets with two overs to spare. In a tight game at Lowestoft, Walsham were bowled out for 216 (Paul Woods 46). In reply, Lowestoft scored 194-8 as they collapsed from 124-2, but Chris Woods (6-19 in 7 overs) led Walsham to victory in an overs-based game. However, Caister proved to be too strong for Walsham. Facing 182-8 (Scales 49), they cruised to a five wicket win with several overs to spare, despite Pyer claiming three wickets.

After the tour of Essex, it was a struggle to field even nine players, including eleven year-old debutant Dan Scales, against Gooderstone, who were reduced to 68-7 before recovering to 156-8. Chris Woods bowled exceptionally well to take 5-12. However, with a weak batting side, and Johnson and Moore both falling for early ducks, Walsham not surprisingly lost the match making only 110. This was followed by a low-scoring game against Halvergate for the Graham London Memorial Trophy when more good bowling from Chris Woods (4-27) saw the home side collapse to 94 all out. Walsham cruised to a six-wicket win just after tea. However, in the penultimate game of the season Bradenham were easy victors totalling 209-4, with three wickets for Johnson, before dismissing Walsham for 112. The traditional final game of the season saw the President's side score 244, but 104 not out from Johnson and 79 from Watkins saw Walsham home by eight wickets, before the traditional adjournment to the Upton White Horse for another splendid evening, courtesy of 'President Ray'.

Neil Johnson and Millie 'The Boundary Hound'

Jon Moore's second and final season as captain had been successful with twelve wins, eight defeats and five draws. It was another high-scoring season, the 200 mark being passed on thirteen occasions. Johnson (846 runs) topped the batting averages, while Scales (725), Watkins (598) and Paul Woods (483) also scored heavily. In the bowling department, Chris Woods led with 43 wickets at 14.51, Greg Loades took 40 while Paul Woods took 27. Paul Woods and Scales impressed with their catching taking 15 and 14 respectively.

Press Cuttings 2005/06

Loades and Futter Walsham's weekend men

SOUTH Walsham played two matches over the weekend, drawing with touring side Belhus and then beating Billingford by 77 runs.

Belhus batted first and were soon hitting the Walsham bowling to all parts, reaching 80 in the first 10 overs.

Neil Johnson and Greg Loades brought a bit of control to proceedings and Loades in particular picked up three wickets to halt Belhus' progress.

Shaun Corcoran also picked up three wickets but the batting was good and the Walsham bowlers were pleased when Belhus declared on 238-6, five minutes before the scheduled tea interval.

After tea Walsham openers set about chasing the target but David Watkins (12) and Andy Scales (26) fell chasing quick runs.

Neil Johnson hit three sixes in his excellent 48 but wickets kept falling.

As the tourists maintained some tight bowling with 20 overs left Walsham still required 145, which was beyond them.

Despite a few big hits the game slipped towards a draw. Walsham finished on 105-8 with the honours going to the visitors.

Walsham were more upbeat on a sunny day at Billingford.

After a difficult start on a damp wicket Watkins soon fell for three but Andy Scales (37) and Richard Whiteside (43) got the innings moving with some fine shots.

Corcoran and Johnson fell quickly but Garth Futter (57) took the game away from the Billingford bowlers with a typical hard hit 50.

Jon Moore (23 not out) and Sean Corcoran (17) hit some useful runs at the end and Walsham were well pleased with their total of 219-7 off the allotted 40 overs.

After tea the Billingford batsmen started steadily against an accurate attack of Futter and Corcoran and after they had both completed their opening spells Billingford were only 48-2 from 18 overs.

From that point Billingford were never really in the game although P Ellis showed some resistance scoring 50 not out.

Loades and Corcoran picked up two wickets each and aided by two run outs, Billingford finished on 142-8 after 40 overs to give Walsham a win by 77 runs.

Upton White Horse Man of the Match: Greg Loades against Belhus, excellent bowling spell; Garth Futter against Billingford, fine attacking half-century.

Cricket

Boundary hound is kept busy

IN the blazing conditions it was not a day for a lot of running in an extravaganza of runs at South Walsham's superb home ground on Sunday.

A total of 50 fours and 14 sixes were struck to the boundary where the Labrador Millie was kept in full action, hunting out the balls from the hedgerows.

In a rarely-played time game it was set up for Shannon Dunnett to show his batting skills and prowess.

But not before the young ones had a go at the crease. David Mann batted solidly and made a good 36 from the opening berth.

Luke Caswell, fast emerging as a talented all-rounder, scored 18. Twelve-year-old Michael Johnson made double figures and Colt Sam Whittaker made 17 before the gladiator Dunnett stole the show with a great knock of pulverising power making 102 not out from the No 7 berth.

His first seven scoring shots were all fours and he followed this with three more plus six huge sixes that included one way over the South Walsham pavilion and into the adjacent park.

It allowed skipper Nathan Garrod, who also joined in the fun to score 17, to declare on 235-7, which Town thought was enough.

But South Walsham had other ideas, mainly through Neil Johnson (33), Andy Scales (40) and finally a bludgeoning batting show by Paul Woods with 54 (six fours and four sixes).

As Walsham went for the target some Town bowlers took some stick, but Luke Caswell (2-22) and Shannon Dunnett (2-8) held their nerve late on with Walsham finally out for 214 with two overs left of the mandatory 20 in the final hour.

A great game to watch in the sunshine, played in admirable spirit and friendliness.

Sgt Peppers Man of the Match: Shannon Dunnett.

Stuart G Baker

Runs flow in tourist match

SOUTH Walsham enjoyed an exciting win on a superb home batting track against touring side Belhus from Essex.

Belhus decided to bat first in excellent conditions and after a few careful shots early on, openers Lincoln and Turner put the Walsham bowlers to the sword, adding 123 for the first wicket off 19 overs.

Shaun Corcoran bowled Lincoln for 53. Kieran Robinson dismissed the impressive Turner for 94, but all the Belhus batsmen took a liking to the bowling and declared on 256-5 off just 35 overs.

Chris Woods was the most successful bowler with 2-36, but Garth Futter bowled the steadiest against the fierce hitting of the Belhus batsmen. The Walsham fielders came in a little downcast at tea knowing they were in for a battle to make a game of it.

Despite Walsham losing an early wicket, Andy Scales (44) and Neil Johnson (37) started crashing the ball to the boundary as the run rate rattled along at eight an over.

Shaun Corcoran (16), Paul Woods (20) and Chris Woods all played cameo innings to maintain the impressive run rate.

Woods Senior and Garth Futter, who top scored with 50, added 79 in just nine overs and kept Walsham in the hunt of an unlikely victory.

Robinson came in and hit three splendid boundaries to see Walsham home on 260-8 with just under four overs remaining.

A splendid game against an opposition who had enjoyed a great five-day tour in Norfolk.

Upton White Horse Man of the Match: Garth Futter, an excellent 50 and a steady bowling performance.

Watkins on form

SOUTH Walsham batted first on a hot Sunday at Halvergate and openers David Watkins (77) and Andy Scales (56) took full advantage of the excellent conditions to add 98 runs for the first wicket. Scales was the first to go, well caught by Brooks on the boundary.

Instead of increasing the run rate, the Walsham batsmen faultered against tidy Halvergate bowling. Although Richard Whiteside scored 16, no other Walsham batsmen reached double figures and by tea the score had reached 185-7, about 30 runs short of a good total on an excellent wicket.

After tea, Walsham took an early wicket with Garth Futter dismissing Stephen Cooke for a single.

But Ben Key (36) and J Gill (66) went on the attack. Walsham's catching was not up to scratch, and when skipper Steve Clarke was bowled for 27 only a few runs were needed for victory.

Halvergate timed their reply well as they coasted home by four wickets with 16 balls to spare and Walsham were left to rue their dropped catches.

Upton White Horse Man of the Match: David Watkins, a return to form with the bat.

Walsham cruise to big win

SOUTH Walsham cruised to an eight-wickets victory against Aylsham St Giles.

An early start, so players could watch the England match in the tea interval, saw Aylsham batting first and they were soon in trouble against the medium pace of Paul Woods, with both openers falling early on.

Greg Loades dismissed Bryant for a duck as Aylsham slipped to 27-3.

Pegg went on the offensive hitting 36 but some excellent spin bowling by Dav Roff had the batsmen and wicket keeper Evans in trouble with the turning ball.

Roff picked up 3-11 off six overs as Aylsham fell away to 72 all out off 27 overs.

Alex Evans made a rare appearance at the top of the order for Walsham but it was Dave Watkins who was going to try and win the game before the start of the football.

The fifty came up in 12 overs at which point Evans fell for eight. Liam Corcoran didn't trouble the scorers, but Watkins hit a couple more fours to win the game off 18 overs. Watkins finished 60 not out as Walsham got home with a comfortable win.

Upton White Horse man of the match: Dave Watkins - excellent hard hitting half century.

Walsham reverse

SOUTH Walsham suffered their first defeat of the season when they lost to Happisburgh by three wickets.

Happisburgh put South Walsham in on a damp wicket and opening bowlers Catchpole and Peck had the Walsham batting in all kinds of trouble.

Walsham batsmen could hardly lay bat on ball as they slipped to 18-4 off 19 overs.

David Watkins stood firm but it was not until the second string bowlers came on that the Walsham score got going.

Watkins and Paul Woods added 42 for the sixth wicket before Watkins was caught on the boundary for 38. Paul Woods then fell for 23.

Garth Futter and Chris Woods both scored 20 to lift the score beyond three figures, but an all-out total of 132 at tea was going to be difficult to defend.

After tea the Walsham bowlers quickly picked up two early wickets. Wayne Catchpole then attacked and hit a quick 35.

With wickets falling at regular intervals Walsham were still in with a chance as Happisburgh slipped to 92-7.

After that, although the batsmen hit the ball in the air, nothing really went to hand and a stand of 41 between Cousins (25 not out) and Mash (16 not out) saw Happisburgh home with eight balls to spare.

Upton White Horse MoM: Paul Woods (23 runs, 3-39).

Pyer shows good form

SOUTH Walsham were second best to a good Caister side when they went down by five wickets.

Walsham batted first and soon lost Dave Watkins for three. Walsham batsmen found it quite tough against accurate bowling but a good third-wicket partnership between Neil Johnson (38) and Andy Scales (49) added 60.

Again the middle order failed to deliver, but good contributions from the lower order, Paul Woods (17), Chris Wood (20) and Greg Loades (25 not out), lifted the score to a reasonable 182-8.

After tea Caister impressed with good running between the wickets and S Kerrison hit the ball well before he was stumped for 38. R Brown guided Caister towards victory with 81 not out.

Chris Pyer picked up three wickets and Walsham were in with a chance when Caister were 86-4, but a half-chances were missed and Caister eased home. Pyer finished on 3-57 off 12 overs to be Upton White Horse MoM.

Sporting gesture comes back to haunt Lowestoft

SOUTH WALSHAM visited Lowestoft on Sunday and came away with a narrow 22 run victory.

Skipper Greg Loades won the toss and elected to bat in a 45 over match. Walsham were indebted to Lowestoft for giving them one of their spare players, R Karrion who performed admirably scoring 11 runs, two catches and a wicket.

Dave Watkins and Andy Scales started the innings at their usual tempo, but Sales misjudged a drive and was well caught by Dunnett for nine with the score on 30.

Neil Johnson then came in and made a few spectators move rather quickly with a few hard hit boundaries. Watkins fell for 44 and the middle order fell away rather badly slipping for 103 for one to 154 for eight. Players were rushing round for their pads as a wicket seemed to fall every over. Johnson played on for 39 and with the score on 158 with 15 overs to go, Walsham were in trouble.

A typical hard hitting display from Paul Woods (46) and a careful innings of 20 from Greg Loades lifted the score to beyond 200, as Walsham were bowled out for 216 in the 40th over. Walsham feared the total might not be coming on a good wicket and a fast outfield.

After tea, Brice and Goldspink quickly got into their stride adding 45 for the first wicket before Goldspink went for 17 off Paul Mercers first ball of the season. Brice and Dunnett then got together and started moving the ball round the field well with the occasional big hit. With the score on 144 for one all seemed lost, but Lowestoft still had to score at six an over. Brice fell for 88 bowled by guest Karrion and then Dunnett was brilliantly caught by Scales in the deep, a fine driving effort for a 43-year-old off the bowling of Chris Woods.

The inexperience of the Lowestoft middle order caused problems with the run rate and extremely tight bowling from Woods saw Lowestoft slip further behind the rate, a few county hits from John Jenner couldn't bring Lowestoft back into the game and the home side finished on 194 for eight. Chris Woods led the team in following his superb bowling with six for 19 from seven overs and he was deservedly the Upton White Horse Man of the match.

Extras thwart a brave chase

SOUTH Walsham went down to a narr defeat against Billingford on Sunday.

Skipper Loades won the toss and Billingford into bat on a dry wicket an quick outfield. Opening bowlers Ga Futter and Paul Woods kept things ti, with only 19 run coming from the first overs.

Good batting and some erratic bowlin then saw Billingford take charge and goo 50s from A Lake and P Fuller lifted the ru rate. J Bidewell came in and hit a quic 45. Greg Loades picked up three wicket; but with 18 wides and seven no ball: Walsham allowed Billingford to reach 22! 6 when a total of 200 was probably abot the limit Walsham could chase.

After tea Walsham set about the tas well with Andy Scales and David Watkin adding 45 for the first wicket in nin overs. Scales was well caught and bowle by Johnson for 22.

Watkins and Johnson then added 100 in good time before Watkins was bowled for 58. All seemed under control as Waisham needed 120 off 20 overs with nine wickets left.

Very tight bowling from the Billingforc spinners made life difficult for the Walsham batsmen and smart keeping from Ellis also made it difficult. Neil Johnson fell for 77, Richard Whiteside for 20 as Walsham battled really hard for victory.

It was not to be however and Billingford held on to win by 13 runs. It was the extras column where the game was lost.

Upton White Horse Man of the Match. Neil Johnson, a fine effort of 77 to try and get Walsham home.

Johnson hits a century

SOUTH Walsham hammered Rackheath in a very one-sided friendly at South Walsham on Sunday. Batting first, Walsham were soon in their stride with Dave Watkins and Andy Scales batting carefully against a steady opening attack. Scales was bowled by Heyhoe for 31 and that was the last wicket Rackheath took as Watkins and particularly Neil Johnson steadily built up a formidable total. By tea they had added 181 unbeaten for the second wicket as Walsham declared on 226-1 once Johnson had reached his 100, finishing on 103 not out, while Watkins finished on 60 not out.

After tea Rackheath lost four quick wickets, two to Steve Hollis and two to Greg Loades. Rackheath's No 3 JoJo was hitting the ball well but no-one could stay with him as Hollis finished his spell with 3-3 from six overs. Loades finished with 2-24 from seven overs.

Garth Futter then came on to mop up the tail with 3-14. JoJo stayed in until the end when he was well caught by Scales on the boundary off the occasional bowler Jonny Moore for 50. Unfortunately with seven extras and only 11 coming from the other batsmen, Rackheath were dismissed for just 68. Upton White Horse MoM: Neil Johnson.

CHAPTER THIRTY NINE Loades For A Year...
The Woods era opens 2007/08

There were two changes for the 2007 season: Greg Loades took over from Jon Moore as skipper and one new player - Steve Hollis - was welcomed. A very good medium-paced, left-arm bowler who could also whack the ball to good effect, Hollis played for two seasons before leaving the area.

The first match saw a comfortable victory over St Andrews. Walsham were bowled out for 162, Garth Futter top-scoring with 33 but, on an uncharacteristically dusty early-season pitch, the Saints collapsed from 64-1 to 105 all out, Loades (5-23) and Chris Woods (3-32) leading Walsham to victory by 57 runs. The winning start was maintained as Eaton scored 175-7, with three wickets for Futter and two for Hollis on his debut. Walsham were in trouble at 73-6, but an unbeaten 104-run partnership for the seventh wicket between Garth Futter (76*) and Chris Woods (23*) saw Walsham home by four wickets. Rain spoiled the game against Old Catton; a halt to proceedings came with Walsham on 92-4. A draw was achieved against Billingford, who finished on 134-8 (Loades 3 wickets) in reply to Walsham's 178-8 (Hollis 34*).

Greg Loades

Against Rocklands, Scales (83) and Watkins (69) put on 157 for the first wicket, but even after a collapse to 205-9. Walsham still seemed to be in charge as they did for the majority of the opposition's innings, but the last-wicket pair added thirteen to give them an improbable victory. Much more unfortunate were the implications of the collision between Scales and Paul

Woods. While chasing the ball in the field, they ran into each other and Scales broke his collar bone putting him out for the season - a big blow for both player and club. A rare appearance from Steve Belton against St Andrews saw him make the top score of 54 in a total of 169-7, Paul Woods also producing a typically hard-hit fifty with three sixes and five fours. In reply, the Saints struggled to 104-8, Chris Woods taking four wickets.

In a very tight game at Aylsham St Giles, the home side managed 110-8 from their 40 overs, but at 78-8 the game looked lost. However, a ninth wicket partnership between Loades and Evans led to a dramatic victory. Billingford were superior in a 40-over game as they hit 153-3; Walsham, missing a few regular players, never looked like getting close and lost by 40 runs. The game against Hemsby resembled that against Aylsham, as Walsham bowled them out for 80 and looked to have the game won at 42-0, only to lose eight wickets for 24 runs before Robinson and Evans knocked off the final fifteen runs to cross the line by two wickets. There was another close finish against Lowestoft who were beaten by eight runs in a rather strange 40-over contest. Walsham scored 185-9, with a splendid 98 not out by Paul Woods, and Lowestoft struggled against tight bowling finishing on 177-3, all three wickets falling to Hollis. The return match with Aylsham St Giles saw Walsham recover from 83-8 to 135-8 at tea. However, Aylsham also found run-scoring difficult and finished on 96-5 from 43 overs.

A splendid 101 for David Watkins was the highlight of Walsham's total of 230-4 against Eaton who were never in the hunt after they reached 12-3 off the first 14 overs. It was then Walsham's job to winkle out the remaining batsmen, but they failed as Eaton finished on 100-7. There was a terrific game with Happisburgh even though it ended in defeat. Walsham scored 233-5 with a century from Scales, but Happisburgh hit back with Wayne Catchpole and Ivan Andrews scoring heavily to lead them to victory by five wickets, another three wickets for Hollis being the only bowling highlight.

Walsham were well beaten in the Graham London Memorial Trophy when Halvergate chased down a reasonable total of 177-8 in 37 overs with only four wickets down. Bradenham also proved to be too strong scoring 219-9 and winning by 57 runs, although Walsham's reply included another fifty by Scales. The final game of the season saw the President's side gain a rare victory. They were all out for 185 (Keith Denton 77), Chris Woods taking

4-19. However, in reply, only Scales with a fifty and 25 from Chris Woods really troubled the scorers as Pennington and Hollis proved too good for the Walsham line-up who were bowled out for 149.

In a wet season only sixteen games were completed: five wins, seven defeats and four draws. This was reflected in the run-scoring with no one passing the 500 mark. Scales (467) and Watkins (454) topped the charts while, in the bowling, only Chris Woods (26 wickets) passed the 20 mark.

Over the close-season, Greg Loades found a new job in Peterborough and, as the appointed vice-captain, Paul Woods took over the reins. The club were sorry to lose Greg, who had been an excellent player and clubman for the previous six seasons, but the 2008 season was reasonably successful for the new skipper. The first fixture, against Halvergate, was lost to the weather so the first match was against St Andrews. Walsham batted first and reached an excellent total of 216-7, both Scales and Gilbert hitting 57. The latter's innings was the more dramatic as it contained five sixes and five fours. It was his day as he bowled six overs without conceding a run and took the important wicket of Keith Hunt for seven. The Saints were well beaten, bowled out for 141 - three wickets each for Chris Woods and occasional player Ollie James. The good work continued against Eaton, who made 180-7, with another three wickets for Chris Woods, but hard hitting from Johnson and Gilbert put Walsham well ahead of the run-rate and eased to a five-wicket victory in 37 overs.

However, there was a reality check in the next game when Lowestoft scored 231-3 from their 40 overs and, in reply, Walsham collapsed to 32-8. The final two wickets managed 90, Chris Woods hitting 62, but it was a poor all-round performance. There was a four-wicket defeat at home to Billingford, despite making 183 (Denton 60). However, this was followed by a big win against Rackheath who suffered as Walsham hit 226-1, Johnson hitting a 'ton' and Watkins 60 not out in an unbeaten 181-run partnership for the second wicket. Although one of the Rackheath batsmen hit fifty, no-one else scored above five as they were bowled out for just 68, Hollis and Garth Futter taking three wickets each. However, the next match against St Andrews was more of a struggle as Walsham scored 133-9, only Watkins passing thirty. The Saints found it equally difficult to score runs on a slow, low pitch and could only muster 80-7 off 45 overs.

There was an excellent game against Aylsham St Giles as Paul Woods (70) led the way in a total of 217-6. A century from the Aylsham opener Bingham put them in with a chance of victory, but the other batsmen couldn't support him as the game finished in a draw with Aylsham on 203-9, Gilbert bowling very well to take 4-46 from 14 overs. The return match with Lowestoft saw Walsham gain revenge for the defeat earlier in the season. In trouble at 61-6, a maiden half-century from Loades, making a rare appearance, and 34 not out from Garth Futter lifted the score to 187 all out. The youthful Lowestoft side never got going as Garth Futter and Chris Woods both picked up early wickets and they were bowled out for just 92. However, Billingford completed the double in a 41-run victory. Both Gilbert and Pyer took three wickets as they scored 171-9 from 40 overs. Despite an eighth wicket partnership of 52 between Paul Woods and Gilbert, Walsham were always behind the run-rate and were bowled out for 130.

This was followed by another high-scoring game with tourists Belhus, who declared on 250-7 from 40 overs, but Walsham hit back with fifties from Scales, Denton and Johnson and passed their total in 35 overs with just five wickets down. This form was maintained against Bradenham who were beaten by four wickets. There were four run outs in the Bradenham innings, three of them from excellent fielding by Scales as they reached 180-8 at tea. Fifties from Scales and Johnson helped Walsham home by four wickets, but not before a collapse from 132-1 to 135-6. Garth Futter and Paul Woods completed the job.

A draw against Southtown included a Watkins half-century in a total of 168-9. Chris Pyer then took control of the game bowling sixteen overs taking 8-38. Unfortunately, Southtown hung on at 143-9, but it was a brilliant display by the slow left-armer. The final game before the bi-annual tour was at Aylsham St Giles with the home side scoring 162-6 but, with probably the strongest batting line-up of the season, Walsham failed miserably and were bowled out for 121, only Scales with fifty making an impression.

Back in Norfolk after the tour of Kent, Walsham were missing a few players for the game against Eaton. Having been put in on a slow, low wicket the batsmen struggled to 80-9 until Chris Woods (64) and Evans added over 50 for the last wicket to lift the score to 134. However, Eaton cruised home by nine wickets from 35 overs. There was a return to winning ways by 36 runs against Happisburgh, Walsham scoring 218-6 (Jon Fudge 74), before the opposition made a good effort after recovering from 82-8 to 182 all out which included an 88-run partnership between Woolston and Peck. The 200 mark was again passed against Old Catton, as Walsham scored 203-7 (Paul Woods 82). Old Catton never really challenged this total, finishing on 165-9 to draw the match.

Walsham then narrowly beat Southtown at the Beaconsfield, the home side struggling to 121-9, Hollis 7-20 in 6 overs exploiting the damp conditions. Walsham also had their problems and, at 88-7, it was anybody's game, but Hollis came in and capped a man-of-the-match performance with a quick 28 not out to ensure victory.

This was followed by an extremely tight game against Halvergate for the Graham London Memorial Trophy. Walsham were bowled out cheaply for 102, only Watkins passing twenty. Halvergate were soon in difficulties as Pyer took two wickets in his first over. They recovered to 52-3, only to collapse against the bowling of Gilbert and Hollis who cleared them out for 99. The final game of the season saw Walsham defeat the President's side. Gilbert and Chris Woods took three wickets each as the opposition were bowled out for 182, Walsham cruising to victory by three wickets with Johnson making 89

In a mixed year, Walsham won ten and lost eight while six games were drawn. Johnson (637) topped the run charts while Paul Woods (451), Watkins (366) and Scales (366) also had successful seasons. Hollis (25 wickets) topped the bowling averages while Pyer, Garth Futter and Chris Woods also passed the 20 mark. Paul Woods continued to be brilliant in the field with 22 catches.

Press Cuttings 2007/08

Hares at their Sunday best on a social occasion

HALVERGATE'S Sunday team had a very enjoyable game against old friends and local rivals South Walsham at the Playing Field on Sunday when a good all-round performance saw the Hares win the game by six wickets, after the visitors had set a target of 178 to beat from their 40 overs.

South Walsham won the toss and decided to bat first on what looked a lovely, flat batting surface, with their experienced pair David Watkins and ex-Hare Andy Scales opening their innings.

With the Hares two young opening bowlers Tom Booth and Shaun Howley both bowling a lovely line and length, the batsmen were finding runs hard to come by.

Then a stunning one-handed catch by Scott Foreman, off Shaun's bowling saw Scales (16) dismissed in the 10th over with the score on 24.

New batsman Richard Whiteside joined Watkins and together they had an excellent partnership of 91 runs, before a good catch by Shaun Howley off a skier saw Watkins' very good innings of 59 come to an end in the 26th over, when the score had reached 115.

Just six runs later another catch by Shaun, this time off Tim Crane's bowling, dismissed J Moore for five and in the very next over Whiteside's patient innings of 29 was ended when he was bowled by Howley with the score on 120.

Garth Futter (11) and Peter Woods then added a quick 19 runs together, before a catch by 12-year-old William Howley off Tim's bowling ended Futter's brief cameo.

Two more wickets went down on 149, when K Robinson (4) was run out and Tom Booth bowled S Hollis without scoring to give Tom a wicket his bowling deserved.

However, there was still a sting in the South Walsham tail as C Woods (11 not out) and G Loades (15 not out) plundered 28 runs in the last three overs as the innings ended on 177-8 after 40 overs.

Shaun Howley had figures of 3-40 runs from his 10 overs, while Tom in spite of going for 13 runs in his last over, took 1-23 from his 10 overs, and Tim Crane had 2-40.

Aaron Brooks was the other wicket taker as he finished with one for 41 runs from his 10 overs.

When the Hares began their reply skipper Stephen Clarke and Stephen Cooke gave the team an excellent start as they put on 88 runs before Cooke was out to a superb catch by Andy Scales way out on the square leg boundary.

This was in the 22nd over after he had scored 38 runs in a very good innings that contained four fours as well as several other attractive shots.

Three overs later the skipper also departed after he too had played very well in scoring 46 runs, with seven boundaries, before he was caught and bowled by Greg Loades after the total had reached 104.

William Gilder then came in to join Scott Foreman who was playing very fluently as he stroked the ball around in his quick-fire innings of 33.

He hit two huge sixes and three fours before he was caught way out at deep long on. They had added 32 runs in only four overs to take the score to 136 in the 19th over.

Tim Crane and Williams then added another 16 runs before scoring 12, which left Tim 24 not out and David James 10 not out, to knock off the remaining 24 runs needed for the six-wicket win with two overs to spare.

Veteran Chris Woods was South Walsham's most successful bowler taking 2-34 from his 10 overs.

Thanks went to Mike and Stephen for the excellent barbecue to round off a most enjoyable day for all.

This Sunday's game is the final league match, at Worstead with a 1pm start.

Hollis takes five wickets

FOLLOWING the washout against Happisburgh, South Walsham were keen to get back on the field of play and enjoyed a splendid game with Rocklands on Sunday.

Batting first, openers Dave Watkins and Andy Scales gave Walsham a flying start, putting on 157 for the first wicket before Watkins was bowled for 69.

Scales soon followed being stumped for an excellent 83. With the stand of 157 coming up in 31 overs it looked as though South Walsham would get a score of 240.

It was not to be however, as the batting collapsed to 205-8 mainly through good bowling from Sakthi, who took 4-18 in 13 overs.

On a smallish outfield, 205 was going to be a difficult total to defend.

Puttock and Pearce added 60 for the first wicket before Chris Woods bowled Pearce for 17.

Sakthi then came into bat and crashed the ball to all parts for 31, before falling to Chris Woods. By this time Rocklands were well up with the run rate, needing just 80 from the last 20 overs.

Steve Hollis was brought on to bowl and stopped Rocklands in their tracks, picking up 5-20 from eight overs, all his victims bowled.

Once his spell had come to an end however, tail-ender Lusher and Dodgson took a liking to the bowling and brought Rocklands back into the game.

With the last two together, Rocklands needed 10 runs from the last two overs. They reached victory with one ball to spare.

Unfortunately, Andy Scales broke his collar bone as he and Paul Woods tried in vain to prevent the winning run. They ran into each other and landed in a heap.

Upton White Horse MoM: Steve Hollis, excellent display of medium pace bowling with 5-20.

Tailenders deliver surprise win

IT was a tense affair as South Walsham narrowly defeated Aylsham St Giles by two wickets.

Skipper Loades won the toss and put the home side in on a damp wicket, and it soon became clear it was going to be a game for the bowlers.

Garth Futter quickly sent back two of the Aylsham batsmen for ducks and after 20 of their allotted 40 overs Aylsham were 38-3.

Pegg and Cocks both hit 30 as they tried to increase the run rate, but with Loades regularly changing the bowlers and some sharp fielding, South Walsham always kept a stranglehold on the batsmen. Garth Futter and Jack Belton both picked up two wickets as Aylsham reached 110-8 off their 40 overs.

It was quite clear that South Walsham were going to find it equally difficult to score runs as openers Dave Watkins and Richard Whiteside added 23 for the first wicket off 15 overs. When Walsham tried to increase the tempo wickets began to fall and only Paul Woods with 31 made any impact.

All looked lost as Walsham reached 77-8 with just six overs to go, but to the surprise of the Aylsham and Walsham players alike tail enders Greg Loades and Alex Evans started crashing the ball to all parts as well as picking up a few crafty singles. They added 34 in under six overs, and when Evans guided the ball through the vacant slip area for two Walsham were home with a ball to spare.

A very enjoyable competitive friendly.

Upton White Horse man of the match: Greg Loades excellent 20 not out and he captained well in difficult conditions.

South Walsham find Lowestoft too tough in friendly

SOUTH Walsham suffered a crushing friendly defeat at the hands of Lowestoft, going down by 109 runs.

Lowestoft batted first and got off to a quick start, scoring 45 in the first six overs for the loss of Bishop, who fell to an outstanding catch by Paul Woods off Ollie James.

The second wicket took a long time coming, but Chris Woods finally trapped Moore for 47 as he took one liberty too many against the veteran spinner.

T Brice was hitting the ball extremely well and it was only eight overs from Kevin Gilbert who gained any sort of control against the Lowestoft batsmen, with his eight overs just going for 18 runs.

Chris Pyer bowled Aldred for 29 and Brice finally reached his century in the final over.

Walsham battled hard but in the heat and the large outfield it was hard work as Lowestoft finished on 231-3 from their 40 overs.

After tea Walsham had to get off to a good start to make a game of it, but Scales unluckily played on for two in the first over and things went from bad to worse as the Walsham batsmen found it almost impossible to play the youthful Lowestoft attack.

Once the two opening bowlers had finished their five over spells Walsham were 32-8.

Chris Woods then took charge and started attacking the Lowestoft bowling and with Chris Pyer added 41 for the ninth wicket.

Woods continued the good work when Alex Evans came to the crease and another 49 was added before Woods was finally out caught behind of Bishop for an excellent 62.

Walsham were all out for 122, but it was a crushing defeat. Upton Man of the Match: Chris Woods.

SOUTH WALSHAM had two excellent victories against Belhus, a team from Essex on Friday, by five wickets, and defeated Bradenham on Sunday by four wickets in two very entertaining friendlies.

The Belhus match saw the visitors batting first in a 40 over match and they got off to a steady start before Garth Futter dismissed both openers, caught by the wicket-keeper. Belhus increased the run rate and on a good wicket and fast outfield the Walsham bowlers were struggling. K Whisker (116) and T Thompson (37) added 108 for the fifth wicket, and although Jack Belton picked up two late wickets, Belhus' total of 250-7 in their 40 overs was quite a formidable one.

Openers Andy Scales and Keith Denton really got after the Belhus bowling, reaching the 100 partnership in just 11 overs. Denton was batting very fluently and it was a bit of a surprise when he gave a catch to point when on 51. Andy Scales soon followed for 50 but Neil Johnson by then was in his stride, hitting the ball to all parts, before falling for 65.

Walsham had maintained a pretty impressive run rate as Garth Futter 27 not out and Woods 12 not out saw Walsham home with more than five overs to spare.

Upton White Horse MoM: Keith Denton for his fluent half century.

On Sunday, Bradenham batted first and were soon in trouble thanks to some excellent bowling from Paul Woods who took 2-32 from nine overs.

The Bradenham No 4 M Hunter took control, hitting 84 before he was well held in the deep by Andy Scales. It was Scales' day in the field as he ran out three batsmen, two with direct hits, as well as taking two catches. Gilbert and Hollis kept things tight in the bowling department and when the declaration came at 180-8 Walsham were well pleased with their afternoon's work.

Walsham openers Watkins and Scales found it difficult to get the ball away on a damp pitch. They finally broke free, adding 40 before Watkins was caught for 10. Scales and Neil Johnson then took complete charge of the game, adding 92 for the second wicket before Scales went for one big hit too many and was caught for 52. Johnson fell in the next over for 55 and Walsham slipped from 132-1 to 135-6.

Skipper Woods and Garth Futter then pulled things back Walsham's way with an excellent stand of 49 to give Walsham victory by four wickets with three balls to spare.

Upton White Horse MoM: Andy Scales good batting, brilliant fielding.

Home start to season for Walsham

SOUTH Walsham CC are due to start their 2008 campaign with a home game against Halvergate on Sunday.

The squad for the season remains largely the same with three players, Alex Evans, Dave Watkins and Garth Futter, clocking up over 30 years service and another three Neil Johnson, Andy Scales and Richard Whiteside over 20 years.

It is hoped they don't suffer the number of injuries they had last year, with Neil Johnson and Chris Pyer out all season, while Andy Scales and Jon Moore both missed a part of the season with cricket-related injuries.

Batting should be okay, bowling will be spin and guile rather than pace while fielding will be good in parts.

Paul Woods takes over from Greg Loades as captain, with Greg now working away, which might affect his availability.

All the other officers in the club were re-elected at the AGM and there was a big thank you in particular to Dave Watkins who continues to produce an excellent wicket.

It is tour year this year, with Walsham off to Kent in late July to play five games in the Margate area. This is Walsham's 16th tour since the first one to Sussex in 1974.

Sponsors were thanked for continuing to support the club – Ray Norman, the president at the Upton White Horse, and Eastern Telephones.

Latest news can be found on the web site www.southwalsham.play-cricket.com

Friendly victory for Walsham

SOUTH Walsham managed to beat a young Lowestoft side by 95 runs in a friendly played at home.

Walsham batted first and were soon in trouble against the excellent bowling of the Brice brothers who had the top order in all sorts of trouble. At 26 for five the game looked like finishing early but skipper Paul Woods pulled a master stroke by promoting Greg Loades up the order with orders to hang around for 20 overs, this Loades did with great aplomb and once the opening attack finished their spells batting became a little easier.

Loades with Kevin Gilbert added 35 for the sixth wicket, Loades then opened out a little and with the help of Jack Belton added 64 for the seventh wicket with Belton scoring his highest score for the club with 23.

Loades was finally bowled by B Brice who was back for a second spell for an excellent 53, his first 50 for the club. Garth Futter then took over in typical fashion with some lusty blows, scoring 34 not out. The tail hung around as Walsham, with the help of a few extras as well, were able to lift their score to a respectable 187 all out. Lowestoft bowler B Brice was a most impressive bowler taking 7-29 from 14.5 overs.

After tea the young Lowestoft batting line up were soon in trouble against the steady Walsham bowlers with both Loades and Futter picking up an early wicket. T Brice batted well for a while adding 31 before he was well caught by Loades at mid-wicket.

Loades then took two more mid-wicket catches in quick succession as Lowestoft slipped to 50 for five. Garth Futter reached 600 wickets for the club as he took three for 15 while Chris Woods was whipped off after two maidens following three more quick wickets. Lowestoft slipped to 67 for nine and despite a spirited last-wicket stand of 25 Lowestoft were well beaten in the end. Jack Belton had an excellent all-round game, taking 2-15.

Upton White Horse MoM: Greg Loades.

Denton hits out but it's not enough

SOUTH Walsham suffered another defeat, at the hands of Billingford.

Walsham batted first and lost Watkins, fourth ball of the game for nought. Johnson and Paul Woods quickly followed and at 18-3 Walsham were in trouble.

Former skipper Keith Denton, playing one of his rare games these days, and the ever-reliable Chris Woods added 59 for the fourth wicket before Woods went for 17.

Denton finally fell for 60 when the score had just passed the hundred mark and with 25 from Richard Whiteside and 21 from Jonny Moore and a few boundaries from Garth Futter and Kevin Gilbert, Walsham posted a reasonable score of 183 all out about 10 minutes before the normal tea interval.

After tea Billingford got off to a steady start with A Lake and J Bidewell coping well with the Walsham attack adding 68 for the first wicket.

Not for the first time this season Chris Woods slowed the run rate and immediately took the first wicket with Bidewell well stumped by Whiteside for 38.

The run rate was maintained and the Walsham bowlers were a little out of sorts as Billingford kept control of the game with Lake scoring 50 and Websdale 30.

Chris Woods took 2-22 from 12 overs while Ollie James picked up 2-27, but the Walsham bowlers were never able to put enough pressure on the batsmen and Billingford got home by four wickets with four overs to spare.

Upton White Horse Man of the Match: Keith Denton for his fine innings.

Gilbert is star man

SOUTH Walsham and Aylsham St Giles enjoyed an excellent game at South Walsham on Sunday. Batting first Walsham were soon on the back foot, losing Keith Denton to the second ball of the game. Neil Johnson and Dave Watkins quickly put things right adding 70 for the second wicket before Johnson went for 36. Paul Woods played a typical attacking innings with 12 boundaries in his 70, while Watkins 26, Chris Woods 20 and a quick 46-run stand between Kevin Gilbert and Steve Hollis lifted the score to 217-6 declared at tea.

After tea, the Aylsham St Giles openers found runs easy to come by against the Walsham bowlers and quickly added 64 in the first 15 overs. Pegg went for 32 and Cocks for 10 both falling to catches behind the wicket, but it was Bingham who was proving difficult to remove as he crashed the ball to all parts.

Aylsham looked as though they were going to win the game at a canter when Keith Denton finally bowled him for 109. From then on wickets began to fall as Aylsham tried to maintain their chase.

It wasn't until they lost their ninth wicket and with two overs to go that they played defensively and hung out for the draw. Kevin Gilbert was the star man with the ball with 4-46 from 14 overs, ably supported by Keith Denton with two for 23.

Upton White Horse man of the match: Kevin Gilbert for his accurate bowling when the ball was being hit to all parts.

Growing old gracefully:
Club with a rich heritage bucks league trend

Walsham determined to uphold traditions

A club which helped former England Test star John Edrich to cut his cricketing teeth is batting for an altogether more genteel aspect of the game.

For in these days of intense wall-to-wall league and cup cricket at every level South Walsham are a throwback to a bygone era. They have stoically maintained their long-held tradition of Sunday friendlies – with an onus on fair play and getting everybody involved.

Winning is encouraged but a win at all costs attitude is not. Many games are still played according to time and the honourable draw is still achievable.

Judging from the length of service of many of the players it's a formula that has worked well at South Walsham.

The list of hardy annuals includes Andy Scales, who has scored about 12,000 runs in 20 years, while club chairman John Vaughan had the satisfaction of passing the 10,000 runs milestone before retiring from playing.

Another club stalwart David Watkins, who has been turning out since 1974, has amassed 25,000 runs. Bowler Garth Futter, a regular since 1979, is now closing in on 600 wickets after passing the 470 milestone of previous club record holder Terry Ogden.

"We have got a squad of about 17 players," said Alex Evans, who has been playing since 1970 and has kept meticulous records since 1967.

"A lot of us are getting old together but we have got a few younger players who are the sons of existing members," "Every year we have a vote on whether we want to change things," said the 57-year-old veteran.

"We get invited into the Mid Norfolk Sunday League but it's always been decided that we want to carry on as we are."

The club has strong links with the famous Edrich cricketing family, including former England Test opener John Edrich.

"John Edrich played for us in 1953 when he was about 14 and lived in Blofield. We are mentioned in his autobiography," said Evans.

Former Walsham player Pat Hood had a bet with Ingham legend Jack Borrett that John Edrich would play for England by the time he was 21 but lost because John didn't play for the national team until he was 23. He went on to score 12 centuries in 77 Tests.

The club owes a huge debt to George Edrich who got a team together in 1948 after preparing the pitch which became his "pride and joy."

In the days before limited overs cricket Walsham would compete with many of the top clubs in the region.

Sometimes there would be six Edrich's in the side with Edwin Edrich umpiring and one of the Edrich wives doing the scoring.

Evans revealed that Walsham did have a brief flirtation with a more intense brand of cricket but decided it was not for them.

"We were in the first year of the Carter Cup. We bowled Sprowston out for about 50 and they then bowled us out for 25. We decided it was probably a bit too strong for us.

"We like our friendlies to be competitive though and we'll always go for the win rather than block out for the draw. We try to give everyone a game if we can."

Gentlemen and players: Two of Norfolk's finest, John Edrich, aged 16, left and Peter Parfitt.
Photo: EN LIBRARY

CHAPTER FORTY *Two Good Years - 2009/10*

Paul Woods continued as captain in 2009. He was clearly beginning to enjoy the job, was extremely enthusiastic and the responsibility never seemed to affect his batting or fielding. The only debutant was Markus Leak, son of former player Fred, who seemed to be an enthusiastic and talented young player. In the usual opener, against Halvergate, the rustiness showed as Walsham lost by 68 runs, managing only 132 - Watkins and Garth Futter getting into the forties - in response to Halvergate's 200-7. In a cracking match against St Andrews, Walsham hit an impressive 234-3, with fifties from Watkins and Scales, but could not contain the Saints' batsmen as they won by two wickets, despite a good spell from Gilbert (3-34 from seven overs).

The first win of the season came against Eaton. Three wickets from Futter restricted the opposition to 156-6 at tea and this was easily knocked off for the loss of four wickets led by Watkins (80*). There was a close 40-over game at Lowestoft. Walsham struggled to 128 and the hosts were looking well-placed at 60-2, but a good spell from part-timer Keith Denton (3-14 from 8 overs) and a tight spell from Garth Futter ensured that Lowestoft finished on 122-8 from their 40 overs to give Walsham victory by six runs. A 73-run win was gained against Billingford with a century from Johnson and good bowling from Futter. A fourth consecutive win - by two runs in a 40-over game - was achieved against Happisburgh. Walsham hit 204-5, with fifties from Scales and Watkins, and Jack Belton held his nerve to bowl the last over as the home side finished on 202-7.

Markus Leak made his debut against Old Catton and, after a bad start, Walsham recovered to 227-8, Gilbert (47) and Futter (71*) adding 101 for the seventh wicket. The Catton batsmen took the Walsham bowlers to task adding 121 for the first wicket and were always in control winning by eight wickets in the fortieth over. Another high-scoring game saw Aylsham St Giles try to chase down the Walsham score of 213-7 (Futter 58*). They got off to a great start, but a lower-order collapse against the bowling of Gilbert and Dan Scales saw them slip from 110-1 to 191-7, the game finishing in a draw. It was five wins out of six when Southtown could only muster 156-7 in 40 overs. Watkins (77) led the way to a six-wicket victory in just 32 overs.

A magnificent 109 from Paul Woods was the highlight of a total of 233-6 against Lowestoft and three wickets for Dan Scales led Walsham to victory as the opposition collapsed from 112-4 to 149 all out. Another 40-over game saw Walsham gain a rare victory at Billingford. Although only mustering 135 (Chris Woods 36), tight bowling particularly from Futter (2-6 in eight overs) saw Billingford restricted to 115-9. Regular Essex visitors, Belhus, controlled the next match as Walsham were disappointed to be dismissed for 173. It was never going to be enough as the tourists got home by three wickets despite a good effort from Futter (3-33). Aylsham St Giles could only manage 124-9 on a wet day, and a quick 50 from Johnson made sure of victory in just 32 overs.

Walsham totalled 180-3 in the home game against Southtown, although Johnson batted well with 85 not out. However, on a good track, the opposition batsmen made the total look very small as they won by eight wickets. A third game with Aylsham St Giles saw another Walsham victory after hitting 193-6 in a 40-over game, Paul Woods and Futter adding 81 for the seventh wicket to achieve a respectable total. Although wickets were hard to come by for the Walsham bowlers, Aylsham were never in it and finished on 158-4.

There was a tight affair against tourists Old Parkonians who looked a useful side when hitting 234-7. However, Walsham attacked from ball one and, despite the loss of two early wickets, Watkins, Denton and Paul Woods all made good contributions. A collapse from 188-4 to 216-9 ensured a nail-biting finish, but Futter and Evans held their nerve and - with Futter hitting and Evans blocking - the final twenty runs were scored to give Walsham victory. As usual, Walsham struggled on the Eaton track and were bowled out for 136, although it took the home side 43 overs to pass the total to win by seven wickets. Against Happisburgh, after only scoring 30 runs from the first fifteen overs, Walsham recovered to 221-8 which turned out to be too many for the opposition who reached 162-6 from 42 overs to secure the draw.

A game with Aldborough was arranged to cover for a called-off fixture and it proved a little unlucky for Chris Gould who hit the leg stump of opener Waters early in his innings. The bail stayed on and the batsman went on to score a valuable 73 not out in a total of 181. Walsham found the variable bounce difficult to handle, although a second wicket stand of 77 between

Andy Scales (55) and Chris Woods (31) opened up a chance. However, Denton got a grubber, and despite a quick 28 from Futter, Walsham finished fourteen runs short of victory in a tight finish. Against Crusaders, whose strength seemed to be in their batting, Walsham hit 238-4, Scales and Johnson both scoring 72. It looked like a draw until a clatter of wickets towards the end. Chris Woods bowling (5-62) and three excellent catches from Futter ensured that Crusaders were bowled out in the final over for 207.

Probably the highlight of the season was the day out at Castle Rising in the west of the county, transport courtesy of a minibus driven by one of the more responsible players. The day started for him around 11am, driving round half of Norfolk to pick up the squad and it was a good effort to arrive for a 2pm start. The game - a high scoring draw - was a good one. Walsham hit 244-7 with fifties from Denton and Watkins. On a good wicket and fast outfield the home side looked favourites, but Mallett (3-45) and two wickets each from Loades and Gould kept the batsmen in check. Indeed had one or two more catches been held, a draw might have been turned into victory as the home side finished on 226-8. The highlight of the day was an absolutely breathtaking catch from Richard Whiteside who managed to dive full length about ten yards from the bat to grasp a thunderous shot from a Castle Rising batsman. Of course, the day didn't end there; after a few drinks with the opposition, driver Mallett made his way to Dereham where the squad enjoyed themselves for a couple of hours in a very busy pub in the town centre, only leaving as it approached midnight. The heroic chauffeur finally got to bed after 2 am having seen the whole squad safely home.

In the penultimate match of the season Walsham were outclassed by Bradenham, who knocked off 172 for the loss of four wickets in just 25 overs. The final match was the usual President's game which turned out to be another excellent day climaxed when, at tea, President Ray Norman presented the club with a pavilion clock - a great gesture. As for the game, the President's side only made 177 (Gilbert 5-37). With Johnson (67) leading the reply, Walsham won the game easily before the traditional enjoyable evening in Upton White Horse.

In terms of results, it was a successful season: twelve wins and eight defeats from the twenty-three games completed. Watkins (744) topped the run charts with Johnson (668) and Scales (590) not far behind. Garth Futter had an outstanding year - topping the batting averages with 53.14 in scoring 372 runs, taking 26 wickets and 14 catches - and was deservedly player of the season. In the bowling department Kevin Gilbert took 24 wickets at an average of 15.04, while Paul Woods and Stewart Mallett both reached the 20 mark.

Paul Woods was deservedly re-elected as skipper for the 2010 season with Neil Johnson as his deputy. In the previous year, vice-skipper Chris Pyer had not been able to play much so he agreed to stand down. Unfortunately, the curse of the vice-skipper's job continued as Johnson only played seven games during 2010. It was a strange year for team secretary Garth Futter; sometimes he would have seventeen players available while, on other days, he would have only nine. David Jones was the only debutant of note, moving from Halvergate, while Markus Leak and Rob Burling played their first full seasons. Defeat against Halvergate by six wickets in the first match was followed by a cracking victory against St Andrews. This was the first game between the two clubs playing for the Ian Gilmore Trophy. Ian had been a Saints player for many years but, sadly, had died of cancer. He had always enjoyed his games against Walsham, so it seemed appropriate that the two clubs should compete for a trophy in his name every season. The Saints scored 193-9 with soon-to-be Walsham tourist Keith Hunt hitting 82, although another future tourist - Louis Bellchamber - was dismissed for a duck. Andy Scales was in great form in reply, hitting 100 not out as Walsham won comfortably by seven wickets to take the trophy.

With only ten players against Eaton on a miserable day, the opposition posted 193-3, far too many for a weakened Walsham side. Jack Belton showed promise in the struggle to draw at 110-5. John Chilvers also remembers that day *'the inhuman weather in the game at South Walsham in 2009 - I umpired with five layers, woolly hat, scarf and gloves. Only two bunches of lunatics would have played cricket in those conditions; perhaps that says it all.'* In rather more clement conditions, Hemsby scored 150 (Dan Scales 4-48), but it was never enough as Chris Woods (55) led a successful chase to a five-wicket victory. Happisburgh edged to a two-wicket win as they chased down Walsham's total of 175-9, although Dan Scales shone again with 3-35. The first game against Horsford for many years ended in a draw, as Walsham hit 208-6 (Scales 63). In reply, Horsford struggled to 137-6.

The return game with St Andrews was played in miserable conditions as

Scales hit 60 not out in a total of 168-7. Had it not been for Louis Bellchamber it would have been enough, but the young left-hander hit 139 not out in their reply of 169-6. No other batsmen passed 10 as Futter and Mallett took five wickets between them, but the Saints regained the Ian Gilmore Trophy. In an enjoyable game against Sprowston, they scored 211 all out and, despite 56 from Paul Woods, Walsham slipped to a narrow defeat being bowled out for 190. Southtown turned up with just nine men and suffered for it as Walsham scored 202-4 with a fifth wicket stand of 101 between Whiteside and Chris Woods. Southtown made a really good effort, but were bowled out for 175.

An entertaining draw against Old Catton followed, Walsham hitting 246-2, with Johnson thrashing 113 and Watkins 88 not out. Catton replied with 232-7 with another three wickets for Futter. Aylsham St Giles looked odds on winners when they scored 252-4 and had Walsham 5-3, but Paul Woods counter-attacked and hit a brilliant 116 before Gould and Mallett were left to block out the last five overs to draw the game on 185-9. On another super batting wicket, touring side Belhus declared on 221-4, but it was nowhere near enough as Paul Woods (80) and Denton (71*) saw Walsham home in just 26 overs to record a five-wicket win. The return fixture with Hemsby was very similar to the first; they scored 158 with an excellent bowling spell from Markus Leak, but fifties from Watkins and Scales saw Walsham win easily by eight wickets.

An equal-score draw followed against Crusaders. Jack Belton hit 71 - his highest score for the club and his first fifty - out of a total of 207-5, but some wayward bowling made the game a bit closer than it should have been, as the opposition finished on the same total with eight wickets down. A similar game followed against Sprowston, as Walsham were bowled out for 188, Paul Woods top-scoring. Sprowston responded with 184-8 with more wayward bowling leading to lots of extras. Dan Scales impressed again with a four-wicket haul.

Probably the lowest point of the season came in the next game, away at Eaton, in a crushing 90-run defeat. They managed 149-9 from 49 overs with Markus Leak (3-17) bowling very well. In reply, the Walsham batting failed completely and collapsed to 59 all out. The batting struggled again in the next match, as only three Walsham players managed double figures. Luckily,

Andy Scales and Paul Woods both hit sixties in a total of 197. However, lots of dropped catches meant that Happisburgh won the game by six wickets, despite a good bowling spell from Futter (3-26).

After a successful tour of Northampton, it was back to Norfolk to play Felthorpe and another failure to muster enough runs, being bowled out for 155. Felthorpe won the game with five wickets down and eight balls to spare. The next game was probably the best win of the season. With several members of the squad unavailable for various reasons, Walsham turned up at Aylsham St Giles with just ten players, including the now semi-retired author and Steve Belton who had not played for two years. Fielding first and battling well, Jones and Mallett took two wickets apiece in Aylsham's total of 194-7. After sixteen overs Walsham were struggling on 30-4, with a total of around 120 the best that could be expected. However, Belton looked as though he had never been away and, when he was joined by Paul Woods, they turned the game on its head, adding an amazing 162 in just 22 overs, creating a new fifth-wicket club record. The game was won by four wickets with an over to spare, Woods finishing on 99 not out and Belton 55. What a game!

Woods certainly deserved a century, but he made up for it in the next game scoring 100 not out in the Walsham total of 205-9 against St Andrews. The Saints were never in the game, but battled out to draw on 49-8 from 44 overs and retain the Ian Gilmore Trophy. As usual, the final fixture was another fantastic day with the President's side taking the honours in a drawn game. They scored 257-3 with a century from Neil Johnson and 95 from tourist Keith Hunt. Walsham were soon struggling at 6-3, but a maiden half-century from Jones and runs from Scales and Futter meant that Walsham, probably undeservedly, held on to draw on 205-9. Another great evening followed down at the White Horse, with a few speeches and much alcohol!

The season's statistics: nine wins, nine draws and seven defeats in the twenty-five games completed. Paul Woods had an excellent season scoring 761 runs at 42.28, Andy Scales scored 663 at 34.89 while David Watkins and Chris Woods also passed 400 runs. As usual, the wickets were shared around: Garth Futter took 30 at 21.77, while Stewart Mallett took 27 at 22.44. Dan Scales and Markus Leak both showed a lot of promise to finish first and second in the averages.

CHAPTER FORTY ONE *Not The End Of The Story...2011/12*

Paul Woods continued as skipper in 2011, for an almost unprecedented fourth season. He enjoyed the role and was good at it, involving all the players but still trying to win games. It was a year when the weather was kind: all twenty-six games were started, although the home match against Sprowston was rained off at the halfway point.

The first game was a surprising win over Halvergate, always regarded as a warm-up occasion. Halvergate recovered from a poor start to record a respectable 173 and Walsham also lost early wickets, with the usually prolific Watkins and Scales both being run out. The game seemed to be drifting towards a draw when Paul Woods suddenly started hitting the ball to all parts with an amazing 99 not out to force a win by four wickets. Watkins scored a century in the next match against St Andrews, but the rest of the batting struggled to total 193. Yet again, this probably would have been enough had Louis Bellchamber not been in the St Andrews side; he hit 122 to win the game by five wickets. The usual early-season draw occurred against Eaton with Chris and Paul Woods as well as Stewart Mallett all hitting half-centuries before Eaton finished on 159-7.

In a 40-over match with Felthorpe, Andy Scales led the way with 103 in a massive 251-9. Walsham were always in control, Felthorpe finishing on 193-9. However, Sprowston proved to be too strong as Walsham struggled to 143, which would have been worse had youngsters Dan Scales and Markus Leak not added 36 for the last wicket. Sprowston coasted home by five wickets. Andy Scales (65) and Garth Futter (45) ensured that Walsham passed the 200 mark against Happisburgh and it was just enough in a 40-over game as the opposition finished on 190-6. A 40-over game against Old Catton saw another victory, Paul Woods hitting 62 as Walsham won by five wickets.

Another three wins followed: revenge against St Andrews by five wickets with a strong all-round performance from Paul Woods; a good chase to overhaul Hemsby's 192 with Scales (49) and Keith Denton (52*) helping in a six-wicket win; and a comfortable success against a youthful Thetford Saxons side as Scales made 90 in a score of 208-4. The return match with Old Catton was drawn, but Walsham took a hammering against Aylsham St Giles. Mustering only 165-9 on a good wicket, the opposition won with ease in 34 overs and by eight wickets. The usual enjoyable game with Belhus ended in victory, Robert Bean (106*), more well known in South Walsham Football Club circles, scoring his first century for the club in a total of 211-5 when chasing the tourists' 207-6 declared.

Horsford proved too strong and won by 54 runs, despite a battling 84 not out from Andy Scales who carried his bat through the innings. 2010 tourists Keith Hunt and Louis Bellchamber helped out with fifties as Speldhurst - a touring side from Kent - were beaten by seven wickets. Fifties from Watkins, Denton and Paul Woods provided the basis for a win against Felthorpe by 73 runs, but Walsham lost narrowly to Eaton when attempting to chase down 200. The opposition bowlers Luke Billington and Michael Barker proved to be the difference as Walsham lost by 17 runs, despite another fifty from Scales. The scores finished level against Happisburgh; both sides made 177-7, Kevin Gilbert's late burst of 4-27 saving Walsham from defeat. A very young team, by Walsham standards, turned out against touring side Kibworth who recovered from a poor start to post 153. Walsham also started well, but fell away to 139 all out, despite an excellent 49 from youngster Will Jennings.

Caleb Futter, son of Kim and nephew of Garth, hit his first half-century for the club against Southwold in a score of 220-5; the Suffolk opposition were unable to match this and were dismissed for 130. There was an exciting game against Buxton as Walsham hit 204-6 declared. After a poor start, these new opponents recovered - Bunn hitting 77 - but another collapse saw Walsham home by 22 runs, Garth Futter taking 4-26. A rain-affected draw with Thetford Saxons was followed by a poor defeat against Acle when Walsham could only muster 111.

The season finished in its usual way against Ray Norman's President's XI, strengthened by Keith Hunt from Drayton and Tom Booth from Norwich. The President's side scored 250-8, Hunt hitting 124 and Gilbert 32. Walsham recovered from a very poor start and, with Scales and Bean adding 188 for the sixth wicket, the side came to the brink of victory, but Booth (5-25) and Gilbert (3-49) ensured that Walsham finished twelve runs short with one wicket left. As ever, the day was not all about the cricket. 'President Ray', put on his usual excellent spread and the drinking and merriment went on into the early hours. At the AGM in October, Ray was elected Honorary Life President, a well-deserved tribute which was much appreciated by the recipient.

It had been a successful season: twelve wins, five draws and eight defeats. Andy Scales (707) led the run-scoring, while David Watkins (628) and Paul Woods (569) also scored heavily. In addition, Keith Denton and Jack Belton both made over 200, but there were a few batting collapses when the main men failed or were unavailable. Stewart Mallett, usually regarded as a bowler, scored his first two half-centuries for the club as well as taking 23 wickets and these performances led him to be recognised as the player of the year. Markus Leak, just sixteen, was the highest wicket-taker with 33 - an excellent effort from a young bowler - while veteran Chris Woods took 24 and David Jones 19. Garth Futter claimed 17 victims as he approached ever closer to 700 wickets for the club.

President's Day 2012

In 2012, after four seasons of Paul Woods' leadership, the captaincy passed to David Jones. He had only been with the club for a couple of seasons, having previously played for Halvergate, but had quickly fitted in with the ways of South Walsham. No new players joined the club but, with Richard Whiteside and Robert Bean not playing at all and Neil Johnson turning out for only one game, the batting was fragile. However, the main problem with 2012 was the weather: seven games were called off, one game was abandoned after twenty overs and two more were cancelled by opponents unable to raise a side. Even in a tour year, Walsham played just twenty-one games, winning six, drawing five and losing ten, albeit two games by just one run.

Only one game was played in an exceptionally wet April. Halvergate had much the better of a draw, Walsham finishing on 128-6 chasing 208-4. After being soundly beaten by both Felthorpe and Old Catton, Andy Scales led the way with a magnificent 121 in a total of 201-8 against Happisburgh who held on for the draw on 166-8. One of the best performances saw Sprowston beaten as Walsham chased down 213, Scales and Keith Denton both hitting half-centuries.

One game almost certainly shouldn't have been played. With Chris Gould captaining for the first time, Luddenham - a touring side from Leicestershire - were entertained to a 20-over game despite the incessant rain. Scales and Watkins stayed 'in the hutch' as Walsham chased 130 for victory, finishing on 128-6 to lose by one run. The tourists were very appreciative of the efforts to stage a game and a good time was had by all in the White Horse! The second win of the season came against another touring side Brasted and Sunridge Exiles from Kent. They were not strong and nine bowlers were used as they were dismissed for 147. Walsham were in trouble at 86-6, but an unbroken partnership of 66 between Scales and Gould ultimately produced a comfortable victory.

A narrow, two-wicket defeat at Southwold was followed by a close draw with Bradenham. The match with Mattishall was an exciting affair. Walsham posted 222-5, Watkins and Scales hitting fifties, and all seemed under control as they moved steadily along to 146-6. However, M. Taylor came in and smashed seventy in no time to win the game with two balls to spare. Old Catton again proved to be too strong as Walsham held on for the draw with eight wickets down and this was followed by another poor performance and defeat against Felthorpe.

It was tour year - Leicestershire in early August - but returning to Norfolk, Walsham were thwarted from gaining a victory by the last pair at St Andrews - a fifty from Denton and four wickets from Jones were the highlights. Probably the most amazing game of the year, was Walsham's first-ever visit to Elsing. Batting first, the home side scored 161 on a wicket which could politely be described as 'variable'. With a weakened side, it was going to be an uphill struggle and so it proved with Walsham on 95-9. Enter new skipper Jones: in four overs he hit 46 not out. The home side were getting edgy when Dan Scales called for a reasonable single which Jones turned down - Scales junior was run out and Walsham lost by ten runs. However, the response was two wins - against Bradenham and Aylsham St Giles - with 66 from Paul Woods against Bradenham and 82 not out from Andy Scales against Aylsham.

As usual, the final fixture was the President's game. In the previous fortnight, President Ray had finally retired after thirty years as landlord of the Upton White Horse, so the main festivities took place at the ground before we returned to the pub for a few more beers.

The match was a exciting with Keith Hodds and Fred Leak rolling back the years to put on 78 for the first wicket. The amazing Hodds scored 50 before 'retiring tired'; only a couple of years earlier, he had been at death's door with a serious illness and his innings delighted his friends who were so pleased to see him well and cheery. The President's side hit 236-8, Walsham's reply slipping to 45-6, before Woods and Denton added 122 for the seventh wicket. The innings fell away again in another 'magic moment' from the near-heroes of Elsing, as Jones and Dan Scales, running a quick single, managed to crash into each other and Jones was left flattened by the considerably slimmer Scales junior. The President's side was victorious by one run!

The statistics of the season didn't make great reading, except for Andy Scales who scored a magnificent 740 runs at 46.2. Keith Denton hit 246 in his eight innings, while only Paul Woods (533) and David Watkins (236) also passed the 200 mark. The wickets were well spread: Stewart Mallett took 29, David Jones 25 and Chris Woods topped the averages with 20 at 18.3.

CHAPTER FORTY TWO *Still Touring But Rather Less Boisterously*

The club maintained its tradition of a biennial tour throughout the first decade of the new century. However, as the squad aged, the 'antics' of earlier years - without ever disappearing altogether - did begin to subside. The Belvoir Valley (Leicestershire) was the setting for the first adventure of the third millennium, billeting in a country hotel/pub close to Belvoir Castle. The side were completely outclassed in the first match, managing only 136-7 (Vaughan 52) against Belvoir who made quick work of winning inside 31 overs and losing just three wickets. The second match was a 20-over evening contest - always rather 'unpredictable' when the squad have all day to test the local hostelries. However, in a good performance against Croxton Kerrial, Scales (38) led the way to a total of 136-7; the opposition only managed 117-6 in reply. Outclassed again in the third match against Egerton Park, Walsham made a modest 162, no-one passing 40; the hosts replied with 166-1 in 35 overs.

Dave Watkins celebrating his 10,000th run in 2000

In the Thursday game at Bottersford, the opposition scored 187-6 and Walsham were struggling on 94-4 but recovered to 150-6 (Watkins 59*) to secure a draw. However, the highlight of the game was the celebration for David Watkins as he passed 10,000 runs for the club. It was a night to remember as he consumed all sorts of coloured drinks and, in many ways, it was fortunate that he reached the milestone when on tour, as leading the school assembly the following morning in his capacity as a headteacher could have been problematic had this happened in term-time. The 'lively' evening meant only the driver was unable to join in the merriment as he negotiated the minibus down the narrow country lanes on a foggy night.

Being based in the country rather than close to a big town did limit opportunities to enjoy late-night festivities. The final game was a fun 18-over contest against Pedigree Foods, Walsham making 128-3 and always being in control as the hosts finished on 102-9. Indeed the degree of control was such that the author, in his thirty first season, was given the final over and took the second wicket of his Walsham career.

Wiltshire in 2002: based in the army town of Warminister, which was rather more lively in the evenings than the rural

South Walsham Touring Party to Wiltshire 2002

environs of Belvoir Castle two years earlier. The first game, against the town club, was not particularly satisfactory, as they turned up with just seven players. Having not been selected, Garth Futter and the author had adjourned to a local pub and wandered up to the game late, only to be told they were playing for the opposition. Both were able to provide advice to the Warminister side and took catches, Futter also claiming two wickets, as Walsham were dismissed for 146. However, once the author had been dismissed early in the innings, Warminster had little trouble knocking off the runs.

In the next game against Trowbridge, who fielded two Australian professionals, Walsham battled hard to reach a total of 135. Pennington struck with two early wickets and Trowbridge were in trouble at 106-8, but one of the Aussie pros ensured their win without further loss of wickets. Moving on to Devizes, on a very wet day, the hosts were keen to play and this was possible by using their all-weather wicket in a 30-over contest. Their ground had very small boundaries and Walsham's 201-6 was never enough, the home side winning the game in the twentieth over. They were excellent hosts - many clubs would have just called the game off - and a good night was had by all.

On the Thursday, the opposition were Westbury, the game being played on one of Wiltshire's county grounds. They scored 231-7 in 40 overs and, despite Watkins hitting 74, Walsham only managed 190-7. Once again, Garth Futter was loaned to the opposition and he responded by bowling out Watkins! The final game at Frome produced a win by 29 runs, Johnson hitting 75 out of a total of 205 and Frome replying with 178-6 in their 40 overs. The weather had generally been good and all five games had been played - another excellent tour organised by Terry Ogden.

Yorkshire 2004 - with the base at The Crown in Harrogate - a very wet week in which only two games were played: on the first day and a 20-over game on the Friday. It was disappointing that the host clubs made no attempt to put on some kind of game rather than leaving the squad to kick their heels.

However, a trip to Derby gave the opportunity to watch the West Indies play Derbyshire. For entertainment, the squad decided to 'adopt' a West Indian spinner called 'Dave' and, in a half-empty ground, gave him a howl of approval every time he touched the ball much to his astonishment and amusement of others. Both games that were played were won. The only full contest of the week was against a young Alltofts side, who bowled out Walsham for 175 in 40 overs. Despite a good start, they fell behind the clock and finished on 148-9 to lose by 27 runs. In the 20-over game on the way home at Stamford, Walsham scored a respectable 123-7 and soon had the hosts in trouble as Garth Futter took 5-5 in 4 overs. They never recovered and limped along to 99-6.

For Essex 2006, the squad was based in Chelmsford but, thankfully, the weather was kinder than it had been two years earlier in Yorkshire. In the first match Walsham scored 244 all out against Hadleigh and Thundersley, with an excellent maiden century for Graham Yallop but, as the final two batsmen walked off the field, it was thought that this was about sixty runs short of a decent total on a good wicket and a small ground. This proved to be an accurate assessment as the home side raced to victory in only 34 overs to win the game by seven wickets.

The second game included a fine example of the art of captaincy by the Ardleigh Green skipper. The home side scored 206-4 and, in reply, Walsham got to 136-2, but the home skipper kept dangling the carrot to keep Walsham going for the win. Jon Fudge hit a splendid 83 as Walsham finished on 197-7 - a draw, but an excellent game of cricket. Walsham proved to be too strong in a first visit to the home of regular Norfolk tourists, Broomfield Hospital. On a difficult track, they were dismissed for 114, Yallop (47) helping Walsham to a seven-wicket victory. Belhus - also annual visitors to Norfolk - were the hosts in another tight run chase. They hit 204-6 and, after recovering from 84-6, Yallop and Paul Woods added 96 for the seventh wicket to lead Walsham to a one wicket win. Veteran Kim Futter hit the winning single in the final over. Another great match!

Dave Watkins in full flow in 2006

The final game of the 2006 tour was against a useful side of experienced cricketers from Brentwood Victorians. They scored 229-9 as Walsham struggled to keep the runs down, but all was set up for a good chase. Again, the home skipper was very experienced and was quite happy to encourage Walsham to go for the runs. It all fell apart when one of the tourists, who will remain nameless but no longer plays for the club, batted for eighteen overs for a score of less than twenty. Falling behind the required run rate and causing the other batsmen to fling the bat, 188 all out was a sad end to a brilliant tour. The home skipper weighed up the situation and we had a good evening, but many of the Walsham players remained disappointed about the way the day had gone.

Kent 2008: based in Margate with a large squad of twenty - the usual regular Walsham tourists plus Jon Fudge, Kim and Caleb Futter, Ed Marjoram and John Pennington. The first game was against Minister who batted in very cavalier style and were bowled out for 198 in just 32 overs, Garth Futter and Jon Fudge taking seven wickets between them. However, Walsham were never in the hunt, subsiding to 109, with no one passing the twenty mark.

The second game against a quality Sandwich side was no better. They fielded two overseas players, including a West Indian called Leroy Johnson who was to play for West Indies 'A' against England a few months later. Luckily, against Walsham, he bowled off only two paces! They were a class side up against a village team, and despite excellent spin bowling from Loades and Pyer which kept some control, still reached 242-5 from 40 overs. After tea, the bowling and fielding standards were much higher than normal for Walsham games and, not surprisingly, the side were close to embarrassment at 57-6. However, Jon Fudge hung in with 52 and a late flurry from Pyer saw the reply reach 115-8 at the close.

The size of the squad caused a few headaches for team selector Garth Futter and the side were not at its strongest when playing Goodnestone Park. It was a game that might have been won; the opposition made only 183-9, but the Walsham batting collapsed from 86-2 to 139 all out, only Watkins and Johnson making an impression. The best game of the tour was at Mersham, as Walsham scored 212-5 with 72 not out from Fudge and some big hitting by Paul Woods and Hollis. The home side batted in an enterprising manner as the game was kept open and they required fifteen runs to win with two wickets and two overs left. Both teams went for the win, but Mersham finished on 204-9 in a very honourable draw. Caleb Futter, aged twelve, played his first game and looked a very useful performer. In the final game, Walsham only managed to make 164 against Chestfield when it might have been 200 and the hosts cruised home by seven wickets.

Unbelievably, Andy Scales dived to try and stop the winning boundary and broke his collar bone, which put him out of action for the second consecutive season. Abandoning the end-of-tour festivities, he was driven straight back to A&E at the Norfolk and Norwich University Hospital. The phone call to his wife, Margaret, was a little difficult; until she arrived at the hospital, she wasn't convinced that she was not the victim of a tour hoax.

This mishap aside, it had been an excellent tour. This may seem a strange statement as, unusually, Walsham had failed to win a game. In addition, Margate was not a place to which anyone would rush back and the accommodation could generously be described as 'modest' - a local café was found that offered superior breakfasts. However, socially, it had been an enjoyable week: the squad peaked early on Monday evening, drinking at a Margate pub of dubious reputation, although all made it back to the hotel safely while, at Goodnestone Park, the entertainment in a local pub involved some of the younger players in dressing up - which they seemed to enjoy!

Northampton 2010: an area Walsham had toured some twenty years earlier, but it was thought to be long enough for the locals

South Walsham Touring Party to Northampton 2010

to have forgotten! The party of nineteen contained the usual suspects, plus David Jones for the first time and three guests: Keith Hunt from St Andrews, Louis Bellchamber , who was enjoying success in senior cricket with Horsford and Robert Bean from Ashmanhaugh. The first game was against Newbold-on-Avon in Warwickshire. They were a mixture of youth and older players but soon reduced Walsham to 7-2, whereupon Bellchamber (125) and Hunt (43) compiled a record third wicket partnership of 158 to secure a 40 overs total of 237-5. In response, Newbold reached 156-1, but they slipped behind the run rate and, as they tried to attack, wickets began to fall. David Jones and Bellchamber picked up three wickets each as they slipped to 195 all out. The second game, against Abington, saw another record broken as the team made a highest ever score of 297-6 from 40 overs, with another century from Bellchamber and fifty from Denton. In reply, it was always going to be hard for the home side, particularly as they slipped to 3-2. Chris Gould took 3-38, but it was Stewart Mallett who was man-of-the-match with 5-36 as Abington were bowled out for 174.

The best game of the week was against West Haddon. Like all tour games, you never know what you are going to get. However, the opposition set the scene when they rang a few days earlier to ask if this set of tourists could drink a barrel of real ale. The challenge was taken up and the barrel was finished about 6pm - well before the game was completed! Meanwhile, on the field, the home side were dismissed for 215, Paul Woods chipping in with four wickets. Their bowlers were determined to make it tough for the Walsham batsmen, but Hunt (60), Bellchamber (55) and a late dash from Denton (49 not out), which included a six from the fourth ball of the final over, saw Walsham home by five wickets. A great game followed by an excellent evening: lots of drinking, a few songs and a few games leaving the West Haddon secretary wishing he had got in a second barrel. Needless to say, they were also running short of lager and cider by the end of the evening!

It was then off to Great Houghton on a rather damp day, for a time game, in which the hosts made 194-9 (Futter 4-38). The reply was a struggle, but Walsham finished on 148-8 to secure the draw. The final game at New Bradwell was all but rained off. Despite great efforts from the home side, a 20-over game was attempted but was abandoned. It had been a great tour, enjoyed by the whole squad.

South Walsham Touring Party to Market Harborough 2012

It was off to Leicestershire in 2012. A decision had been made not to travel too far and Market Harborough turned out to be a good choice. The weather in 2012 had been nothing short of awful, so the squad was concerned that the tour might be a washout as it assembled at the usual breakfast stop at Red Lodge on the A11. All the usual suspects were there, supplemented by the youth policy of the younger Scales and Leak, although it was disappointing to be without Denton and Bean, and also 'President Ray' who was unwell.

The Three Swans turned out to be an excellent base and Market Harborough also had a good selection of other pubs, all of which were visited by the squad, sometimes into the early hours. Monday was grey in the village of

Great Glen where the opposition turned out to be a super bunch. Invited to bat first with a wet, slow outfield but on a good wicket, Walsham scored 163-2 from 41 overs, Scales top scoring with fifty. Skipper Jones declared and seemed to have got it right when opposition wickets fell regularly, as they slipped to 118-7. However, a mixture of good batting and lacklustre bowling and fielding saw the home side fight back, the eighth wicket pair seeing their side home with three overs to spare. A lively night followed in their clubhouse after what had been an excellent day.

On Tuesday, the local hostelries were given a good airing as Fleckney had called off in the morning. It had rained overnight and it was not unduly surprising when the call came. Ed Marjoram showed up a day late, making excuses about collecting thousands of eggs, and got the party started having brought a chicken outfit with him. Greg Loades and Dan Scales were early victims, wandering around looking rather silly. The third day saw a visit to Kibworth, a very big club in the area.

There was a county second XI game between Leicestershire and Northants on the adjoining ground, as Walsham were entertained by a young Kibworth side. At 31-6, the hosts were in trouble, but two of their youngsters scored fifties and they reached respectability at 186-8. In reply, despite losing two early wickets, all was plain sailing at 141-2 and 168-3. The opposition had all but given up as they brought on a 'lob' bowler. He proceeded to take 5-1 and Walsham were dismissed for 174. Disappointment was an understatement; the squad was unusually quiet, most of the opposition had gone home and, although we made an effort with the fines, the mood was sombre.

The third game was against the village of Cosby. Like Great Glen, they were very much part of the community and it was a pleasure to play against them. They went off 'like a train' and it looked as though Walsham would be chasing over 250. However, Chris Woods came on and immediately slowed the run rate taking 4-20 from ten overs, before they declared on 181-9. All looked rosy in an excellent opening partnership of 130 between Scales senior and Woods junior, both of whom hit fifties before being stumped, but another batting collapse ensued. Fortunately, Keith Hunt steadied the ship to secure a three-wicket win. Visiting the local hostelry, not for the first time the bar staff became confused with our watering can, selling litres when they thought they were selling pints. The barman was almost apologetic about charging for five pints, when he had supplied five litres; Walsham cricketers are too polite to argue!

The final game was really out in the sticks, at Gumley. All through the week, when we mentioned Gumley to the locals, their comment was, *'you're going to Gumley, then?'* and smiled. We had heard there was a road running through the ground, quite close to the square; cars would wait until the end of the over and then come through. We thought it would just be the odd car but it was quite a regular occurrence. Gumley had let it be known they only had eight players, so we gave them our 'youth policy': the junior members of the Leak, Scales and Belton families. None of them troubled the scorers too much as Gumley scored a reasonable total of 169-8, but Dan Scales was really fired up as he cleared out Watkins, Loades and Woods senior all for ducks. Once again, it was Keith Hunt who steadied the ship with 70, ably supported by Paul Woods and Andy Scales. Walsham got home by four wickets.

Two wins and two defeats had made for a most enjoyable tour. No longer does the squad stay out until 5.00 am, although Garth Futter and Chris Gould can still drink with the best of them! We would have been struggling without the runs of Andy Scales and Keith Hunt, and it was a pleasure to see Garth Futter taking his 700th wicket for the club against Crosby, when Woods senior took an amazing catch. Although many of the players were getting older, the spirit was still there for a few more tours yet.

CHAPTER FORTY THREE *The Friendly Alliance... And The Future*

As is apparent in earlier chapters, towards the end of the 1990s South Walsham appeared to be a cricket club that was 'swimming against the tide'. League cricket dominated the priorities of other clubs on Saturdays, while it had edged into Sunday cricket in the form of the Mid-Norfolk Sunday League. Although some cup competitions had faded from the scene, the traditional friendly - preferably time-based - which was Walsham's favoured format appeared to be in jeopardy. The club continued to maintain a full fixture list from mid-April to mid-September, but the range of potential opponents was reducing. Over the next few years, this situation seemed to be gradually worsening, not only for South Walsham but for other clubs whose preference was for competitive friendlies on Sundays.

And so, on a dark, November Sunday night in 2003, eight men gathered in the Upton White Horse to discuss the way forward. South Walsham had convened the meeting - hence its remote setting - but common interest drew together the other representatives. The outcome was the birth of the Friendly Alliance. The concept was simple: the provision of a forum to discuss matters of mutual concern and to arrange fixtures. A decade on, five clubs - South Walsham, Eaton, Happisburgh, Old Catton and St Andrews - continue to provide the core membership. Three others have fallen by the wayside - Lowestoft, Beccles and Caister - opting either for league cricket or reducing their Sunday commitments but, by 2012, they had been replaced by twelve other clubs whose conversion or, in some cases, re-conversion to a traditional format of the game has strengthened the group's belief in its value. Indeed, even the Norfolk Cricket Board, with its emphasis on league cricket, youth cricket, Focus Clubs and implementation of bureaucratic ECB directives has seen fit to invite the 'Alliance' to be represented on its Recreational Committee.

However, this entanglement with officialdom has not compromised the autonomy of the 'Alliance' - or its member clubs - or undermined its many strengths:

- there is no hierarchy/pecking order of clubs - it is an association of equals

- it has simplified the task of fixture secretaries, who can co-ordinate on an annual basis

- there is an agreement that the home team determines the format - this has enabled those clubs who retain a preference for time-based cricket, rather than the formulaic overs-based win/lose format, to continue to champion this traditional form of the game

- the standard of cricket - and the absence of points-chasing - has allowed clubs to field balanced sides consisting of:

    - a small core who want to play twice a weekend and enjoy the Sunday format

    - a few players who do not possess the ability to compete successfully in league cricket but who, nevertheless, can make a solid contribution at a slightly lower standard

    - a group of older players who have 'stepped across' from league cricket

    - younger players who, playing alongside those who are more experienced, are exposed to and absorb the ethos of the game as well as developing their talents; the framework provided by the 'Alliance' has been particularly helpful in sustaining this philosophy

- clubs can play as many or as few 'Alliance' opponents as they wish, retain traditional fixtures against sides outside the circle and continue to entertain touring sides

- playing many of the same oppositions every year, rather than diminishing the enthusiasm of players, has enabled really good cricketing relationships to be established between a growing number of clubs. One of the most encouraging features of the ten-year history of the 'Alliance' is that it has been joined by four established senior clubs - Mattishall, Sprowston, Thetford and Bradenham - who have either grown weary of league cricket on Sunday or seen the benefits of running an additional side to meet the cricketing needs of their members. Moreover, in recent years, two Friendly Alliance clubs - Winterton and Old Catton - have, in terms of their league status, moved from the junior to senior ranks - clearly a sign that they are flourishing. The core continues to consist of junior clubs, some that only play on Sundays and others that recognise the value of running complementary sides on bothdays of the weekend.

Whether the steady growth of one additional club every year will continue is unclear, but at present it is evident that there is a gradually awakening realisation to the positive aspects of the 'Sunday friendly' format of the game. If more clubs could be 'reconverted', this would be highly advantageous to the health of the game in Norfolk and beyond. In 2012, Friendly Alliance clubs made a joint submission to the Norfolk Cricket Board highlighting their commitment to this form of the game, with a plea that it should be given wider official recognition. One of the most telling contributions to this submission came from Geoff Sutton, secretary of Felthorpe CC:

'Club/Village/Friendly cricket needs to survive because it is a leisure outlet for the enthusiast rather than the result-orientated performers who seek their release in competitive cricket. If cricket loses 'us' (ie the enthusiasts), its popularity will take a dive as it's the enthusiast who - more often than not - runs clubs, turns up on a short-notice call-up, supports the Test and international teams and keeps the 'Barmy Army' going!'

Despite the money flowing into the game at the top level, cricket as a national sport is ultimately dependent on the enthusiasm of volunteers. In the past twenty years, much of this drive has been directed towards coaching schemes and the growth of youth cricket. This is the way the ECB and the county boards perceive to be the correct route to underpinning the game. Perhaps........but what is the purpose of youth cricket? If it is merely to nurture the talents of an elite group of players, then the wider game will gradually wither. The modest performer at youth level needs to have a natural route to retain his enthusiasm and friendly cricket can offer this, provided that the 'league/cup only' mentality has not invaded his thinking by the age of fifteen.

From the perspective of South Walsham, whose commitment to younger players has always been reflected in their selection and encouragement directly through the adult game, the future is broadly encouraging. Like all clubs there is a degree of dependence on the efforts of the 'hardy annuals' to sustain its health. But new players have been absorbed who respect the ethos that has been developed in almost a century of cricket. There is no reason to suppose that the club will not be there in a further hundred years, still battling against Eaton and enjoying the end-of-season President's Day. Perhaps a century is an over-lengthy time-span upon which to speculate but, for the immediate future, the story continues. Season 2013 beckons........and the good news: Upton White Horse, after a brief period of closure, has reopened!

CHAPTER FORTY FOUR *Recollections*
*40 Years Of
South Walsham Cricket*

Contrary to popular belief, I did not appear in the first South Walsham game in 1908. After leaving school, I had been umpiring for CEYMS on Saturdays and, although I loved playing, I never really considered myself good enough for what I thought was a high standard. However, I was persuaded to turn out for South Walsham by school and life-long friend John Westgarth and made my debut against St Barnabas on May 31st 1970. I remember fielding in the slips and was pleased to hold on to two good catches and dropping a third, the easiest of the three. I batted at number nine and didn't last long, being bowled for a duck by Colin Crisp, one of his haul of 6-34.

In the return game with St Barnabas a month later, I fared little better making just four. I tended to play only when we were short - after all, in many of the games we continued to come up against county players. Sometimes I had to respond to a late call. On one occasion - at Attleborough - having being contacted after the game had started, I arrived to find the scoreboard reading 43-8 and scored two not out in a total of 63. We lost by five wickets!

However, I enjoyed the camaraderie and became hooked on cricket - especially South Walsham cricket - and never looked back. In 1970, the club was at a low ebb, seeking through its fixtures to punch above its weight. The Edrich era had ended and the new generation struggled weekly against superior opposition. Defeat followed defeat until the memorable day in 1972 when we achieved a draw against UEA. This was Trevor Johnson's debut and, for me, the first time that I reached double figures. I was batting at number eight and came in at 8-6. The opening bowlers returned figures of 2-6 from 10 overs and 3-15 from 13 overs. I battled for well over an hour - the longest I had ever batted in my life - and made twelve. Trevor and I advanced the score to 27-6. We were both dismissed but, with just two overs to go, the final pair held out, as we finished on 43-9 from 39 overs. It may sound boring, but it showed we had a bit of character and it was the match that changed our attitude. It taught us to fight a little more. The corner had been turned. The subsequent years, although they have had their ups and downs, have to be measured from this benchmark.

My contributions continued to be modest, but I had the thrill of taking part in a large stand against Dersingham. Coming in at 32-6, I put on 71 for the seventh wicket with Keith Hall (64), a lovely lad who died from cancer a few years later at an early age. I only made 19, but was beginning to prove my worth in a crisis. However, my real breakthrough came against Hoveton and Wroxham in 1979 when I kept wicket for the first time. I claimed a stumping off Malcolm Hill - demolishing the stumps rather than removing one bail. I was not particularly confident about doing the job, but the club had been searching for someone to take it on for some time. It turned out to be my niche role, one in which, although never elegant, I could be effective. I kept wicket for over thirty years: stopping most things, holding on to the straightforward chances and catching the occasional good one. My stumpings were very much the same: some good, some easy and quite a few missed.

Where did the forty years go?

However, alongside the cricket was the social side of the game. When I first started playing, we went to the King's Arms, whose landlord also provided the teas. We moved to the Ship in the early 1970s and stayed there for about twenty years.

John Chilvers from Eaton remembers happy days: *'After a game at South Walsham we always 'concluded' in The Ship, where ex-Norwich City player Graham Paddon was mine host. The post-match atmosphere was excellent against most oppositions in that era. Less so nowadays, although SWCC and ECC remain honourable exceptions.'*

When entertaining touring sides it wasn't unheard of to end up at the Ranworth Country Club which had a quite 'flexible' attitude to closure times. When the new Village Hall and pavilion were built we did make an attempt to use the bar facilities, but it didn't really work. There was very little atmosphere and, in the early 1990s, we moved to the Upton White Horse which has been the club's HQ ever since.

Touring, which became a biennial venture, provided many of the highlights of South Walsham cricket. One of the most touching moments for me came on the tour of Essex (2006) when 'President Ray' marked up the minibus on front, back and sides with the slogan 'Alex Evans Testimonial Tour'. Perhaps, after 36 years, I had finally arrived, if only to be recognised as my career was moving towards its close. In 2006, it was a little premature for time to be called but, by 2010, injury and age made me take more of a back seat in the playing department. I 'helped out' in four matches, but recognised that, after playing over 700 games in 40 years, it was time to ensure the younger members had the opportunity to play.

In 2011 and 2012, my single performances were against South Walsham - for the President's side - but I am delighted that the club's spirit continues to be excellent. The younger players are making progress while the more mature continue to make their mark. Having been a very moderate cricketer, I am lucky to have had such a great career for such a wonderful club. I would like to think that, in a hundred years time, someone might pick up this book and think 'that sounds like a great little cricket club'. My thanks to all the players, officials and everyone connected with the club who have made my Sundays so enjoyable for over forty years.

OFFICERS OF THE CRICKET CLUB FROM 1949

Year	President	Chairman	Captain
1949	Maj H R Broughton	George H Edrich	Pat Hood
1952	Maj H R Broughton	Pat Hood	George H Edrich
1953	J Bond	Pat Hood	Ronnie Hewitt
1954	F Rayns	Pat Hood	Ronnie Hewitt
1955	F Rayns	Pat Hood	Ronnie Hewitt
1958	R Youngs	Pat Hood	Ken Mayhew
1967	John Mack	Pat Hood	Derek Blaxell
1968	George H Edrich	Pat Hood	Derek Blaxell
1969	George H Edrich	Derek Blaxell	Derek Blaxell
1970	George H Edrich	Arthur Edrich	Gladney Wrag
1971	George H Edrich	Barry Loades	George Heward
1972	George H Edrich	Barry Loades	Peter Fisher
1973	George H Edrich	Barry Loades	Rod Burdett
1974	George H Edrich	Barry Loades	Rod Burdett
1975	George H Edrich	Barry Loades	Rod Burdett
1976	George H Edrich	Alan Robinson	Rod Burdett
1977	Alan Robinson	John Vaughan	Ken Kerry
1978	Alan Robinson	John Vaughan	Mike Conrad
1979	Alan Robinson	John Vaughan	Mike Conrad
1980	Alan Robinson	John Vaughan	Dave Watkins
1981	Ken Kerry	Alex Evans	Dave Watkins
1982	Ken Kerry	Alex Evans	John Westgarth
1983	Ken Kerry	Dave Watkins	Dave Watkins
1984	Ken Kerry	Dave Watkins	Dave Watkins
1985	Ken Kerry	Terry Ogden	Dave Watkins

1986	Ken Kerry	Terry Ogden	Derek Gorrod
1987	Ken Kerry	Terry Ogden	Derek Gorrod
1988	Barry Battersby	Terry Ogden	Derek Gorrod
1989	Barry Battersby	Terry Ogden	Garth Futter
1990	John Westgarth	Terry Ogden	Garth Futter
1991	John Westgarth	Terry Ogden	Garth Futter
1992	John Westgarth	Terry Ogden	Kim Futter
1993	John Westgarth	Terry Ogden	Kim Futter
1994	John Westgarth	Terry Ogden	Steve Belton
1995	John Westgarth	Terry Ogden	Andy Scales
1996	Neville London	Terry Ogden	Andy Scales
1997	John Westgarth	Terry Ogden	Richard Whiteside
1998	John Westgarth	Terry Ogden	Richard Whiteside
1999	Ray Norman	Terry Ogden	Keith Denton
2000	Ray Norman	Terry Ogden	Keith Denton
2001	Ray Norman	Terry Ogden	Keith Denton
2002	Ray Norman	Terry Ogden	Neil Johnson
2003	Ray Norman	Terry Ogden	Neil Johnson
2004	Ray Norman	Terry Ogden	Neil Johnson
2005	Ray Norman	Terry Ogden	Jon Moore
2006	Ray Norman	John Vaughan	Jon Moore
2007	Ray Norman	John Vaughan	Greg Loades
2008	Ray Norman	John Vaughan	Paul Woods
2009	Ray Norman	John Vaughan	Paul Woods
2010	Ray Norman	John Vaughan	Paul Woods
2011	Ray Norman	John Vaughan	Paul Woods
2012	Ray Norman	John Vaughan	Dave Jones

SOUTH WALSHAM CRICKET CLUB TOURS

Year	Area	Base
1974	Sussex	Brighton
1977	Yorkshire	York
1978	Yorkshire	York
1980	Yorkshire	York
1982	Worcestershire	Worcester
1985	Wiltshire	Cirencester
1988	Shropshire	Shrewsbury
1990	Northamptonshire	Northampton
1992	New Forest	Brockenhurst
1994	Sussex	Arundel
1996	Somerset	Illminister
1998	Derbyshire	Derby
2000	Belvoir Valley	Belvoir
2002	Wiltshire	Warminister
2004	Yorkshire	Harrogate
2006	Essex	Chelmsford
2008	Kent	Margate
2010	Northamptonshire	Northampton
2012	Leicestershire	Market Harborough

SOUTH WALSHAM CRICKET CLUB
Averages 1949-2012
Qualification 10 innings,
50 overs, 5 catches
(except in the earlier years where the number of games played was much less).
For Key see page (vii)

1949	P15	W6	D0	L7	A2
	I	NO	Runs	HS	Ave
P Edrich	11	2	200	61*	22.22
F Atkins	10	2	128	33*	16.00
R Hewitt	10	1	119	27	13.22
J Gunton	10	0	95	38	9.50
J Lang	8	1	66	32*	9.43
G H Edrich	8	0	74	31	9.25
	O	M	Runs	W	Ave
G H Edrich	87.2	20	216	29	7.4
G C Edrich	53.4	10	137	16	8.6
P Edrich	103	28	252	27	9.3
W Wheeler	41.1	15	115	12	9.6

Catches - J Gunton 5

1950	P13	W10	D1	L2	
	I	NO	Runs	HS	Ave
F Atkins	10	0	155	43	15.50
P Hood	9	0	137	41	15.22
R Hewitt	9	0	131	55	14.55
G C Edrich	11	1	142	28	14.20
G H Edrich	11	2	123	33	13.88
	O	M	Runs	W	Ave
P Edrich	123.5	34	252	50	5.04
G C Edrich	100.2	27	206	32	6.44
G H Edrich	111.1	33	232	33	7.05
F Atkins	40.1	9	98	11	8.91

Catches - A Hawkshaw 8 & 10 st P Edrich 5

1951	P 14	W6	D3	L5	
	I	NO	Runs	HS	Ave
F Atkins	12	1	345	95	31.4
J Webb	8	1	168	60*	24.0
G H Edrich	12	3	163	37	18.1
A Hawkshaw	12	2	179	29	17.9
P Hood	9	1	115	61	14.4
P Edrich	11	0	88	25	8.0
	O	M	Runs	W	Ave
P Edrich	162.1	58	318	41	7.7
J Webb	80	26	140	15	9.3
G H Edrich	118.4	20	317	23	13.8
F Atkins	61	7	184	11	16.8
P Hood	41	7	157	7	22.4

Catches - A Hawkshaw 9 & 10 st G H Edrich 5

1952	P14	W9	D2	L2	A1
	I	NO	Runs	HS	Ave
J Edrich	10	2	218	52*	27.25
F Atkins	10	0	241	59	24.10
P Hood	10	0	219	58	21.90
R Hewitt	10	0	169	47	16.90
P Edrich	13	1	197	46	16.41
	O	M	Runs	W	Ave
G C Edrich	170.2	46	375	43	8.72
P Edrich	164.3	37	376	43	8.74

Catches - A Edrich 7 & 2 st P Edrich 9

1953	P18	W11	D3	L4	
	I	NO	Runs	HS	Ave
J Edrich	15	3	471	109*	39.25
I Stringer	7	0	183	59	26.43
R Hewitt	11	0	223	55	22.02
	O	M	Runs	W	Ave
G C Edrich	233	70	397	66	6.02
P Edrich	209	54	437	41	10.65
K Mayhew	41	8	120	11	10.91
G H Edrich	101	20	233	20	11.65

Catches - J Edrich 8 & 1 st G H Edrich 7
R Perkins 6 G C Edrich 6 P Edrich 6
R Hewitt 5 J Gunton 5

1954 P22 W11 D4 L4 A3

	I	NO	Runs	HS	Ave
J Edrich	13	7	512	101*	85.3
I Stringer	11	3	333	51*	41.6
R Perkins	9	2	188	59	26.8
P Edrich	7	2	116	57	23.0
P Hood	12	1	233	50	21.1
R Hewitt	14	2	217	78	18.0
G H Edrich	11	1	156	53	15.6
G Head	15	0	192	45	13.8

	O	M	Runs	W	Ave
G C Edrich	253.2	90	437	56	7.8
P Edrich	207.5	58	418	48	8.7
G H Edrich	78	18	183	14	13.0

Catches - G Head 11 G H Edrich 8 A Eades 6

1955 P19 W5 D5 L7 A2

	I	NO	Runs	HS	Ave
G Head	13	1	394	65*	28.1
G H Edrich	13	2	252	50*	22.9
P G Edrich	13	1	270	124*	22.5
F Atkins	10	1	167	76*	18.5
P Hood	14	0	248	51	17.7
R Hewitt	12	1	164	42*	14.9

	O	M	Runs	W	Ave
G C Edrich	297	75	622	61	11.0
P Edrich	218	37	527	41	12.8
P Hood	48	8	148	9	16.4
G H Edrich	52	6	188	9	20.9

Catches - G C Edrich 6 G Head 5 & 2 st
F Atkins 5 R Hewitt 5

1956 P20 W11 D3 L5 A1

	I	NO	Runs	HS	Ave
J Edrich	6	2	390	116*	97.5
K Mayhew	9	4	156	50	31.2
F Atkins	9	3	166	55	27.6
I Stringer	14	3	300	64*	27.3

	O	M	Runs	W	Ave
R Tomkys	61	18	147	21	7.0
P Edrich	262	69	567	64	8.9
K Mayhew	84	24	205	22	9.0
G C Edrich	95	33	200	19	10.5
G H Edrich	117	24	268	17	16.3

Catches - G Head 5 & 6 st P Edrich 8 I Stringer 5

1957 P18 W6 D4 L6 A2

	I	NO	Runs	HS	Ave
I Stringer	14	3	300	64*	27.3
G H Edrich	13	2	196	67	17.8
B Tibbenham	11	0	196	67	17.8
I Stringer	14	1	219	55	16.9
B Cator	13	2	164	25	14.9

	O	M	Runs	W	Ave
P Edrich	185.2	38	418	48	8.7
A Pennington	49.2	5	140	16	8.8
G C Edrich	56.5	19	108	12	9.0
K Mayhew	113	34	285	22	12.9
B Cator	120.1	25	305	21	14.5

Catches - B Tibbenham 7 K Mayhew 6
A Edrich 5 B Saull 5 A Pennington 5

1958 P20 W7 D5 L5 A3

	I	NO	Runs	HS	Ave
P Edrich	16	3	387	67	29.8
K Mayhew	11	1	181	40	18.1
F Atkins	8	1	125	36	17.8
B Tibbenham	16	0	251	105	15.7
B Cator	13	0	159	33	12.3

	O	M	Runs	W	Ave
B Cator	80	25	217	21	10.3
G C Edrich	151	47	348	31	11.2
P Edrich	211	68	484	41	11.8
A Pennington	163	29	421	33	12.8
K Mayhew	41	7	132	10	13.2

Catches - G H Edrich 6 P Edrich 6
P Hood 5 A Edrich 2 & 3 st

1959 P19 W8 D2 L7 A2

	I	NO	Runs	HS	Ave
K Mayhew	7	1	167	84	27.8
P Hood	14	0	365	120	26.0
W Hopkins	9	1	174	43	21.7
B Tibbenham	16	2	284	66	20.3
P Edrich	17	1	305	65	19.1
B Cator	15	2	187	64	13.4

	O	M	Runs	W	Ave
P Edrich	233	55	577	58	9.8
B Cator	123	13	332	24	13.4
A Pennington	98	13	334	22	15.2
G C Edrich	140	33	390	23	16.3

Catches - P Edrich 9 A Edrich 8 & 1 st
A Pennington 6 B Tibbenham 5

1960	**P16**	**W7**	**D5**	**L4**	
	I	NO	Runs	HS	Ave
B Tibbenham	13	2	390	76	33.5
P Hood	13	0	272	44	20.9
B Cator	13	0	241	42	16.0
F Atkins	12	1	172	33*	15.7
P Edrich	10	1	132	48*	14.6
	O	M	Runs	W	Ave
P Edrich	141.3	30	364	45	8.1
G C Edrich	115.2	37	264	21	12.6
B Cator	92.5	19	263	16	16.4
F Atkins	76	4	298	14	21.3

Catches - B Tibbenham 9 A Edrich 6 & 1 st
K Mayhew 5 G H Edrich 5 P Edrich 5

1961	**P20**	**W6**	**D7**	**L5**	**A2**
	I	NO	Runs	HS	Ave
R Beeney	9	1	241	97*	30.3
P Hood	8	0	186	68	23.3
F Atkins	13	2	218	79*	19.8
P Edrich	13	1	219	40	17.7
R Hewitt	9	0	152	76	17.6
B Cator	18	1	290	31	17.0
	O	M	Runs	W	Ave
J Syrett	59	16	174	17	10.2
A Pennington	132.3	28	371	31	12.0
P Edrich	210	66	540	44	12.3
F Atkins	72	12	197	14	14.1

Catches - B Cator 9 J Syrett 7 A Edrich 3 & 2 st

1962	**P20**	**W7**	**D4**	**L5**	**A4**
	I	NO	Runs	HS	Ave
P Edrich	14	5	218	58*	24.2
J Syrett	10	2	173	71*	21.6
R Beeney	8	0	147	62	18.4
P Cator	9	1	130	82	16.2
B Cator	16	1	193	74*	12.9
J English	10	2	102	57*	12.8
A Hammond	15	0	187	39	12.5
P Hood	11	0	123	27	11.2
F Atkins	9	2	37	15	5,3
	O	M	Runs	W	Ave
P Edrich	218	49	519	53	9.8
B Cator	59.1	13	160	7	22.9
G C Edrich	107.2	23	300	11	27.3

Catches - A Hammond 6 & 1 st A Edrich 6

1963	**P16**	**W2**	**D4**	**L7**	**A3**
	I	NO	Runs	HS	Ave
J Tomlinson	11	0	424	128	38.6
P Edrich	10	3	229	71*	32.7
P Cator	14	3	207	48*	29.6
P Hood	11	1	211	41	21.1
J Syrett	10	3	104	33	14.9
B Cator	14	0	102	40	7.3
A Hammond	12	1	66	23	6.0
	O	M	Runs	W	Ave
A Pennington	84	25	222	17	13.1
K Mayhew	73	16	194	13	14.8
J Syrett	53	11	194	12	16.2
P Edrich	185.1	46	454	24	18.9
B Cator	92.1	20	339	16	21.2
J Tomlinson	68	12	234	7	33.4

Catches - P Cator 5 & 1 st J Tomlinson 5
A Edrich 5

1964	**P19**	**W3**	**D7**	**L5**	**A4**
	I	NO	Runs	HS	Ave
N Owers	11	2	305	78*	33.9
P Edrich	8	2	167	82*	27.8
A Hammond	15	0	320	55	21.3
B Cator	15	2	209	40	16.0
P Hood	8	0	127	34	15.9
D Balls	10	1	90	24	10.0
	O	M	Runs	W	Ave
K Mayhew	62	11	192	15	12.7
P Edrich	121	29	213	24	12.9
R Hardesty	104	20	277	18	15.4
B Cator	103	18	323	18	17.7

Catches - A Hammond 5 & 2 st A Edrich 5

1965	**P 19**	**W4**	**D6**	**L6**	**A3**
	I	NO	Runs	HS	Ave
P Edrich	11	4	453	118*	64.7
N Owers	12	3	200	43*	22.0
B Cator	11	2	141	70*	15.6
	O	M	Runs	W	Ave
T Ridley	74	15	195	17	11.5
B Cator	95	18	266	17	15.6
R Hardesty	162.4	23	454	26	17.4
P Edrich	70	19	178	10	17.8
G C Edrich	57	14	140	7	20.0

Catches - A Edrich 5 & 1 st P Edrich 5

1966	P 17	W2	D1	L10	A4
	I	NO	Runs	HS	Ave
K Wright	10	1	185	93	20.5
R Hardesty	10	2	157	41*	19.6
B Cator	14	2	154	44	12.8
J Sizeland	10	0	77	21	7.7
	O	M	Runs	W	Ave
B Cator	87	17	253	20	12.6
R Hardesty	141	29	426	25	17.0
T Ridley	81.3	16	286	16	17.7
R Attoe	94	18	285	15	19.0

KEY

P - Played	I - Innings
W - Won	NO - Not Out
D - Drawn	HS - Highest Score
L - Lost	A - Average
A - Abandoned	O - Overs
T - Tie	M - Maidens
	W - Wickets
	st - Stumped

Catches - B Cator 8 P Edrich 3 & 2 st A Edrich 4 & 1 st

1967	P22	W10	D4	L5	A3
	I	NO	Runs	HS	Ave
K Wright	12	2	412	65*	41.20
M Owers	15	6	140	33*	15.55
B Cator	15	3	176	51*	14.66
M Moreland	19	1	251	38	13.95
P Shorten	12	1	90	30*	8.12
	O	M	Runs	W	Ave
M Owers	124	26	403	42	9.53
R Hardesty	136.2	34	388	26	14.92
B Cator	158.3	26	481	30	16.00
D Blaxell	131	28	349	15	23.27
K Wright	107	21	343	12	28.58

Catches - K Wright 8 M Moreland 8 R Hardesty 7 B Cator 6

1968	P21	W2	D8	L10	A1
	I	NO	Runs	HS	Ave
M Moreland	18	3	282	74	18.80
I Sidell	18	1	298	70*	17.53
R Hardesty	11	4	122	40	17.46
G Wragg	15	0	229	66	15.27
B Cator	10	2	102	54*	12.75
P Shorten	16	3	83	15	5.53
	O	M	Runs	W	Ave
R Hardesty	170.5	49	394	28	14.07
M Moreland	50	5	171	10	17.10
D Blaxell	100.3	20	313	18	17.38
B Cator	98.5	10	328	13	25.23
K Wright	88.2	20	282	9	31.33

Catches - I Sidell 11 G Wragg 9 & 4 st

1969	P23	W2	D3	L13	A5
	I	NO	Runs	HS	Ave
G Wragg	17	4	338	66	26.00
D Clark	10	6	74	27	18.50
I Sidell	14	1	235	75	18.08
S Smart	13	0	161	40	12.38
M Moreland	16	1	125	23	8.33
P Shorten	10	1	72	26	8.00
	O	M	Runs	W	Ave
M Moreland	99	7	409	13	31.46
S Smart	87	12	325	6	54.17

Catches - G Wragg 7 & 1 st M Moreland 5 S Smart 5

1970	P19	W0	D2	L16	A1
	I	NO	Runs	HS	Ave
P Fisher	17	0	311	49	18.29
A Sheppard	10	0	155	37	15.50
J Westgarth	15	2	184	71*	14.15
D Bane	13	2	144	32*	13.09
S Smart	16	0	175	35	10.94
D Clark	12	3	92	27	10.22
G Heward	12	1	78	42	7.09
	O	M	Runs	W	Ave
G Worth	100	22	248	21	11.81
G Heward	125.5	24	378	22	17.18
A Sheppard	115.3	12	438	23	19.04
S Smart	71.2	10	291	10	29.10

Catches - J Westgarth 14 & 4 st P Fisher 12 D Clark 6

1971 P24 W4 D5 L15

	I	NO	Runs	HS	Ave
S Smart	11	1	183	74	18.30
K Hall	10	1	111	51*	12.33
D Bane	14	1	147	32*	12.25
G Heward	17	2	148	30	9.86
P Fisher	24	1	215	46*	9.34
T Johnson	13	5	66	21	8.25
A Evans	14	1	105	28	8.07
J Denton	13	1	70	18	5.83
G Worth	12	3	47	14	5.22
R Lusted	16	6	41	15	4.10

	O	M	Runs	W	Ave
T Johnson	235.1	51	653	47	13.89
G Heward	195.2	36	578	34	17.00
G Worth	171.2	33	556	25	22.24
D Ellis	64	7	188	6	31.33
R Lusted	78	2	398	13	36.15

Catches - P Fisher 20 & 3 st J Denton 8 T Johnson 6

1972 P21 W5 D5 L10 A1

	I	NO	Runs	HS	Ave
J Denton	14	2	247	67	20.06
R Burdett	16	1	297	54*	19.80
D Russen	10	3	58	17	8.28
A Evans	13	3	64	16*	6.40
T Johnson	13	6	38	9	5.53
R Lusted	11	1	55	30	5.50

	O	M	Runs	W	Ave
T Johnson	236.1	54	632	52	12.2
R Burdett	85	12	263	17	13.5
M Cross	79.1	15	246	16	15.4
G Worth	96	17	299	13	23.0

Catches - D Russen 11 & 3 st T Johnson 9 J Denton 7

1973 P21 W6 D6 L5 A4

	I	NO	Runs	HS	Ave
J Denton	11	2	315	79*	35.0
D Palmer	10	0	174	55	17.4
R Burdett	12	0	203	36	16.9
J Vaughan	16	1	211	46	14.1
G Coan	13	1	141	31	11.8
R Lusted	11	4	60	16*	8.6
A Evans	11	3	55	13*	6.9
C Thomas	10	1	58	18	6.4

	O	M	Runs	W	Ave
T Johnson	175.1	46	395	36	10.9
R Burdett	67	10	187	15	12.5
G Worth	90	21	219	17	12.9

Catches - P Fisher 7 J Denton 7 T Johnson 6
A Evans 5 M Sidell 5 R Lusted 5

1974 P32 W7 D6 L13 A6

	I	NO	Runs	HS	Ave
J Denton	24	2	393	63	17.8
R Burdett	19	1	269	48	14.9
J Vaughan	16	0	219	34	13.7
L Lowe	12	3	88	25	9.8
P Fisher	25	0	234	46	9.4
A Evans	13	2	55	19	5.0
G Worth	12	5	35	11*	5.0
C Denton	13	0	61	12	4.7
R Lusted	15	2	58	17	4.4
G Coan	13	1	46	13	3.8
T Johnson	14	8	14	8*	2.3
P Robinson	14	5	15	7*	1.7

	O	M	Runs	W	Ave
J Vaughan	96	19	242	25	9.7
T Johnson	246	63	620	42	14.8
G Worth	116	29	269	18	14.9
R Lusted	80	6	253	16	15.8
K Kerry	56	4	267	17	16.8
R Burdett	126.1	26	334	19	17.6
P Robinson	77	14	211	12	17.6
C Denton	55	4	228	12	19.0

Catches - P Fisher 18 & 6 st T Johnson 13 A Evans12
J Denton 9 J Vaughan7 R Burdett 6 K Kerry 6

1975 P22 W4 D9 L8 A1

	I	NO	Runs	HS	Ave
J Denton	21	2	479	72*	25.26
M Conrad	19	3	386	68*	24.12
B Dwyer	11	0	217	47	19.73
J Vaughan	21	2	361	57	19.00
D Watkins	20	4	283	87	17.69
R Burdett	15	0	197	66	13.13
P Robinson	10	6	49	21	12.25
C Denton	17	4	134	26*	10.31

	O	M	Runs	W	Ave
T Johnson	212.5	51	608	31	19.6
R Burdett	83.5	9	292	13	22.5
M Conrad	135	27	423	18	23.5
C Denton	142.5	13	615	26	23.7
P Robinson	99.3	13	327	12	27.3
J Vaughan	74	8	302	9	33.6

Catches - J Denton 8 & 3 st M Conrad 7
P Robinson 6 J Vaughan 5 A Evans 5
B Dwyer 5

1976 P22 W13 D7 L2

	I	NO	Runs	HS	Ave
J Denton	19	4	646	98*	43.06
M Conrad	18	6	437	57*	36.42
J Vaughan	16	4	351	47	29.25
B Dwyer	11	1	258	49*	28.50
D Watkins	19	0	228	68	12.00
C Denton	14	6	91	23*	11.38
K Kerry	12	2	109	39	10.90

	O	M	Runs	W	Ave
T Johnson	267.5	69	617	55	11.22
M Conrad	74.1	24	195	16	12.19
J Vaughan	157.2	43	429	28	15.32
C Denton	113.2	15	425	26	16.35
K Kerry	56	5	216	12	18.00
P Robinson	146	38	401	20	20.05

Catches - J Denton 12 & 1 st R Lusted 12 & 1 st
M Conrad 11 D Watkins 9 K Kerry 9 A Evans 7 P Robinson 7
B Dwyer 5 & 1 st C Denton 5 T Johnson 5

1977 P30 W11 D12 L6 A1

	I	NO	Runs	HS	Ave
M Conrad	26	4	703	79	31.87
J Vaughan	25	4	604	64	28.76
C Denton	27	4	567	88*	24.65
K Kerry	18	2	289	88	18.06
D Watkins	22	1	300	49	14.29
B Dwyer	11	2	114	26	12.66
R Lusted	11	7	49	12*	12.25
A Evans	13	6	73	15*	10.43
M Hill	20	4	158	33*	9.87
C Reeson	13	2	31	11	2.82

	O	M	Runs	W	Ave
M Conrad	161.2	39	443	33	13.42
J Vaughan	240.5	56	637	43	14.81
C Denton	168.4	18	634	40	15.85
T Johnson	298	77	753	44	17.11
K Kerry	62	7	216	10	21.60
P Robinson	111.5	18	397	18	22.06
M Hill	94.1	6	405	13	31.15

Catches - C Denton 16 K Kerry 11 B Dwyer 10 & 1 st
A Evans 10 J Vaughan 10 M Conrad 10
D Watkins 7 P Robinson 5

1978 P28 W8 D9 L4 A7

	I	NO	Runs	HS	Ave
M Conrad	18	3	552	90	36.80
M Stevens	12	1	245	74	22.36
D Watkins	19	5	297	41	21.21
J Vaughan	20	3	320	57*	18.82
D Palmer	16	3	223	39*	17.15
C Denton	14	3	156	28*	14.18
K Kerry	18	0	188	51	10.44

	O	M	Runs	W	Ave
M Hill	77.4	8	215	17	12.65
D Palmer	149.3	27	396	27	14.66
T Johnson	185.2	40	465	29	16.04
M Conrad	77	22	210	13	16.15
C Denton	197.1	26	612	34	18.00
K Futter	57	9	186	7	26.57
R Lusted	64.3	2	269	10	26.90
J Vaughan	84.1	16	253	8	31.62

Catches - M Conrad 18 & 1 st C Reeson 11 & 4 st K Kerry 10
C Denton 9 D Watkins 5 & 1 st A Evans 6 D Palmer 5

1979	P24	W3	D10	L9	A2
	I	NO	Runs	HS	Ave
M Conrad	16	3	724	107*	55.69
M Sidell	10	1	231	55	25.66
J Vaughan	20	1	472	51	24.84
C Denton	22	5	371	83	21.82
K Denton	12	8	81	24*	20.25
D Watkins	16	3	234	57*	18.00
D Palmer	11	1	111	32	11.10
A Evans	10	3	48	13	6.86
R Lusted	10	4	29	13*	4.83

	O	M	Runs	W	Ave
T Johnson	72.1	23	164	16	10.25
J Vaughan	96	17	265	13	20.36
K Futter	151.4	39	415	20	20.75
D Palmer	142.2	42	360	17	21.17
C Denton	181.5	16	723	26	27.81
M Hill	69	3	285	10	28.50
R Lusted	115	4	472	14	33.71

Catches - C Denton 10 A Evans 8 & 2 st M Conrad 8
J Vaughan 8 D Palmer 5

1980	P28	W9	D14	L5	
	I	NO	Runs	HS	Ave
J Vaughan	26	7	806	101*	42.42
D Watkins	18	5	298	73*	22.92
D Palmer	16	2	254	73*	18.14
C Denton	23	0	352	51	15.30
T Kinsley	25	1	326	57	13.58
A Evans	11	6	61	16*	12.20
K Futter	12	5	83	26	11.86
K Denton	16	3	116	29	8.61
S Munday	15	3	96	36	8.00
C Reeson	14	2	69	25	5.75
S Royal	10	0	51	24	5.10
M Sidell	11	0	52	22	4.73

	O	M	Runs	W	Ave
C Denton	250.4	52	770	57	13.51
M Hill	51.1	7	197	14	14.08
D Palmer	154.3	52	367	24	15.29
J Vaughan	104	29	291	14	20.86
T Johnson	78	26	197	9	21.89
G Futter	78.2	15	229	10	22.90
R Lusted	69	2	325	13	25.00
K Futter	181	40	533	21	25.28

Catches - C Denton 15 T Kinsley 14 K Denton 10 & 5 st
A Evans 10 & 3 st J Vaughan 11 D Watkins 6 R Lusted 5
M Conrad 5

1981	P19	W3	D10	L5	A1
	I	NO	Runs	HS	Ave
J Westgarth	14	0	359	63	25.55
T Kinsley	12	1	200	49	18.17
J Vaughan	17	0	307	37	18.06
D Watkins	12	0	146	48	12.17
A Evans	13	2	130	39	11.82
K Denton	15	2	137	36	10.54
K Futter	10	4	50	21*	8.33
S Munday	12	6	46	22*	7.67
D Gorrod	14	3	80	17	7.27

	O	M	Runs	W	Ave
K Futter	156.2	39	422	32	13.19
S Munday	137.2	19	410	28	14.79
D Gorrod	66	11	180	11	16.36
K Denton	64	10	196	8	24.50

Catches - A Evans 10 D Watkins 8 J Vaughan 7
S Munday 6 J Westgarth 6 T Kinsley 5

1982	P24	W7	D8	L5	A4
	I	NO	Runs	HS	Ave
C Denton	10	2	269	66	33.62
J Westgarth	19	3	440	108*	27.50
D Watkins	16	1	290	72*	19.33
J Vaughan	18	1	313	52	18.41
K Denton	18	3	268	55	17.87
T Kinsley	15	2	206	54	15.85
M Sidell	11	2	112	30	12.44
K Futter	15	0	90	20	6.00
A Evans	13	0	71	13	5.46
S Munday	11	3	31	9	3.88

	O	M	Runs	W	Ave
C Denton	81.5	13	244	26	9.39
M Sidell	61.2	15	200	19	10.53
S Munday	160.2	22	544	37	14.70
K Futter	161	45	452	24	18.83
K Denton	50	12	160	5	32.00

Catches - J Westgarth 12 & 2 st A Evans 10 & 2 st K Futter 7
T Kinsley 6 & 3 st K Denton 5 M Sidell 5 G Futter 5

1983 P20 W3 D8 L5 A4

	I	NO	Runs	HS	Ave
J Vaughan	16	1	494	75	32.93
D Watkins	16	2	394	69*	28.14
A Evans	10	6	58	24	14.50
S Munday	15	1	141	31	10.66
T Ogden	10	3	63	26	9.00
K Futter	12	4	64	18	8.00

	O	M	Runs	W	Ave
K Parker	56	13	161	14	11.50
K Futter	173.2	35	524	28	18.71
D Gorrod	100	19	355	17	20.88
J Vaughan	63.3	15	190	8	23.75
S Munday	99.3	6	417	15	27.80
G Futter	55.5	6	214	4	53.80

Catches - A Evans 13 & 1 st J Vaughan 6

1984 P21 W6 D7 L5 A3

	I	NO	Runs	HS	Ave
D Watkins	17	3	447	75*	31.93
T Ogden	10	4	160	41	26.26
J Vaughan	15	1	359	77	25.64
S Belton	11	1	247	66	24.70
F Leak	15	1	296	55	21.14
A Evans	11	5	62	22	10.33
B Key	14	2	114	17	9.50
J Abbott	15	2	101	17	7.69
D Gorrod	10	10	15	6*	-----

	O	M	Runs	W	Ave
J Vaughan	91	22	267	17	15.71
T Ogden	85	8	354	20	17.70
G Lewis	87	13	274	14	19.71
G Futter	79	18	285	14	20.36
D Gorrod	129	28	437	17	25.71

Catches - A Evans 15 & 4 st B Key 8 J Abbott 7 F Leak 6
D Watkins 6 J Vaughan 5

1985 P25 W8 D10 L4 A3

	I	NO	Runs	HS	Ave
K Hodds	14	2	551	93*	45.92
J Vaughan	22	1	570	70	27.14
G Futter	17	8	181	31	20.11
D Watkins	21	4	287	39	15.70
F Leak	14	2	188	40	15.66
A Evans	14	7	109	23	15.57
T Ogden	11	1	143	47	14.30
S Munday	17	3	200	56*	14.28
S Belton	13	3	134	42*	13.40
J Abbott	19	1	192	27	10.67
G Lewis	11	1	100	27	10.00

	O	M	Runs	W	Ave
S Munday	153.1	15	504	35	14.40
J Vaughan	132.5	27	370	22	16.82
G Futter	189	39	513	30	17.10
D Gorrod	150	31	460	17	27.06
T Ogden	80	5	325	12	27.09
G Lewis	62	8	209	7	29.86

Catches - J Abbott 11 A Evans 9 & 8 st G Futter 8
F Leak 7 & 2 st D Watkins 7 K Hodds 7
J Vaughan 7 D Gorrod 6

1986 P24 W1 D12 L8 A3

	I	NO	Runs	HS	Ave
K Hodds	14	2	362	89*	30.17
F Leak	16	2	287	59	20.50
J Vaughan	16	2	229	43	16.21
D Watkins	18	0	268	53	14.88
G Futter	11	1	147	39	14.70
S Munday	16	3	159	26*	12.23
S Belton	13	0	132	40	10.15
G Lewis	21	4	162	34	9.53
A Evans	14	5	79	20	8.78
T Ogden	12	3	62	20	6.89
D Gorrod	11	2	50	24	5.56

	O	M	Runs	W	Ave
J Vaughan	132.4	22	463	34	13.62
S Munday	221.4	36	668	40	16.70
T Ogden	63.5	4	280	16	16.85
D Gorrod	154	33	493	22	22.41
G Lewis	67.4	13	230	10	23.00
G Futter	100.5	22	320	7	45.71

Catches - A Evans 25 & 10 st F Leak 8 G Lewis 8
D Gorrod 8 D Watkins 6 J Vaughan 6 T Ogden 5

1987	P22	W2	D5	L13	A2
	I	NO	Runs	HS	Ave
J Vaughan	18	0	467	81	25.94
D Watkins	18	0	424	53	23.56
A Evans	11	9	39	17*	19.50
F Leak	17	4	216	32*	16.61
G Futter	15	2	210	44	16.15
G Lewis	20	1	247	58	13.00
N Johnson	19	2	206	45	12.12
S Belton	21	3	178	40*	9.89
S Munday	16	0	141	64	8.81
T Ogden	15	4	91	17	8.27
D Gorrod	15	5	70	23	7.00
	O	M	Runs	W	Ave
J Vaughan	73.5	9	287	24	11.96
D Gorrod	99	15	314	17	18.35
N Johnson	79	12	302	14	21.57
T Ogden	129.1	16	435	19	22.89
S Munday	149.5	29	447	16	27.94
G Futter	136.2	27	453	16	28.31

Catches - J Vaughan 8 A Evans 4 & 3 st F Leak 4 & 2 st

1988	P27	W9	D11	L4	A3
	I	NO	Runs	HS	Ave
D Watkins	23	3	651	85	32.55
A Evans	15	11	117	22*	29.25
S Belton	22	4	404	82*	22.44
J Vaughan	17	2	304	53	20.27
A Scales	12	0	193	62	16.08
F Leak	21	2	267	57*	14.52
K Futter	12	3	125	24	13.89
N Johnson	13	3	137	47*	13.70
T Ogden	15	2	96	29*	7.38
	O	M	Runs	W	Ave
K Futter	162	40	374	41	9.12
G Futter	76.4	21	155	12	12.92
T Ogden	189.4	39	617	36	17.14
R Ringer	89.5	18	262	14	18.71
D Gorrod	157	26	448	21	21.33
J Vaughan	53	9	188	7	26.00

Catches - A Evans 26 & 9 st D Watkins 12 S Belton 10
F Leak 7 J Vaughan 7 D Gorrod 6 A Scales 6

1989	P24	W7	D9	L6	A2	
	I	NO	Runs	HS	Ave	
J Vaughan	20	3	668	101*	39.29	
M Key	13	3	322	102*	32.20	
F Leak	16	5	330	54*	30.00	
D Watkins	19	0	476	99	25.05	
A Scales	19	2	380	116	22.35	
S Belton	16	3	273	61	21.00	
N Johnson	18	2	258	79	16.12	
K Futter	11	3	107	30	13.37	
G Futter	13	2	142	39	12.91	
	O	M	Runs	W	Ave	
K Futter	215.5	55	598	35	17.08	
G Futter	216	46	720	40	18.00	
T Ogden	159	41	430	22	19.57	
D Kurley	88	8	360	13	27.86	
D Gorrod	86.3	17	261	9	29.00	

Catches - A Evans 15 & 3 st F Leak 12 D Watkins 10
G Futter 8 K Futter 7 A Scales 7 N Johnson 6
S Belton 6 D Kurley 5

1990	P30	W14	D6	L7	T1	A2
	I	NO	Runs	HS		Ave
A Scales	26	5	969	130*		46.14
J Vaughan	23	2	828	93		39.43
D Watkins	24	2	554	75		25.18
S Belton	22	5	424	54*		24.94
G Futter	19	4	347	51*		23.13
N Johnson	22	4	377	45		20.94
F Leak	15	5	177	36*		17.70
R Whiteside	15	3	180	26		15.00
K Futter	14	3	107	19		9.73
T Ogden	11	3	50	11		6.25
D Gorrod	10	6	8	48		-----
	O	M	Runs	W		Ave
K Futter	216.4	45	609	51		11.94
N Johnson	69.3	11	228	13		17.54
D Kurley	115	14	482	27		17.85
T Ogden	252.2	54	780	43		18.14
G Futter	180	35	651	19		34.26
D Gorrod	169	34	540	13		41.54

Catches - A Evans 17 & 9 st J Vaughan 16 G Futter 14
R Whiteside 5 & 2 st S Belton 8 F Leak 6 A Scales 6
T Ogden 5 N Johnson 5

1991 P23 W5 D6 L12

	I	NO	Runs	HS	Ave
R Whiteside	19	5	480	56*	34.28
A Scales	17	1	385	85	24.06
T Ogden	14	4	210	66*	21.00
D Watkins	20	0	399	92	19.95
S Belton	21	5	286	57	17.87
J Vaughan	17	0	303	57	17.82
N Johnson	18	0	287	66	15.94
G Futter	19	4	239	52*	15.93
K Futter	14	4	155	43*	15.50
F Leak	10	0	99	28	9.90
A Evans	10	6	6	3*	1.50

	O	M	Runs	W	Ave
K Futter	193	40	558	36	15.50
T Ogden	186.5	20	674	37	18.22
G Futter	180.4	39	620	25	24.80
D Kurley	105	13	497	14	35.50
R Whiteside	53.4	3	285	8	35.62
D Gorrod	103	21	366	8	45.75

Catches - A Evans 16 & 5 st G Futter 12 J Vaughan 10 D Kurley 9 S Belton 9 R Whiteside 8 & 1 st A Scales 8 K Futter 5 F Leak 5 D Watkins 5

1992 P29 W11 D4 L11 A3

	I	NO	Runs	HS	Ave
J Vaughan	14	1	516	69	39.69
A Scales	22	2	720	86*	36.00
M Key	12	0	298	93	24.83
R Whiteside	20	2	400	70	22.22
N Johnson	18	1	369	135*	21.71
G Futter	21	3	369	52*	20.50
D Watkins	21	0	314	74	14.95
T Ogden	13	3	117	49	11.70
S Belton	21	5	166	32*	10.37
K Futter	14	5	80	17*	8.89

	O	M	Runs	W	Ave
S Belton	98.5	12	447	32	13.97
K Futter	218	52	594	34	17.47
N London	103	22	316	16	19.76
G Futter	154.4	31	507	23	22.04
D Gorrod	116	21	403	18	22.39
T Ogden	160.2	31	532	22	24.18

Catches - A Evans 16 & 13 st A Scales 14 R Whiteside 12 G Futter 11 K Futter 8 N Johnson 8 S Belton 7 M Key 6 C Gould 5 J Vaughan 5 D Watkins 5

1993 P22 W7 D7 L7 A1

	I	NO	Runs	HS	Ave
J Vaughan	15	2	432	87	33.23
N Johnson	15	1	408	102*	29.14
R Whiteside	18	4	383	55	27.36
A Scales	18	0	459	74	25.50
G Futter	14	4	243	70	24.30
S Belton	17	4	281	63	21.62
D Watkins	19	1	386	45	21.44
K Futter	11	2	121	54*	13.44

	O	M	Runs	W	Ave
S Belton	79.5	4	456	28	16.29
K Futter	148.3	42	364	20	18.20
T Ogden	138.2	22	460	24	19.16
N London	93	14	308	16	19.25
G Futter	145.2	26	472	22	21.46
D Gorrod	95	10	393	10	39.30

Catches - A Evans 14 & 7 st N Johnson 10 R Whiteside 7 & 2 st G Futter 7 A Scales 7 S Belton 7 C Gould 6 D Watkins 5

1994 P29 W11 D6 L6 A6

	I	NO	Runs	HS	Ave
A Scales	19	6	822	100*	63.23
N Johnson	16	1	575	132	38.33
G Futter	17	7	360	71*	36.00
R Whiteside	15	4	388	67*	35.27
D Watkins	20	1	520	100*	27.37
S Belton	19	2	303	58	18.94
T Ogden	12	4	92	21	11.50
K Futter	11	3	64	25	8.00
C Gould	12	2	29	6	2.90

	O	M	Runs	W	Ave
G Futter	203.2	38	681	49	13.86
N London	51.3	5	160	11	14.55
K Futter	144	41	360	23	15.65
T Ogden	152.2	34	531	27	19.67
S Belton	82	2	490	20	24.50
D Gorrod	104	23	372	13	28.61
C Gould	95.3	7	460	15	30.67

Catches - A Evans 19 & 2 st R Whiteside 9 & 2 st S Belton 10 C Gould 7 G Futter 6 K Futter 6 A Scales 6 N Johnson 6

1995

	I	NO	Runs	HS	Ave
	P26	W5	D7	L8	A6
A Scales	16	4	651	106*	54.26
D Watkins	20	3	624	106*	36.71
N Johnson	13	3	325	64	32.50
R Whiteside	18	2	441	103*	27.56
A Evans	11	8	48	14*	16.00
S Belton	16	2	209	41	14.93
G Futter	14	3	148	36*	13.46
K Futter	11	1	104	36*	10.40
S Giles	10	4	58	15*	9.67

	O	M	Runs	W	Ave
T Ogden	133.2	23	440	30	14.67
G Futter	148	28	556	25	22.24
C Gould	117	16	478	21	22.76
D Gorrod	89	16	337	12	28.83
K Futter	174.2	37	604	19	31.79

Catches - A Evans 13 & 6 st R Whiteside 9 S Belton 8
A Scales 7 N Johnson 6 G Futter 6 C Gould 5
T Ogden 5

1996

	I	NO	Runs	HS	Ave
	P24	W14	D2	L7	A1
A Scales	19	3	763	101*	47.48
S Belton	18	6	458	54	38.17
R Whiteside	20	4	433	84*	27.06
G Futter	20	3	419	47	24.63
D Watkins	21	3	363	63	20.50
A Evans	11	5	112	37	18.66
T Ogden	10	2	62	16	7.75
C Gould	13	2	51	15	4.64

	O	M	Runs	W	Ave
C Gould	154.3	17	707	39	19.29
D Gorrod	88.2	15	314	14	22.43
S Belton	60.5	2	417	18	23.17
T Ogden	173.5	36	591	25	23.64
K Futter	95	26	312	12	26.00
G Futter	122.3	14	479	17	28.18

Catches - A Evans 11 & 5 st G Futter 13 C Gould 11
R Whiteside 8 & 2 st D Watkins 8 K Byton 7 A Scales 6
S Belton 6 T Ogden 6

1997

	I	NO	Runs	HS	Ave
	P27	W15	D6	L4	A2
K Denton	18	3	743	99*	49.53
R Whiteside	19	7	484	81*	40.33
A Scales	18	2	453	80*	28.31
D Watkins	19	0	499	74	26.26
J Vaughan	16	1	344	45	22.93
J Pennington	11	4	158	43	22.57
K Futter	15	7	155	36*	19.37
G Futter	19	3	296	65	18.50
T Ogden	11	6	39	11*	7.80
D Gorrod	14	6	56	8	7.00

	O	M	Runs	W	Ave
J Pennington	143.2	24	475	28	16.85
G Futter	177.5	38	669	39	17.15
T Ogden	184	36	639	31	20.61
K Futter	163.4	49	513	23	22.30
D Gorrod	116	25	426	14	30.42

Catches - A Evans 15 & 10 st K Denton 13
R Whiteside 11 K Futter 9 G Futter 9
D Watkins 8 A Scales 6 J Vaughan 5

1998

	I	NO	Runs	HS	Ave
	P29	W6	D4	L12	A7
A Scales	20	3	699	97	41.11
K Denton	17	6	405	70*	36.82
J Vaughan	13	2	344	72	31.27
G Futter	14	5	267	88	29.66
S Belton	15	0	347	70	23.13
D Watkins	19	0	419	64	22.05
R Whiteside	16	1	312	61	20.80
N Johnson	10	0	132	37	13.20
J Pennington	11	2	96	35*	10.67
A Evans	11	7	22	11	5.50

	O	M	Runs	W	Ave
K Futter	84.1	11	349	25	13.96
J Pennington	146.2	34	476	26	18.31
G Futter	148	33	494	24	20.58
S Belton	54.5	5	279	11	25.36
T Ogden	130	24	505	17	29.71
D Gorrod	87.4	18	331	11	30.91
D Pennington	67	3	309	7	44.14

Catches - A Evans 12 & 10 st J Pennington 13
K Denton 12 A Scales 8 G Futter 7 R Whiteside 7

1999 P23 W12 D6 L2 A3

	I	NO	Runs	HS	Ave
K Denton	16	7	481	69	53.44
S Belton	15	6	340	76	37.78
A Scales	20	1	624	90	32.84
D Watkins	20	3	494	75	29.06
R Whiteside	17	1	402	65	25.12
N Johnson	17	2	317	56	21.11
J Vaughan	12	2	173	49*	17.30
G Futter	12	1	157	54	14.27

	O	M	Runs	W	Ave
S Belton	72.4	5	348	28	12.43
G Futter	68	15	189	15	12.60
J Vaughan	50	12	150	10	15.00
T Ogden	180.3	39	545	33	16.52
D Gorrod	151	35	411	21	19.57
N Johnson	84	16	271	10	27.10
S Burns	50	5	234	6	39.00

Catches - A Evans 15 & 8 st K Denton 12 A Scales 10
R Whiteside 8 & 3 st N Johnson 8 G Futter 8
J Vaughan 6 S Belton 6

2000 P29 W11 D7 L9 A2

	I	NO	Runs	HS	Ave
J Vaughan	18	3	644	110	42.93
K Denton	21	9	497	80	41.42
N Johnson	12	2	365	101	36.50
A Scales	24	2	762	115	34.64
D Watkins	22	3	524	59*	27.57
R Whiteside	17	4	289	60*	22.23
T Ogden	10	4	85	37	14.17
G Futter	15	4	128	22*	11.64
A Evans	14	4	102	38	10.02
Jon Moore	10	0	36	11	3.60
S Burns	11	2	21	7	2.33

	O	M	Runs	W	Ave
T Ogden	165	39	442	33	13.39
G Futter	122.5	20	357	24	14.88
R Whiteside	71.2	7	320	19	16.84
J Pennington	66.1	10	194	10	19.40
D Gorrod	163	35	487	24	20.29
S Burns	116.2	20	550	23	23.90

Catches - A Evans 5 & 12 st G Futter 12 A Scales 12
K Denton 11 R Whiteside 8 N Johnson 8 T Ogden 7
D Watkins 7 S Burns 6 J Pennington 6 J Vaughan 6
M Smith 5

2001 P23 W8 D2 L4 A9

	I	NO	Runs	HS	Ave
D Watkins	13	1	656	102	54.50
R Whiteside	13	3	299	58	29.90
G Futter	10	5	144	40*	28.80
A Scales	12	1	304	70	27.63
N Johnson	13	1	212	107	17.50
K Denton	11	3	134	41*	16.75
Jon Moore	14	2	40	10	3.33

	O	M	Runs	W	Ave
D Gorrod	53.1	10	174	10	17.40
A Scales	73	7	352	18	19.56
T Ogden	91	15	296	13	22.77
S Burns	75	6	312	12	26.00
G Futter	116	32	397	13	30.53
M Smith	67	5	245	4	61.25

Catches - A Evans 5 & 6 st R Whiteside 4 & 2 st
K Denton 6 M Smith 6 A Scales 5 N Johnson 5
G Futter 5

2002 P25 W12 D1 L7 A5

	I	NO	Runs	HS	Ave
N Johnson	21	3	902	150*	50.11
G Futter	13	6	341	63*	48.71
R Whiteside	16	4	406	80*	33.83
D Watkins	21	1	617	109	30.85
A Scales	21	1	612	105*	30.60
S Belton	12	2	159	54	15.90
A Evans	10	5	74	41	14.80
Jon Moore	10	0	67	21	6.70

	O	M	Runs	W	Ave
J Pennington	109	30	356	19	18.73
G Futter	163.4	35	549	28	19.61
M Smith	73.1	4	311	13	23.92
T Ogden	63	13	187	7	26.77
S Burns	77	14	310	9	34.44

Catches - A Evans 9 & 6 st R Whiteside 12 & 2 st
G Futter 10 A Scales 8 J Moore 8 S Belton 4 & 1 st

2003	P25	W13	D7	L4	A1	2004	P27	W11	D4	L5	A7
	I	NO	Runs	HS	Ave		I	NO	Runs	HS	Ave
N Johnson	21	1	826	109*	43.47	G Futter	11	5	251	68*	41.83
S Belton	14	4	308	86	30.80	D Watkins	20	0	691	86	34.55
D Watkins	24	2	646	83*	29.37	A Scales	18	3	479	73	31.93
P Woods	12	4	229	55*	28.62	P Woods	15	6	276	67*	30.67
A Scales	22	1	525	105	25.00	N Johnson	20	0	560	96	28.00
G Futter	17	6	196	33	17.82	R Whiteside	13	2	195	48	17.73
R Whiteside	15	1	200	35	14.28	Jon Moore	13	4	112	34*	12.44
Jon Moore	18	1	235	54*	13.82	C Woods	13	3	114	22	11.40
A Evans	11	5	76	19	12.66						
Jim Moore	10	1	33	15	3.67						
	O	M	Runs	W	Ave		O	M	Runs	W	Ave
C Woods	56	6	199	15	13.27	G Futter	121.4	32	323	23	14.04
G Futter	220	55	597	42	14.21	G Loades	156	33	489	32	15.28
G Loades	95	13	374	15	24.93	P Woods	112	19	349	21	16.62
S Burns	57	7	156	6	26.00	C Woods	124	18	468	27	17.33
P Woods	100	16	342	13	26.31						
N Johnson	75	10	270	10	27.00						

Catches - A Evans 19 & 4 st G Futter 10 A Scales 10
N Johnson 9 Jon Moore 9 D Watkins 9
R Whiteside 8 P Woods 8 G Loades 7
S Belton 4 & 1 st

Catches - P Woods 10 A Scales 9 Jon Moore 9
R Whiteside 7 & 2 st A Evans 3 & 5 st N Johnson 8
C Woods 8 D Watkins 7 G Futter 5 G Loades 5
M Corcoran 4 & 1 st

2005	P25	W8	D7	L7	A3	2006	P29	W12	D5	L8	A4
	I	NO	Runs	HS	Ave		I	NO	Runs	HS	Ave
A Scales	21	2	957	153*	50.37	N Johnson	22	1	846	117	40.29
N Johnson	22	3	647	125	34.05	A Scales	20	2	725	98	40.28
P Woods	18	4	461	54	32.93	R Whiteside	11	4	241	83*	34.43
R Whiteside	17	2	395	48	26.33	P Woods	17	2	483	117*	32.20
G Futter	13	5	204	57	25.50	D Watkins	22	1	598	86	28.48
D Watkins	22	0	488	77	22.18	G Futter	15	6	202	50	22.44
C Woods	18	7	188	33	17.09	G Loades	14	7	113	25*	16.14
M Corcoran	16	0	71	19	4.44	C Woods	14	4	154	32	15.40
						K Robinson	10	3	84	25	12.00
						Jon Moore	13	0	93	35	7.28
						M Corcoran	13	2	72	17	6.55
	O	M	Runs	W	Ave		O	M	Runs	W	Ave
N Johnson	100.5	12	424	26	16.71	C Woods	181.4	30	624	43	14.51
G Futter	174	44	478	24	19.92	G Loades	180	19	736	40	18.40
C Woods	103.1	14	412	20	20.60	K Robinson	53.5	6	282	10	28.20
G Loades	158	10	707	31	22.81	P Woods	186.5	26	804	27	29.78
C Pyer	64	7	233	9	25.55	G Futter	191	50	597	17	35.12
P Woods	113.4	13	514	14	36.71	C Pyer	77.1	4	360	6	60.00
K Robinson	87	4	482	9	53.55						

Catches - A Evans 11 & 6 st A Scales 12 G Loades 11
G Futter 11 N Johnson 8 P Woods 7 D Watkins 7
K Robinson 6 M Corcoran 5 & 1 st

Catches - P Woods 15 A Scales 14 A Evans 6 & 7 st
G Futter 10 G Loades 8 N Johnson 8 D Watkins 7
C Woods 6 M Corcoran 6

2007 P22 W5 D4 L7 A6

	I	NO	Runs	HS	Ave
A Scales	12	1	467	102	42.45
G Loades	11	7	134	38*	33.50
D Watkins	16	4	454	101	28.38
P Woods	15	2	318	98*	24.46
R Whiteside	11	1	186	60*	18.60
C Woods	14	5	162	25	18.00
G Futter	12	2	170	76*	17.00
K Gilbert	11	0	100	26	9.09
Jon Moore	12	0	73	25	6.08
K Robinson	10	2	42	18	5.25

	O	M	Runs	W	Ave
K Gilbert	65	20	144	11	13.91
C Woods	119	19	390	26	15.00
G Futter	111.5	35	243	16	15.19
S Hollis	75.3	11	221	13	17.00
G Loades	90	11	367	15	24.47
P Woods	82	12	334	8	41.75

Catches - R Whiteside 8 G Loades 7 C Woods 7
Jon Moore 7 P Woods 6 A Evans 2 & 3 st

2008 P28 W10 D6 L8 A4

	I	NO	Runs	HS	Ave
N Johnson	22	1	637	103*	30.33
G Futter	16	6	253	42	25.30
D Watkins	16	1	366	60	24.40
A Scales	15	0	343	57	22.87
P Woods	23	2	451	82	21.48
S Hollis	14	6	153	33*	19.13
C Woods	19	3	269	64	16.81
K Gilbert	13	1	183	57	15.25
J Belton	16	0	143	27	8.94
Jon Moore	12	1	58	21	5.27

	O	M	Runs	W	Ave
S Hollis	111	26	371	25	14.84
C Pyer	99	15	411	26	15.81
K Gilbert	110	26	285	18	15.83
C Woods	119.1	14	481	28	17.18
G Futter	135.4	27	488	22	22.18
P Woods	123.5	7	514	17	30.24

Catches - P Woods 22 A Evans 9 & 3 st C Woods 10
G Futter 10 N Johnson 8 A Scales 6 G Loades 6
Jon Moore 6 C Pyer 5 D Watkins 5

2009 P24 W12 D3 L8 A1

	I	NO	Runs	HS	Ave
G Futter	14	7	372	71*	53.14
D Watkins	20	2	744	80*	41.33
N Johnson	19	2	668	105*	39.29
A Scales	19	1	590	77	32.77
P Woods	19	3	428	109	26.75
K Gilbert	11	3	185	47	23.13
R Whiteside	11	2	163	35	18.11
C Woods	15	3	191	36	15.92
J Belton	12	2	72	41	7.20
S Mallett	10	2	41	15	5.12

	O	M	Runs	W	Ave
K Gilbert	104.5	21	361	24	15.04
G Futter	177	47	505	26	19.42
S Mallett	87.5	5	428	20	21.40
D Scales	70	8	329	13	25.31
C Woods	94.4	13	416	16	26.00
P Woods	137.1	10	640	20	32.00
N Johnson	74	11	271	8	33.88

Catches - P Woods 21 & 1 st G Futter 14 A Evans 7 & 7 st
K Gilbert 9 N Johnson 6 R Whiteside 4 & 1 st

2010 P27 W9 D8 L7 A2

	I	NO	Runs	HS	Ave
P Woods	22	4	761	116	42.28
A Scales	23	4	663	100*	34.89
K Denton	12	2	341	71*	34.10
C Woods	19	4	432	55	28.80
D Watkins	21	3	451	88*	25.06
J Belton	16	6	237	71*	23.70
R Whiteside	11	4	120	55*	17.14
G Futter	13	1	93	36	7.75

	O	M	Runs	W	Ave
D Scales	78.2	11	316	16	19.75
M Leak	74.4	12	346	17	20.53
G Futter	192	34	653	30	21.77
S Mallett	114.3	8	606	27	22.44
C Woods	115.4	7	518	19	27.20
K Gilbert	75	9	311	11	28.27
D Jones	98	13	387	13	29.75
P Woods	80.4	4	459	14	32.78
C Gould	87	10	402	8	50.25

Catches - A Scales 13 & 4 st R Whiteside 9 & 4 st
G Futter 13 P Woods 7 D Watkins 6 D Jones 6 C Gould 5
L Bellchamber 5 J Belton 5 R Bean 4 & 1 st

2011	P26	W12	D5	L8	A1	2012	P28	W6	D5	L10	A7
	I	NO	Runs	HS	Ave		I	NO	Runs	HS	Ave
A Scales	20	1	707	117	37.21	A Scales	18	2	740	121	46.25
D Watkins	19	1	628	101	34.89	K Denton	8	2	246	52	41.00
P Woods	21	4	569	99*	33.47	P Woods	22	1	533	82	26.65
S Mallett	11	3	132	56	16.50	R Burling	13	4	188	54*	20.89
R Burling	12	2	161	36	16.10	D Watkins	19	0	336	72	17.68
C Gould	11	5	96	25*	16.00	C Gould	14	4	139	28*	13.90
C Woods	15	3	188	62*	15.67	D Jones	10	5	63	46*	12.60
D Jones	11	4	107	26	15.29	M Leak	11	4	88	24*	12.57
J Belton	17	0	238	49	14.0	J Belton	15	1	173	59	12.36
G Futter	15	5	134	45*	14.00	S Mallett	14	4	122	42*	12.20
M Leak	13	4	51	9	5.67	G Futter	11	2	108	28	12.00
						C Woods	17	2	106	22	7.07
						D Scales	8	1	41	13	5.86

	O	M	Runs	W	Ave		O	M	Runs	W	Ave
C Woods	102.3	14	395	24	16.46	C Woods	80	10	367	20	18.35
M Leak	138.3	15	547	33	16.58	S Mallett	114	7	556	29	19.17
D Jones	128	30	411	19	21.63	G Futter	129	33	367	18	20.39
C Gould	106	10	497	21	23.67	D Jones	136.5	18	530	25	21.20
S Mallett	124.4	12	631	23	27.47	D Scales	91	13	312	13	24.00
G Futter	153.5	19	510	17	30.00	C Gould	94	9	385	12	32.08
D Scales	97	11	329	5	65.80	M Leak	97	5	447	10	44.70

Catches - R Burling 12 C Gould 11 G Futter 11
A Scales 9 & 2 st P Woods 10 K Denton 8
D Jones 7 J Belton 6 C Woods 6 D Watkins 5
M Leak 5 D Scales 5

Catches - P Woods 13 & 4 st D Jones 12 C Gould 11
A Scales 8 & 3 st R Burling 6 & 1 st G Loades 5
J Belton 5

OTHER RECORDS - *Individuals - Top Twenties*

Appearances		Runs		Wickets		Catches/Stumpings	
D Watkins	762	D Watkins	16802	P Edrich	729	A Evans	603
A Evans	740	A Scales	14987	G Futter	706	G Futter	247
G Futter	598	J Vaughan	11059	T Ogden	473	D Watkins	214
J Vaughan	488	N Johnson	9389	K Futter	455	A Scales	213
A Scales	469	R Whiteside	6605	G C Edrich	444	R Whiteside	181
N Johnson	386	G Futter	6283	T Johnson	358	J Vaughan	171
S Belton	368	S Belton	5744	J Vaughan	325	N Johnson	136
D Gorrod	366	K Denton	4379	D Gorrod	309	P Woods	125
R Whiteside	358	P Woods	4564	C Denton	265	S Belton	117
T Ogden	332	P Edrich	3709	C Woods	240	A Edrich	114
K Futter	323	P Hood	3239	B Cator	221	K Denton	109
P Edrich	259	M Conrad	3058	S Belton	215	P Edrich	93
G H Edrich	239	K Hodds	2500	G H Edrich	196	C Denton	73
K Denton	225	A Evans	2388	S Munday	185	P Fisher	69
P Hood	212	C Denton	2369	P Woods	153	D Gorrod	68
P Woods	207	F Atkins	2311	G Loades	150	K Futter	67
B Cator	195	J Denton	2265	N Johnson	147	T Ogden	64
C Woods	188	B Cator	2220	C Gould	144	F Leak	62
G C Edrich	184	M Key	2085	K Mayhew	136	M Conrad	62
F Atkins	180	G H Edrich	2036	A Pennington	129	J Denton	61

Highest Score

A Scales	153*	v Winterton	2005
N Johnson	150*	v Saxlingham	2002
N Johnson	135*	v Cromer	1992
N Johnson	132	v Happisburgh	1994
A Scales	130*	v Presidents XI	1990
N Johnson	128	v Presidents XI	2002
J Tomlinson	128	v William Browns	1963
M Key	127*	v Gothic	1986
M Watts	126*	v Palmers Sch	1959
N Johnson	125	v Rackheath	2005
L Bellchamber	125	v Newbold on Avon	2010
P Edrich	124*	v Hadleigh	1955
K Denton	122	v Great Oakley	1990
A Scales	121	v Happisburgh	2012
M Key	120	v Stewarts & Lloyds	1990
P Hood	120	v Harleston	1959
P Edrich	118*	v St Barnabas	1965
P Woods	117*	v Lowestoft	2006
A Scales	117	v Presidents XI	2011
J Edrich	116*	v Hove & Wrox	1956
P Woods	116	v Aylsham St Giles	2010
A Scales	116	v Saxlingham	1989

Most Wickets in Innings

G C Edrich	10-25	v St Barnabas	1955
P Edrich	10-51	v Ingham	1960
S Belton	9-68	v Dereham	1992
P Edrich	8-8	v Costessey	1950
G C Edrich	8-15	v Overstrand	1953
G C Edrich	8-17	v Gothic	1949
A Pennington	8-20	v Harleston	1959
P Edrich	8-23	v St Barnabas	1959
M Conrad	8-23	v Hov & Wrox	1977
P Edrich	8-26	v Harleston	1953
P Edrich	8-31	v Palmers	1956
C Pyer	8-38	v Southtown	2008
G C Edrich	8-39	v City Police	1953
B Cator	7-5	v Harleston	1959
T Johnson	7-13	v Smallburgh	1977
T Johnson	7-17	v Yarm/Gorl	1976
G H Edrich	7-18	v Overstrand	1951
S Hollis	7-20	v Southtown	2008
D Holyman	7-25	v Tadcaster	1980
J Tomkys	7-26	v Ipswich GH	1956

IN A SEASON

Runs

A Scales	969	in 1990
A Scales	957	in 2005
N Johnson	902	in 2002
N Johnson	846	in 2006
J Vaughan	828	in 1990
N Johnson	826	in 2003
A Scales	822	in 1994
J Vaughan	806	in 1980
A Scales	763	in 1996
A Scales	762	in 2000

Wickets

G C Edrich	66	in 1953
P Edrich	64	in 1956
G C Edrich	61	in 1955
P Edrich	58	in 1959
C Denton	57	in 1980
G C Edrich	56	in 1954
T Johnson	55	in 1976
P Edrich	53	in 1962
T Johnson	52	in 1972
K Futter	51	in 1990

Catches

P Woods	20	in 2009
C Denton	16	in 1977
J Vaughan	16	in 1990
C Denton	15	in 1980
P Woods	15	in 2008
P Woods	15	in 2006
T Kinsley	14	in 1980
A Scales	14	in 2006
G Futter	14	in 1990
G Futter	14	in 2009

Wicket Keepers

A Evans	35	in 1986
A Evans	35	in 1988
A Evans	29	in 1992
A Evans	26	in 1990
A Evans	25	in 1997
P Fisher	24	in 1974
P Fisher	23	in 1971
A Evans	23	in 1999
A Evans	23	in 2003
A Evans	22	in 1998

OTHER RECORDS – Team from 1949

P 1466   W482   D368   T1   L443   A172

Most Runs scored in a season

5228	in	1990
4732	in	2010
4640	in	2006
4536	in	1994
4586	in	2011
4397	in	1997
4358	in	2005
4324	in	2009
4318	in	2003
4168	in	1992

Most Wickets taken in a season

236	in	1977
218	in	199
203	in	1974
202	in	1980
202	in	1988
202	in	1997
198	in	2003
195	in	1994
192	in	2000
187	in	2006
187	in	2008

Highest Team Total

297 for 6	v Abington	2010
289 for 6d	v William Browns	1963
279 for 8d	v Kings College Cambs	1954
269 for 8d	v Hadleigh	1955
265 for 4d	v Palmers School	1959
264 for 6	v Old Catton	2003
261 for 8	v Cromer A	1997
260	v South Wingfield	1998
260 for 8	v Belhus	2006
257 for 6d	v Bradenham	1999

Lowest Team Total

25 v Sprowston		1972
31 v Ingham		1967
31 v Ingham		1969
34 v Eaton		1977
40 v North Runcton		1970
40 v Earlham Lodge		1973
41 v Hadleigh		1968
42 v Lowestoft		2000
43 v Ingham		1952
43 v Norwich Police		1950

RECORD PARTNERSHIPS

1st	228*	A Scales & D Watkins	v	Bradfield	1994
2nd	209*	A Scales & N Johnson	v	Saxlingham	2002
3rd	158	K Hunt & L Bellchamber	v	Newbold on Avon	2010
4th	141	R Whiteside & D Watkins	v	St Andrews	2001
5th	162	S Belton & P Woods	v	Aylsham St Giles	2010
6th	188	A Scales & R Bean	v	Presidents XI	2011
7th	104*	G Futter & C Woods	v	Eaton	2007
8th	109	A Scales & P Woods	v	Caister	2004
9th	81	G Futter & T Ogden	v	Norwich Barleycorns	1991
10th	58	A Evans & D Gorrod	v	Kirkley	1996

SOUTH WALSHAM CRICKET CLUB RECORDS

	Debut	App	I	NO	Runs	HS	Ave	O	M	Runs	Wkts	Ave	Ct/St
Dave Watkins	1975	763	734	60	16802	109	24.93	276.2	13	1437	55	26.13	212/2
Alex Evans	1970	740	402	183	2388	49	10.9	13	1	75	2	37.5	423/18C
Garth Futter	1979	598	443	124	6283	88	19.7	4570.5	988	14529	706	20.58	247
Andy Scales	1988	489	472	50	14987	153*	35.51	272.5	20	1332	64	20.81	204/9
John Vaughan	1972	488	466	47	11059	110	26.33	1710.5	341	5307	325	16.33	171
Neil Johnson	1987	386	369	33	9389	150*	27.94	915.2	120	3494	147	23.09	136
Steve Belton	1983	368	330	65	5744	86	21.68	826.2	69	4306	215	20.03	115/2
Derek Gorrod	1981	366	167	74	633	24	6.81	2354.4	460	7769	309	25.14	68
Richard Whiteside	1988	358	325	62	6605	103*	25.11	433.1	32	2012	93	22.71	155/26
Terry Ogden	1983	332	208	62	1555	66*	10.65	2760	506	9278	473	19.62	64
Kim Futter	1978	323	192	50	1524	54*	10.73	2753.1	649	7940	455	17.46	67
Peter Edrich	1949	259	219	38	3709	124*	20.49	3143	793	7394	729	10.1	91/2
George H Edrich	1949	239	189	26	2010	64	12.33	973.5	183	2739	196	13.97	57
Keith Denton	1979	225	196	53	4379	122	30.62	325.2	47	1181	54	21.87	104/5
Pat Hood	1949	212	197	5	3239	120	16.87	261	44	845	46	18.37	43
Paul Woods	2003	207	184	34	4564	117*	30.43	1012.1	113	4438	153	29.01	120/5
Brian Cator	1951	195	178	19	2220	81	13.96	1240.3	243	3561	221	16.11	46
Chris Woods	2003	188	153	37	2018	64	17.4	1098.5	145	4272	240	17.8	51
George H Edrich	1949	184	109	43	631	33	9.56	2185.5	592	4995	444	11.25	37
Frank Atkins	1949	180	160	20	2311	95	16.51	470	70	1428	94	15.19	32
Ray Lusted	1970	178	108	35	400	30	5.48	531.3	28	2225	95	23.42	45/8
Trevor Johnson	1971	170	76	36	218	21*	5.45	1995.5	498	5098	358	14.24	58
Colin Denton	1974	170	154	27	2369	88*	18.65	1263	168	4575	265	17.26	73
Chris Gould	1990	166	95	27	476	28*	7.01	845.3	90	3813	144	26.48	62
Jon Moore	1997	151	130	13	987	54*	8.44	92.5	2	544	25	22.67	49
Fred Leak	1983	147	137	24	1986	59	17.58	61.4	3	316	19	16.63	58/4
Arthur Edrich	1949	141	103	24	742	49*	9.39	44	11	146	6	24.33	92/22
Steve Munday	1979	140	113	21	898	64	9.76	1025.1	132	3368	185	18.21	22
Tom Mack	1950	135	111	21	591	28*	6.57	13	1	58	1	58	29
Stewart Mallett	1991	115	71	16	627	56	11.4	476.1	39	2365	107	22.1	12
Greg Loades	2002	113	57	25	470	53	14.69	786.5	97	3221	150	21.47	51
Jack Denton	1970	112	110	15	2265	98*	23.84	41.5	7	210	7	35.83	57/4
Mike Conrad	1974	111	109	20	3058	107*	34.36	545	136	1486	96	15.48	61/1
Jack Belton	2002	110	93	13	936	71*	11.7	209.1	9	971	43	22.58	25
Ronnie Hewitt	1949	106	102	6	1601	78	16.68	2.4	0	5	3	1.67	33
Mike Key	1986	99	92	9	2085	127*	25.12	144.4	14	635	39	16.28	28 &1
Ken Mayhew	1953	98	85	11	1268	84	17.14	702.4	164	1950	136	14.43	28
Mike Sidell	1971	96	93	5	1203	73	13.67	127.5	24	485	34	14.26	27
Ken Kerry	1971	90	75	6	894	88	12.96	317.4	27	1276	72	17.72	42

(xxi)

Name	Year												
Peter Fisher	1969	84	80	3	926	49	12.03	38	3	140	5	28	58/11
Keith Hodds	1972	85	83	15	2500	104*	36.76	56.4	4	243	15	16.2	28 & 1
Paul Robinson	1973	83	41	17	124	21	5.17	440	86	1320	63	20.95	21
Alan Eades	1952	80	65	15	554	35*	11.08	101	14	365	18	20.28	19
Colin Reeson	1976	80	57	10	235	25	5	23	3	105	4	26.25	25 & 4
John Westgarth	1970	78	73	6	1391	108*	20.76	24	4	76	7	10.86	43/9
Basil Tibbenham	1957	76	71	4	1405	105	20.97						29 & 2
Jack Foster	1949	76	57	16	173	24	4.22	14	1	64	1	64	7
John Pennington	1994	76	45	12	511	68	15.48	549.4	106	1798	99	18.16	29
Doug Palmer	1973	75	68	10	957	74*	16.5	546.1	132	1425	89	16.01	24
Tony Pennington	1957	72	53	14	381	37*	9.77	646.3	125	1926	129	14.93	22
Rod Burdett	1971	68	66	3	1121	67	17.79	376.5	57	1133	66	17.17	14
Gary Lewis	1984	68	63	8	590	58	10.73	273.4	42	995	38	26.18	15
Roly Hardesty	1957	68	42	12	387	41*	12.9	764.3	173	2004	127	15.78	22
Simon Burns	1999	65	36	11	123	22*	4.92	402.2	58	1647	63	26.14	16
David Jones	2010	61	28	11	271	53*	15.94	367.5	62	1347	57	23.63	26
Mike Moreland	1966	61	54	5	670	74	13.67	186.4	16	730	27	27.04	20
George Head	1950	61	58	3	831	65*	15.11	3	0	14	0		28/13
Tony Hammond	1961	60	57	1	749	55	13.38	15	1	66	1	66	18 & 4
Malcolm Hill	1976	58	47	12	469	51*	13.4	317.1	25	1187	59	20.12	14
Irving Stringer	1950	58	57	7	1299	76	25.98	21.1	3	69	4	17.25	14 & 1
Jack Gunton	1949	57	54	3	503	43	9.86						14
Chris Pyer	2003	57	27	8	167	25*	8.79	402.5	43	1695	73	23.22	12
Keiron Robinson	2005	57	35	6	206	25	7.1	167.2	11	942	26	36.23	10
Kevin Gilbert	2000	57	48	4	617	57	14.02	377.5	78	1184	69	16.78	19
Tony Kinsley	1979	55	53	4	720	54	14.69	23	4	73	1	73	24 & 3
Dan Scales	2006	55	27	7	127	24	6.35	350.2	44	1330	48	27.71	9
Markus Leak	2009	53	33	9	173	24	7.21	311.2	32	1348	60	22.47	10
John Edrich	1951	52	52	16	1932	116*	53.67	11	4	15	2	7.5	25 & 1
John Syrett	1960	52	44	7	495	71*	13.38	254.3	43	929	56	16.59	20
Joe Abbott	1984	51	47	5	411	27	9.79	18	2	89	3	29.67	22
Martin Corcoran	2002	51	44	4	250	27*	6.25						19 & 2
David Bane	1969	50	47	10	469	37*	12.68	32	0	142	4	35.5	5